WHAT PEOPLE ARE SAYING ABOUT

"PHENOMENAL!! The research is fantastic. I really feel I came to know Fannie James. What a gift to Lake Worth and the whole state with *Pioneers of Jewell*." – Jan Tuckwood, reporter for the *Palm Beach Post*

"Ted Brownstein has lifted the veil of mystery surrounding Samuel and Fannie James through unrelenting, in-depth research. Even more remarkably, he has told their story in a thoughtful and entertaining book which is sure to delight the casual reader as well as the serious historian in *Pioneers of Jewell* ." –Debi Murray, chief curator, Historical Society of Palm Beach County

"*Pioneers of Jewell* tells the story of the beginning of our city that includes people of all colors. Black people started things off here. Then other white folks came and helped build the city too. We are all part of history. We are all in this together. We need to pass it on from generation to generation. We don't talk about it enough. Fannie and Samuel James were black. They were the first ones to come to Lake Worth besides the Indians. Especially young people need to know and have pride in our people." – Retha Lowe, first African American commissioner for the City of Lake Worth, Florida

"From its opening pages, *Pioneers of Jewell* is not only the story of a locality, but also a study of the enduring quality of the American spirit." – Lady Hereford, former reporter for the *Palm Beach Post*

"The hardships one faced while settling the West were no more arduous than those Fannie and Samuel faced while establishing what is now Lake Worth. Like the pebble that becomes a pearl in an oyster, they were the foundation for the development of Jewell." – Paul Blockson, first African American fire chief for City of Lake Worth, Florida

"Growing up as a little girl in what was referred to by the adults as the Quarters, Colored Town and Lake Osborne, never allowed my imagination to venture across the railroad tracks let alone the northeast corner of Lucerne Avenue and J Street in downtown Lake Worth where the first settlers were identified as two African Americans, namely Samuel and Fannie James. As I read excerpts from this documentary and became aware of the great contributions of this famous couple, it certainly made my heart sing and feel proud to be a native of Lake Worth." – Delorisa Brown, Lake Worth native, educator, former principal of Barton Elementary School.

Cover art: The opening day of the Jewell Post Office, August 22, 1889. Postmistress Fannie James receives her first delivery via mail boat. No photographs of Jewell or its residents are known to exist. The painting is an artistic recreation, yet strives for historical accuracy. The trees, vegetation, building, and clothing are modeled after what is known from photographs of nearby locations and written descriptions of pioneer life during Lake Worth's Homestead Era. Further detail on the painting's historical backdrop is found in Appendix G.

Painting by Janet Villasmil
Photography by Leonard Bryant

Pioneers of Jewell

A Documentary History
of Lake Worth's
Forgotten First Settlement
(1885 – 1910)

By Ted Brownstein

A Lake Worth Herald Publication

In Commemoration of
The City of Lake Worth's Centennial,
June 4, 2013

Cataloguing in Publication

Brownstein, Ted

Pioneers of Jewell

Local Interest / Palm Beach County

U. S. History / Florida / Palm Beach County

ISBN 978-0-9832609-4-3

Contact author at JewellStories@aol.com.

Photographs are courtesy of the Lake Worth Herald or the Lake Worth Historical Museum, with permission, unless otherwise credited.

Document reproductions are items in the public domain, obtained from the Lake Worth City Clerk, the Palm Beach County Clerk and Comptroller's office or the National Archives.

Net proceeds from the sale of this work will be donated to the Lake Worth Public Library.

Editorial note: This publication uses grammatically correct plural and plural possessive forms of the name James, namely Jameses and Jameses'. Despite their somewhat unusual appearance, these spellings are supported by all English authorities. (See Chicago Manual of Style – 16th edition, p. 354.)

Contents

Foreward by Delorisa Brown ix

Prologue: Digging for Diamonds x

The Lake Worth Centennial Committee and

    How This Book Came to Be Written xi

Acknowledgments xii

Lake Worth Historical Museum xiii

Fannie James, Folk Hero xiv

The Jameses' Slim Biography xvi

Better History through the Internet xvi

Part 1: Jewell Beginnings 1

Chapter 1: Surveyors then Homesteaders 2

Chapter 2: Small Beginnings for the South Florida Homestead Era 5

Chapter 3: Welcome Mat—Canals, Railroads, Steamboats, Stagecoach Line 9

Chapter 4: Arrival of Samuel & Fannie 13

Chapter 5: Homesteading 15

Chapter 6: The Land Dispute 20

Chapter 7: Zooming in on the Jameses' Neighbors 25

Chapter 8: Zooming in on the Pennsylvania Colony 35

Chapter 9: The Founding of Jewell 40

Chapter 10: Samuel James Subdivides His Land 47

Chapter 11: Zooming in on the Site of the First James Homestead ... 50

Chapter 12: Who Were the Jewell Thirteen? 52

Part 2: Jameses in Historical Context 61

Chapter 13: Reconstruction & Backlash 62

Chapter 14: Race and the U.S. Post Office 69

Chapter 15: The Jameses in Tallahassee 71

Chapter 16: The Jameses in Cocoa 73

Chapter 17: Racial Attitudes on the Lake 76

Part 3: Jewell Progress

Chapter 18: Jameses' Second Homestead 82
Chapter 19: Mail Routes 85
Chapter 20: Relocating the Jewell Post Office 89
Chapter 21: A New Batch of Neighbors 92
Chapter 22: The Decline of Jewell 97
Chapter 23: Fannie after Closing of Jewell Post Office 100
Chapter 24: Samuel's Passing 103
Chapter 25: Tracing Samuel's Family Background 105
Chapter 26: Zooming in on Palm Beach Farms Company 107
Chapter 27: Palm Beach Farms Company's Acquisition Strategy 112
Chapter 28: The Pioneer Mystique 114
Chapter 29: Fannie James after 1910 117
Chapter 30: When Fannie Was Not Welcome Here — Segregation Settles in 118
Chapter 31: During Jim Crow, Where Did Fannie Go? 119
Chapter 32: Fannie's Death and Funeral 122
Chapter 33: Samuel & Fannie's Burial Site 124
Chapter 34: Discovery of Fannie's Lockbox Makes Headlines 127
Chapter 35: Through the Probate Door—A Look Inside Fannie's Life 128
Chapter 36: Zooming in on Fannie's Mortgages 136
Chapter 37: Fannie's Sister Contests Her Will 138
Chapter 38: Zooming in on Fannie's Real Estate Holdings 140
Chapter 39: Jameses' Business Acumen 141
Chapter 40: Bird's-Eye View of the Jewell Homestead Era 144

Part 4: Jewell in Historical Context

Chapter 41: How the Lake Became the Intracoastal Waterway 148
Chapter 42: Seminole Community 155
Chapter 43: Fannie's Genealogy 159
Chapter 44: African American Community During the Homestead Era 167
Chapter 45: Zooming in on Segregation Era 174
Chapter 46: Lake Worth Loosens Up 180
    Interview with former Lake Worth Commissioner Retha Lowe 182
Chapter 47: Summing It All Up. What It Means. 184

> Another postoffice has been opened down the lake between Figulus and Hypoluxo, with Mrs. S. James as postmistress and Jewel as its name.

Tropical Sun, September 11, 1889

Appendices 185

Appendix A: Select Newspaper Ads and Clippings 186
Appendix B: History of Postal Offices on the Mail Boat Route 194
Appendix C: Timeline of the James/Fulton Land Dispute 198
Appendix D: James-to-Moore Land Sales Contract................................204
Appendix E: Zoomingin on Surveyors' Maps................................206
Appendix F: Lake Worth Timeline................................209
Appendix G: Historical Basis for Details of Cover Art 220

Citation Abbreviations................................223
Bibliography 225

Last Monday as the "Arthur B." made the Jewell wharf with the mail she capsized. Everything in the boat was soaking wet except the mail, which reached its destination in good order.

Tropical Sun, January 14, 1892

Lake Worth School 1913

Foreward By Delorisa Brown

Lake Worth native and first African American principal of Barton Elementary School

In the words of an unknown songwriter:

I'm so glad I'm from Lake Worth,

I'm so glad I'm from Lake Worth,

I'm so glad I'm from Lake Worth,

Singing Glory Hallelujah, I'm from Lake Worth!

Lake Worth is a city known on the Gold Coast as "The Jewell". However, the untold stories reveal that its history is worth far more than rubies, diamonds or gold!

PioneersofJewell is somewhat like a scene from the *StarTrek* series. It promises to take you on a journey where the mission is to explore a strange new world, to seek out new civilizations and to boldly go where no man has gone before.

The author takes advantage of an opportunity to educate the people of this great City of Lake Worth and share with them some of the rich history which has never been told. This history is research-based, therefore well documented with pictures, legal documents, interviews and newspaper articles, leaving no room for even a speckle of doubt as to the validity of its contents.

Growing up as a little girl in what was referred to by the adults as the Quarters, Colored Town and Lake Osborne, never allowed my imagination to venture across the railroad tracks let alone the Northeast corner of Lucerne Avenue and J Street in downtown Lake Worth where the first settlers were identified as two African Americans, namely Samuel and Fannie James. As I read excerpts from this documentary and became aware of the great contributions of this famous couple, it certainly made my heart sing and feel proud to be a native of Lake Worth.

This documentary reveals how Samuel and his wife Fannie staked their claim to land which is now Lake Worth. It tells how Fannie became the first postmistress and how they both had to endure in times when because of their race, wealth, riches and the pursuit of happiness was not an option for them. It further goes on to share how they both died and were buried on the land they grew to love. This lost history, now rediscovered, certainly deserves to be celebrated during Lake Worth's Centennial.

Mr. Brownstein is to be commended for his tremendous efforts. I am positive that the residents of this community will appreciate this most valuable documentary. He is to be applauded for embarking upon a journey to where "no man has gone before!"

Prologue

Digging for Diamonds

==

DISCOVERING OUR DIVERSE HERITAGE

"Black people have been part of the history of this county and part of the history of this city. People of all colors forget about that. Black people started things off here. Then other white folks came and helped build the city too. We are all part of history. We are all in this together. We need to pass it on from generation to generation. We don't talk about it enough. Fannie and Samuel James were black. They were the first ones to come to Lake Worth besides the Indians. Especially young people need to know and have pride in our people."

- Retha Lowe, first African American Commissioner for the City of Lake Worth, Florida

Unknown woman working at Lake Worth Woman's Club during the 1920s.

The Lake Worth Centennial Committee and How This Book Came to Be Written

Lake Worth, Florida, was founded in 1913. In preparation for its centennial, interested citizens began meeting in early 2012 to plan an exciting series of celebratory events. I began to work with a subcommittee on Lake Worth history. Our mission was to research the city's past and to find ways to incorporate that story in the various events planned for the centennial year.

It soon became apparent that the story of the founding of the city and its subsequent history had been well told. The *Lake Worth Herald* and Lake Worth Historical Museum hold archives of thousands of photographs, articles, maps, and materials documenting the happenings in the city dating back to 1912. In addition, a number of good books showed us that we were on well-trodden ground. Among them are:

Lake Worth—Jewel of the Gold Coast, written by Jonathan Koontz, et. al., published by the Lake Worth Chamber of Commerce.

Images of America: On Lake Worth, a compilation of hundreds of historic photos by Beverly Mustaine, dis-tributed by the Lake Worth Historical Museum.

However, the more we dug, the more we discovered a vast swath of our history had not been told. Besides brief reports about Fannie and Samuel James, the first Lake Worth settlers and African American ex-slaves who opened the Jewell Post Office here in the 1880s, we could find nothing. The era before 1912 seemed to be a blank slate.

Certain obvious questions required answers. If there had been a Jewell Post Office, there must have been a town, a village, or some sort of community for it to serve. Yet the written histories did not provide any history about Jewell, nor name a single resident besides the Jameses. Its roots, its population, and its economic and social life were unknown. Who had lived here? What was life like? What happened to the Jameses and the other inhabitants when the Town of Lake Worth formed in its place? Jewell was like a lost city, forgotten in the mists of time.

With these questions in mind, our research took on a new focus. Rather than retelling well-told stories, we would pursue the lost history, searching out the forgotten people and events from *before* the incorporation of the City of Lake Worth.

We soon discovered that there was an intriguing story to tell and an abundance of new resources that would allow us to dig deeper into the past than had previously been possible. And what we found was a cast of characters who came from across the United States and Europe to create a new life for themselves under the umbrella of the Homestead Act. These people braved the primitive conditions, the swamps, and the mosquitoes. They built homes and cleared fields and thereby acquired land for a nominal fee from the U.S. Government. This earlier period, from the arrival of the first settlers in the mid-1880s until the founding of the Town of Lake Worth in 1912, we dubbed the Homestead Era.

We also discovered that besides the fact that our first settlers were African Americans, issues of race were shied away from. Yet in the wake of the Civil War, the end of slavery, the race-consciousness of Reconstruction and subsequent segregation, there had to be a story to be told. Perhaps due to embarrassment at the sad chapter of racial segregation in our history or perhaps because of a lack of documented sources, our museum does not have an exhibit or materials on the subject. Other resources, while mentioning a "Negro" here and there, had not done much better at telling the story.

Our mission then became twofold. Using Fannie and Samuel James as a springboard, we would bring back to life the lost community of Jewell, Florida, *circa* 1890, with special attention on how issues of race influenced the development of Lake Worth.

To the telling of those untold tales, this work is dedicated.

Acknowledgments

This publication would not have been possible without the skill and generous devotion of time by many who love Lake Worth history. Thanks go to Vickie Joslin, Lake Worth librarian; Helen Greene, local historian and mainstay at the Lake Worth Historical Museum; Debi Murray, curator of the Historical Society of Palm Beach County; Dr. Ginger Pedersen of Palm Beach State College for her help in locating materials in the National Archives; Leonard Bryant for his photographic skills; Betty Resch for spearheading the Centennial Committee; and especially Mark Easton, publisher of the *Lake Worth Herald,* for his tireless work preserving our local history.

Thanks also go to Retha Lowe and Paul Blockson, leaders of Lake Worth's Martin Luther King Committee, as well as others who lent information and inspiration to this project, including Ed Deveaux, Loretta Sharpe, Greg Rice, Harold Grimes, Herman Robinson, Jim and Joanne Kelly, Lori Durante… and anyone whose name inadvertently may have been omitted from this list.

Google Books has been a valuable resource, making older publications, now in the public domain, available online at no cost. Especially useful was James Henshall's *Camping and Cruising in Florida* (1884), which includes dozens of original George Potter sketches.

Of course, the biggest thanks goes to Lake Worth's pioneers who braved the wilderness and helped make our beloved city the little piece of paradise it is today.

Lake Worth Historical Museum

The Lake Worth Historical Museum was established to serve as a repository to preserve the history and culture of the city. It is located in the old City Hall Annex at 414 Lake Avenue.

Librarian Vickie Joslin stands in the doorway of the Archive Room in Lake Worth Historical Museum. Archival files contain thousands of photographs, maps, newspaper clippings, and documents from 1912 to the present.

Overview of display cases and exhibits highlighting the lifestyle of the city's pioneers.

Photographic exhibit of Lake Worth churches, several of which were established during the year of the town's birth.

The History of Lake Worth - From the Beginning

Lake Worth's history, from the time of its incorporation, has been well told. The 100th anniversary edition of the *Lake Worth Herald* chronicled the progress of the city year by year since 1911.

1911

In 1911, the events leading to establishing the townsite of Lake Worth a year later were few and rapid. The idea of locating a town where Lake Worth stands today originated with the Palm Beach Farms company. Paradise was founded by the Palm Beach Farms Company and promoted by the Chicago based firm of Harold Bryant and William Greenwood, who were carrying out a general plan of development and settlement work near Lake Worth.

Fannie James, Folk Hero

Fannie A. James has become something of a folk hero in Lake Worth. As a black woman in an age before the civil rights or women's rights movements, she served as postmistress, successful business-person, and community founder in a white man's world. Along with her husband, she played that most heroic American role of frontier pioneer.

The Jameses arrived in an untamed tropical wilderness with the clothes on their backs and $50 in their pockets. Battling heat, floods, swamps, and mosquitoes—on their own except for a few scattered neighbors who lived miles away—the Jameses overcame one impediment after another to build a small but vibrant community called Jewell.

Professor Dr. Gilbert L. Voss of the University of Miami summarized the Jameses' reputation:

> **Samuel James and his wife were Negroes and settled north of Hypoluxo.... Highly respected by the other settlers, they played a strong role in the development of the area.** (*Pioneer Life in Southeast Florida*, 258.)

Today they are celebrated as trailblazers and champions of the American Dream. In downtown Lake Worth, on the northeast corner of Lucerne Avenue and J Street, near the main post office, stands a granite monument memorializing the Jameses' foundational role in the birth of the city.

"THE BLACK DIAMONDS "

Samuel & Fannie James
This monument stands as a memorial to
Fannie & Samuel James who settled on
the shores of Lake Worth in 1883 [sic]...
Fannie, believed to be an ex-slave,
was the area's first postmaster.
Their land later became the heart of the city.
The Jameses should always be remembered
as the City of Lake Worth's first settlers.

Then again, the City of Lake Worth is not the only voice singing the praises of the Jameses. Each year, the Historical Society of Palm Beach County recognizes Fannie's hero status by giving an annual award in her honor.

Fannie James Pioneer Award Recipients

2003: Laurita Collie Sharpp
    Saved and donated a large collection of images and diaries from the Collie Family.

2004: Robert Hazard
    Worked on the Storm of '28 Memorial.

2005: Roy Rood
    Of pioneer family stock; preserved the history of the towns of Rood and Jupiter.

2006: The Adolf Hofman Family
    Wrote a book about Delray Beach pioneers.

2007: Michael Bornstein
    Barefoot Mailman reenactor and preserver of pioneer history.

2008: Ethel Sterling Williams Family
    Worked to preserve Delray history and founded the Delray Beach Historical Society.

2009: Royal Poinciana Chapel
    Worked to preserve pioneer history with restoration of Sea Gull Cottage.

2010: The Loxahatchee Guild
    Worked to preserve Tindal House and Jupiter pioneer history.

2011: Everee Jimerson Clarke
    Worked to preserve African American history in West Palm Beach and particularly Pleasant City.

The Fannie James Pioneer Award recognizes the achievements of individuals or organizations that have significantly contributed to preserving and sharing the history of Palm Beach County's pioneering days. The award, established in 2003, is named for the late Fannie James, an African American pioneer who served as the first postmistress of the Jewell Post Office (now Lake Worth), which was open from 1889 until 1903. (Historical Society of Palm Beach County website.)

The Jameses' Slim Biography

Despite the acclaim, the awards, and the monuments, our knowledge of the Jameses, up til now, has been modest at best. The little that has been written about them would scarcely fill a couple of pages, and much of it is dubious. Almost everything said about the Jameses has been contradicted by another authority. Even the date of their settlement written in stone as 1883 on Lake Worth's post office monument is off by a couple of years.

Published accounts say they came from Virginia, North Carolina, Georgia, Ohio, and Pennsylvania. Alternatively, some believe them to have been Black Seminoles, escaped slaves who joined the Native American tribes in the early 1800s. If so, they would not have been transplants from any of the aforementioned states. Rather, their families would have come to Florida a generation or two earlier.

As recently as June 1999, a *Palm Beach Post* article commented on the confusion surrounding the Jameses' origins.

> No one knows exactly where the Jameses came from. Some said they were ex-slaves from Georgia; others said they were Black Seminole Indians. (McCabe, "Pioneer's Will Reveals More Surprises.")

Similarly, Samuel James's ethnic background has been a topic of debate. Popular history describes Samuel as of "dark complexion," a negro, and an ex-slave, yet his death certificate shows his race as white.

Published works also differ on an array of other issues, including the location of the Jameses' home, the extent of their land holdings, and the site of their burial. Rumors proliferate when writers merely quote what previous writers have said without going back to primary documents.

Now, some of these riddles can be solved with confidence.

Better History through the Internet

Thanks to the wealth of electronic tools now available, long-buried facts are available to shed historically accurate light on the confusion about the Jameses' story. Previously, researchers would have had to spend long hours sifting through thousands of pages of documents that may have been decades old, stored on dusty shelves, and buried in distant government warehouses. Often, important documents have been, for all practical purposes, impossible to find.

Over the past decade or so, many records of libraries and governmental agencies have been digitized and indexed in searchable databases. Now relevant information often can be found in seconds on the Internet. As a specific example, this author had learned of an 1884 book called *Camping and Cruising in Florida*. Perhaps a used copy might be found online, although it seemed like a long shot for such an old publication. Nevertheless, the book was quickly found in Google's electronic library, and its 300-plus pages, complete with George Potter's handdrawn illustrations, were downloaded, all in less than 15 minutes.

In other cases, electronic searches expedite the ordering of CDs or paper copies. As a result, photographs, maps, and historical documents are now easily obtainable from federal, state, and local sources related to Lake Worth's past in general and to the Jameses specifically. It is remarkable how much the research process has improved with the advent of the computer and Internet.

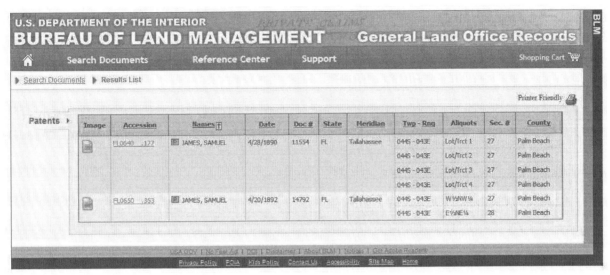

Internet search for Samuel James's homestead property. Copies of land patent certificates are available online at http://www.glorecords.blm.gov/search/default.aspx.

With the aid of these new electronic research tools, we can tell a more accurate and robust story. The improved access to official information not only allows us to clear up earlier confusion, but also provides new insight into the people and history of the early settlers. What emerges is a more complete picture of who Samuel and Fannie were and what life was like on the tropical frontier.

In the course of doing research for this book, we had many eureka moments. New discoveries would emerge from old documents that brought unknown aspects of the Lake Worth story to life. Among topics now published for the first time:

- Biographies of more than a dozen unknown Jewell pioneers.

- Identification of the original site of the Jewell Post Office.

- The land dispute that challenged the Jameses' first homestead claim.

- Why the Jewell Post Office moved west to the Jameses' second homestead.

- The precise location of Samuel James's burial plot, partially under a public sidewalk.

- Fannie's Farmette, the home of her widowhood.

- New insight into the Jameses' slave background.

- History of Fannie James's family, including their flight to Ohio on the Underground Railroad.

- The establishment of the Osborne Colored Addition.

- Klu Klux Klan activity in Lake Worth during the 1920s.

- An in-depth look at the Jameses' financial success.

- The family fight that challenged Fannie James's will.

- The fate of the Jewell pioneers.

GOING TO THE DOCUMENTS

Telling true stories is best done with historical records. Rather than simply telling readers about the results of our research, we prefer to share the experience of discovery. For that reason, this book, to the extent possible, reproduces photographs, maps, excerpts from eyewitness accounts, and copies of contemporary documents that describe settlers' homes, fields, work, and play, allowing readers to see Lake Worth's Homestead Era through an unfiltered lens.

Especially valuable are the voices of those earliest pioneers, including testimony of Fannie and Samuel James, which we now have, for the first time, via transcription of their testimony in court. We can read their description of life on Lake Worth during the Homestead Era in their own words.

Part 1

Jewell Beginnings

===

POPULATION GROWTH, 0 TO 13

"Toward the south lies a panorama of pines, cypresses and saw-grass, with their varying tints of green, amidst which is a network of small streams, glinting in the sunlight like a filigree of silver; while far beyond lies Lake Worth, a burnished shield on a velvet sward. Turning at last toward the east we behold grand old ocean, 'dark, deeply beautiful blue,' stretching away to the vast horizon, where the blue above meets the blue below."

– Dr. James Henshall, 1878

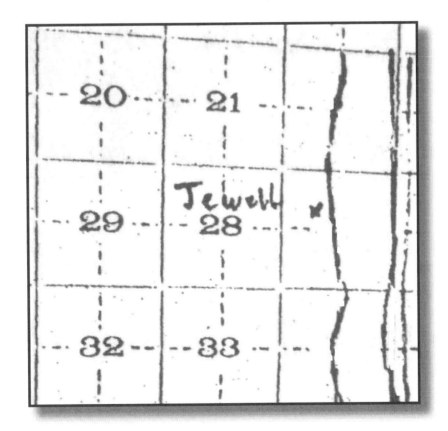

Grid map showing location of Jewell, founded by Fannie and Samuel James on the west bank of the lake, which would grow into the City of Lake Worth, Florida.

Chapter 1: Surveyors then Homesteaders

The history of the Homestead Era begins with a blank slate. The Seminole Wars of the mid-1800s left the land virtually empty of inhabitants. The vast majority of the Seminole population had been marched west on the Trail of Tears to Oklahoman Indian Territory.

South Florida had a reputation as a worthless wilderness. Jacob Rhett Motte, who visited the Jupiter area in the 1830s as a surgeon with General Jessup's army, had second thoughts about deporting the Indians.

> **It is in fact a most hideous region to live in; a perfect paradise for Indians, alligators, serpents, frogs and every other kind of loathsome reptile. The whole peninsula is alluvial, having been formed by successive encroachments of the Atlantic; and offers feeble allurements to an agricultural population... Then why not in the name of common sense let the Indians keep it? (Motte, *Journey into Wilderness*, 199.)**

The U.S. government, however, was of a different mind. As a matter of public policy, it encouraged its citizens to occupy all territories. A first prelude to settlement was division of the land into parcels and lots that could be owned and farmed. Federal survey teams created a grid of numbered ranges, townships, and sectors. The results of their work were published in specialized maps with assigned legal descriptions, such as Range 43 East, Township 44 South, Sector 27.

When homesteaders filed claims, they would use these maps to identify the parcel (usually a 160-acre quarter sector) they wanted. The system was not easy to understand and often created conflicting claims that the Federal Land Office would have to sort out.

After the Second Seminole War, Congress passed the Armed Occupation Act of 1842. The law was designed to encourage settlement in Florida and provide security in lieu of a peace treaty with the Seminoles. It granted 160 acres in the unoccupied regions of Florida to any settler willing to bear arms to defend the property against the remaining Seminoles for five years. Records at the National Archives list 1,184 homesteading permits issued within the nine months that the law was in effect. Most of those were in Central Florida. Less than 25 permits were issued for the southeastern part of the state, nine of which were on the shores of Lake Worth.

DATE	NAME	LOCATION
March 23, 1843	William W. Loring	On Lake Worth, 7 miles from north end
May 14, 1843	James Burroughs and family	Southwest end of Lake Worth
May 14, 1843	Simeon Beaufort and family	Southwest shore of Lake Worth
May 14, 1843	James W. Burnside	East side of Lake Worth
May 14, 1843	B. B. Burroughs	Southwest end of Lake Worth
May 14, 1843	Arba Washburn and family	Southwest end of Lake Worth
May 14, 1843	Henry Otterstraeller	East side of Lake Worth
July 26, 1843	John B. Evans	South end of Lake Worth
August 13, 1843	William A. Cobb	Southwest end of Lake Worth

Report of the Federal Land Office, April 27, 1848, *Early Lantana*, 3.

No existing records indicate who of the permit holders actually took up residence on the land. Those few who attempted to settle, however, did not stay long. By 1870, none of the Armed Occupation settlers remained.

The next wave of settlers arrived in response to the Homestead Act of 1862. Unlike the Armed Occupation Act, the Homestead Act applied to government lands, not only in Florida, but across the U.S. Any citizen or person intending to become a citizen could make an entry application for a 160 acre plot. Construction of a home and cultivation of the land for five years were required to gain title. Land in the Lake Worth area was available under the Homestead Act until around 1920.

Surveyor's map of Township 44 South, Range 43 East showing 40-, 80-, and 160-acre potential homestead parcels. Outline added to mark the original Town of Lake Worth plat.

This map shows Sections 15, 16, 21, 22, 27, 28, 33, and 34. Lake Osborne on the left, the Intracoastal Waterway on the right, swampland on the upper left, and a thick woodland in the middle.

The original 1912 town plat followed section and quarter section lines except for parts of the southern town limits. Those grid lines became major streets within the Town of Lake Worth—A Street, Dixie Highway, Lake Avenue, etc.

See Appendix E for more detail on surveyor maps and methods.

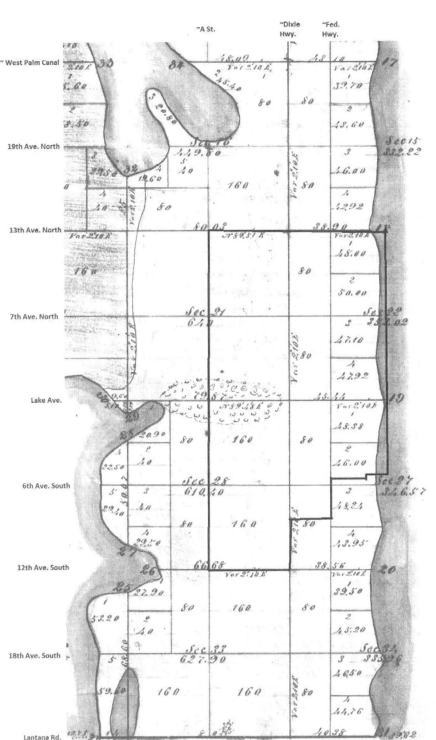

MANY MEANINGS OF LAKE WORTH

The term Lake Worth can be confusing, as it is commonly used in at least four distinct ways.

1) The oldest usage on maps and by surveyors refers to the body of water itself. Originally a freshwater lake, blocked off from the Atlantic by the coastal dunes of Palm Beach Island, the lake was fed by oozing flows of the nearby Everglades. Occasional infusions of saltwater would turn the lake brackish when storms opened up temporary inlets. Later, man-made inlets connected the lake with the ocean, turning the lake into the brackish Lake Worth Lagoon. Canals later connected the lake with the Loxahatchee River on the north and the New River on the south, forming the Intracoastal Waterway. In this sense, the terms Lake Worth, Lake Worth Lagoon, and Intracoastal are interchangeable.

2) The first scattered settlers around the perimeter of the lake, including Hypoluxo and Munyon Islands, would refer to the region as Lake Worth. Until 1891, the *Florida Star* in Titusville was the closest newspaper and ran a regular col-

Inset of Henshall map showing features of the South Florida coast in 1878: Jupiter Inlet, Lake Worth Inlet, Hillsboro Inlet, New River (Fort Lauderdale) Inlet, Miami, and Biscayne Bay. The inlets were all natural outlets of rivers, except for Lake Worth Inlet, which was man-made.

umn titled "Lake Worth," which covered the weather, happenings such as parties and the arrival of new settlers, and other tidbits of community news in the lake area.

3) More confusing yet is the fact that the community at the north end of Palm Beach used the name Lake Worth during the early Homestead Era. The Lake Worth Post Office operated there between 1880 and 1901. Some of the earliest publications were designed to promote what is now known as Palm Beach as a winter resort. With photographs of elegantly clad tourists promenading down coconut tree-lined lanes and decked out in ball gowns, parasols, and tuxedos, hotel owners invited the upper crust to Lake Worth. However, the Lake Worth they were touting was not the City of Lake Worth as referred to today.

4) After Palm Beach gave up the Lake Worth name, a newly formed community farther south on the west shore adopted the moniker. Originally platted and filed with Palm Beach County as theTown of Lucerne, the name was changed to the Town of Lake Worth in 1912 after Lucerne was rejected by the U.S. Post Office Department because it was already in use elsewhere in Florida. In 1949, Lake Worth became a city under Florida statute.

Chapter 2: Small Beginnings for the South Florida Homestead Era

Historically speaking, the Lake Worth area was one of the last places to attract homesteaders, long after more distant places, from Minnesota to California, had been settled. The environment was hostile and full of challenges. The first few brave souls who made an attempt quickly moved on to greener pastures. Even military outposts remained only as long as absolutely necessary and were quickly abandoned after the Seminole and Civil wars. The 1860 and 1870 censuses for Dade County, which then included Palm Beach, failed to list a single resident on the lake.

Before drainage canals were dug, the Everglades lay just west of the future Lake Worth townsite. The waters were so high during the wet season that Seminoles were able to use canoe routes to paddle from the Intracoastal to Lake Osborne. Even after the town was established, flooding continued to be a problem.

During the summer of 1912 Lake Worth experienced a thunderstorm, which caused extensive flooding. After the storm, two men were able to paddle a canoe from Dixie Highway to the lake.

Lake Worth was in trouble and residents of surrounding towns predicted a short life for the new community, because Lake Worth was several feet below lake level. ("The History of Lake Worth—From the Beginning," *Lake Worth Herald*, **May 24, 2012.)**

Mosquitoes presented another major source of discomfort. With wry humor, settlers would joke about swarms of the bloodsucking pests.

Who would not be a "lotus-eater," when the thermometer says 90° in the shade and there are ninety skeets to the cubic inch. The front porch is good enough for me.

Tropical Sun, Lotus Cove Column, August 19, 1891—Ninety mosquitoes per cubic inch.

Big skeeter sketch by George Potter. Courtesy of Historical Society of Palm Beach County.

South Florida pioneers required a special hardiness. Not until the mid-twentieth century after the completion of a network of drainage canals, coupled with the advent of DDT and air-conditioning, did life become bearable for the average person.

JUPITER INLET—GATEWAY TO THE LAKE

The federal government built the Jupiter Inlet Lighthouse in 1860. Although the inlet tended to silt up and close, sometimes for years, it provided the best available inland access. Water routes ran in three directions, northward into the Indian River, westward via the Loxahatchee River, and south through Lake Worth Creek.

From its inception, the lighthouse was truly a lonely place in the wilderness. Except for a small U.S. military base called Fort Dallas in Miami, eighty miles to the south, the lighthouse keeper had no neighbors. Fort Capron at Saint Lucie and Fort Lauderdale had both been abandoned years earlier.

During the Civil War, the Jupiter Light was intended to play a role in the northern naval blockade of southern ports by helping to spot southern blockade-runners. Confederate sympathizers raided the lighthouse early in the war, stole its lens and "took away... enough of the machinery to make it unserviceable." (*Letter of*

Sailing past Jupiter Lighthouse, drawing by George Potter, Henshall 40.

James Paine to Florida Governor Madison Starke Perry, August 1861, as quoted in Snyder, *A Light in the Wilderness*, 118.)

Capt. James A. Armour served as Jupiter's lighthouse keeper from 1866 until about 1909. The well-built lighthouse and keeper's living quarters made it an outpost of civilization and a natural meeting place. Capt. Armour had a reputation as a hospitable man who welcomed Seminoles, explorers, and potential settlers alike. (PLSF, 43; Henshall, 79–81)

Hannibal Dillingham Pierce came south from Chicago in the winter of 1872 and served briefly as assistant lighthouse keeper. During the time of his employment, he lived on site with his wife, Margretta, and his son, Charles.

One the most complete eyewitness accounts of the early Homestead Era comes from the autobiography of this same Charles W. Pierce. *On Wings of the Wind* contains colorful descriptions of life on the lake between 1872 and the coming of Henry Flagler's railroad in 1894. Unfortunately, it is a wordy 690-page unpublished manuscript. Professor Donald W. Curl of the University of Miami abridged Pierce's manuscript down to 200 pages and published it in 1970 under the title *Pioneer Life in Southeast Florida (PLSF)*.

One of the most memorable scenes in the autobiography is Charles's description of his first glimpse of Lake Worth. One day, he climbed the lighthouse tower to get a view of the surroundings. It was one of those eureka moments that set the wheels of history in motion.

> Gazing around in wonder at the panorama spread out in all directions, I saw far to the south something white and glimmering through the green of the trees on the distant horizon. Captain Armour told me that it was the northern end of Lake Worth, a large lake, some twenty-two miles long, and in some places more than a mile wide. He added that no one lived there now, though a German named Lang and his wife had lived there for some time during the Civil War. (PLSF, 31)

AUGUSTUS LANG—PALM BEACH HERMIT (1863)

The only known settler along the shores of Lake Worth during the 1860s was Augustus Oswald Lang. He arrived from Key West in 1861 and worked briefly as an assistant keeper at the Jupiter Lighthouse. When the Civil War broke out, the lighthouse played an important role in enforcing the Union blockade and discouraging blockade runners. As a Confederate sympathizer, Lang conspired with a group of friends to disable the Jupiter Light.

Lang enlisted in the Confederate Army in 1862 and went AWOLa year later. After deserting, he hid out on Palm Beach Island, living as a squatter in a palmetto shack. (*Tropical Frontier*, 321) Rumored to have been a horticulturist to the King of Prussia, he planted impressive tropical gardens around his modest home. When he learned that the Civil War had ended, Lang left Lake Worth for Brevard County, where he eventually married and had a son. Lang died there in 1873. (*Pioneer Days*, 10–11)

Early access to the lake was difficult, a discouragement to settlement. Two water routes were available. Both had inherent difficulties. The outside ocean route required navigating through coral reefs that caused frequent shipwrecks and entrance into the lake through a narrow channel with treacherous currents, and shifting sandbars. The inside route, possible only in smaller boats five feet wide or less, was by way of the southern branch of the Loxahatchee River, known as Lake Worth Creek. The creek was navigable for only about half of the 1 5-miles down to the lake, terminating near a well-used Indian campground. Reaching the open waters of the lake from there required wending one's way through unmarked swamps and alligator crawls, then dragging one's boat over a 300-yard-long "overhaul," a broad path built by the Indians. (PLSF, 43 - 48)

Between 1866 and 1872, a parade of hunters, fishermen, and adventurers tended to prefer the overhaul route to the lake, but no one came to stay.

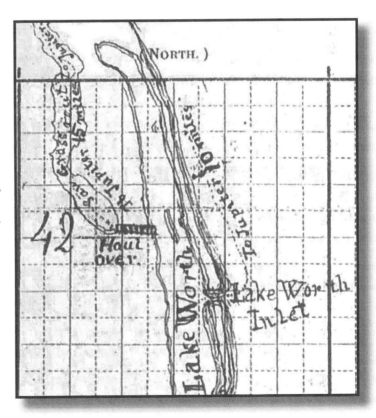

Hand-drawn map showing inside and outside routes, here labeled as "15 mile" "Saw Grass route to Jupiter" with "Haul over" and "10 mile" ocean route. From Lake Worth Post Office Application, 1880.

HANNIBAL PIERCE—HYPOLUXO ISLAND (1873)

After spending some months with Captain Armour at the Jupiter Lighthouse, the Pierce family along with "Uncle Will" determined to take up homesteads on the lake. Will Moore with his friend William M. Butler headed for Munyon Island on the north end of the lake, while the Pierces continued farther south and settled on Hypoluxo Island. At the time of their arrival, they were the only eight people living around the 44-mile perimeter of the lake, stretching over the waterfront sections of what are now Riviera Beach, Palm Beach, West Palm Beach, Lake Worth, Lantana, and Boynton Beach. (PLSF, 50)

Neighbors may have been scarce during those early times, but game was abundant. Deer hunting was excellent in the pinelands across the lake from the Pierce homestead. There were deer trails everywhere. Charles Pierce delighted in his descriptions of hunting as a lone teenager in the solitary wilderness. He seldom came home without venison for the table, which his mother especially craved, but there were times when his mother was disappointed. Charles described one hunting trip to the west shore of the lake, when he shot a panther that confronted him:

> At first I was at a loss as to what to do with my prize. It was too heavy to carry on my back… so I grabbed its tail and started. By dragging for a hundred yards or so and then resting, then another hundred yards, I at last reached the sandy beach of the lake.

> My boat was about a mile up the shore… so I waded up the shore towing the panther in the water.

> When I arrived at the home landing, father was waiting… He thought I had a deer and was certainly surprised when he saw the panther. Mother was disappointed when she heard the news… She wanted some fresh venison… She said, "I wanted some fresh meat for dinner. Now you will have to eat salt bacon."

> I carefully skinned the panther… Sometime later father… traded the skin for a suit of clothes for me. This was the first suit of store clothes I ever earned and I was very proud. (PLSF, 142)

During those early days, the beach was a rich provider. In October of 1879, "a hurricane of extreme violence" hit the Bahamas, causing a number of large shipwrecks. Debris from the ships washed up on the Atlantic beach.

> The beach was a great lumberyard. Heavy timbers such as 4 by 9 planks from twenty to forty feet in length, some 4 by 4 and 6 by 6 and any quantity of big twelve- and fourteen-inch square timber could be found. We combed the beach for more than a week, gathering up and rafting to the island all the planks and small timber we found. After all this lumber had been collected, father decided to build an addition to the house… The house had tremendous strength; while it was not handsome, it was extremely safe in any storm. (PLSF, 144)

Other accounts of beach salvage included cases of varnish, cases of wine, and a shipwreck full of thousands of coconuts that were planted, grew into productive trees, and eventually gave Palm Beach its name. During those early days, settlers had to sail long distances up the coast to Sand Point, Titusville, or Jacksonville to get supplies, making beach salvage all the more a valuable resource.

Chapter 3: The Welcome Mat: Canals, Railroads, Steamboat, Stagecoach Line

As access to the lake improved, the trickle of pioneers became a steady stream.

- In 1877, the first attempt at a permanent inlet between the Atlantic and the lake was opened, improving the "outside route." The inlet was crude and treacherous to navigate. James Henshall's story about using this inlet is harrowing and informative. (See "History of the Inlets" in Chapter 41.)

- The year 1885 saw the completion of the canal connecting the lake with Jupiter, following the course of the old "inside route." It was built by the Florida East Coast Canal and Transportation Company of Saint Augustine. The U.S. government subsidized the construction with a grant of 1,265 acres of land per mile of canal built.

- In 1889, the Jupiter & Lake Worth Railroad, nicknamed the Celestial Railroad, opened, providing service on a narrow-gauge track between Jupiter and Juno at the north tip of the lake.

- Once the railway was operational, steamboat services began to carry passengers to and from the train at both ends of the line. Initially, the schedule was intermittent, but gradually improved. Water routes connected Titusville to Jupiter on the north, via the Indian River, and Juno with the emerging communities on the lake to the south.

Jupiter & Lake Worth Railroad, known as the Celestial Railroad due to its stops at Jupiter, Venus, Mars, and Juno. Courtesy of Library of Congress.

JUPITER AND LAKE WORTH RAILWAY.

27	71	5	Mls	January 1, 1893.		6	66	14
P. M.	P. M.	A. M.		[LEAVE]	[ARRIVE]	P. M.	P. M.	P. M.
†3 30	†3 00	†10 00	0	........Jupiter....... ठ		1 00	†3 35	5 05
3 45	3 15	10 25	4	..........Venus..........		12 40	3 15	4 45
3 53	3 22	10 37	6	..........Mars..........		12 15	3 08	4 38
4 05	3 35	11 00	8	..........Juno....... ठ		†12 01	†3 00	†4 30
P. M.	P. M.	A. M.		[ARRIVE]	[LEAVE]	NO'N	P. M.	P. M.

† Daily, except Sunday; ‡ Sunday only. ठ Telegraph station.

CONNECTIONS.

At Palatka—With Jacksonville, Tampa & Key West Ry., Jacksonville, St. Augustine & Indian River Ry., and Georgia South. & Fla. R.R.

At Juno—With Lake Worth steamers for Oaklawn, Lake Worth, Palm Beach, Figulus and Hypoluxo.

At Bartow—With South Florida R.R. for Sanford, Pemberton and points north.

At Punta Gorda—With Morgan Line steamers for Key West, Havana and New Orleans; with Fort Myers Steamboat Co. for St. James City, Punta Rassa and Myers.

At Gainesville—With Savannah, Florida & Western Ry., Western Div.

At Ocala—With Silver Springs, Ocala & Gulf R.R. for Dunnellon, Inverness, Hernando and Homosassa.

At Leesburg—With Florida Southern steamboats on Lake Harris and Lake Griffin.

At Pemberton—With South Florida R.R.

At Tavares—Connection is made between trains of the Jacksonville, Tampa & Key West and Florida Southern Rys.

Jupiter & Lake Worth Railway schedule, January 1893, showing steamboat connections to points throughout Florida.

- The first road from the lake to Miami was completed in 1892, reducing an arduous three-day hike along the beach to a bumpy two-day ride. Biscayne Bay Stage Line used two hacks (wagons pulled by mules,) and set up a halfway camp at New River (Fort Lauderdale). The wagon ride from Lantana to the camp took 14 hours, while the Miami hack arrived in about seven. The New River was crossed by ferry. Here they exchanged mail and passengers and returned the next

- The extension of Flagler's East Coast Railway reached Palm Beach in 1894 and Miami in 1896.

Tropical Sun – June 1, 1893

CHANGE IS IN THE WIND

During the 12 years between 1873 and the Jameses' arrival in 1885, about 150 people moved to the lake region. Palm Beach was the only concentrated settlement. Located on the barrier island at the easternmost bulge of Florida, it benefited from of its proximity to the warm waters of the Gulf Stream, as well as near access to both the Atlantic Ocean and the lake.

Early settlers appreciated both the beauty and economic potential of their new home. At the time of her arrival at Palm Beach, Ella Dimick wrote:

> This place was nothing but a wilderness when we came here in 1876, but how beautiful that wilderness was. (Dimick, Ella J. "Transportation from 1876 to 1896." *Lake Worth Historian*, 11.)

Adventurer James A. Henshall, who spent two winters cruising the South Florida coast in his private boat, *Blue Wing*, described the lake and its emerging community as he experienced them in 1878:

> Lake Worth is a fine sheet of water, twenty miles long and a fourth to two miles wide. It runs north and south, parallel with the seashore....Originally it was a freshwater lake, but since the cutting of the inlet has become, of course, salty. The head of the lake, near the inlet, is quite shallow, with numerous shoals, snags, and old wrecks. (Henshall, 86)

> The settlement at Lake Worth (Palm Beach) is in the hamak [*sic*] on the east shore, and comprises some twenty-five families, mostly from the northern and western states, who exhibit an amount of pluck, thrift and enterprise, unusual in Florida. Finding the saw-grass route to Jupiter inadequate to their purpose, they built an inlet to the sea... which however, soon fi lled up with sand. (Henshall, 88)

George Potter sketch of sailing on the lake off Palm Beach, *circa* 1884, Henshall 80.

Given today's urban sprawl, it is hard to imagine how scattered the population was during those early settlement years. The 1885 Florida Census listed just 333 inhabitants for all of Dade County, which encompassed the present Palm Beach, Broward, and Miami-Dade counties. Settlers were concentrated in two places: 1) on the lake at the northern end of the county and 2) around Biscayne Bay at the southern end. There were no known settlers in the area in between, comprising what is now Boca Raton, Pompano Beach, and Fort Lauderdale.

There was an ongoing rivalry between Lake Worth and Miami area settlements. Both had a population of around 150 residents and fought a seesaw battle for the Dade County seat, which moved from Miami to Juno and back to Miami between 1888 and 1899.

The eastern shore of the lake, including Munyon, Hypoluxo, and Palm Beach islands, was considered prime land and settled first. Reasons for this are not hard to find. Transportation was more reliable on the ocean side, both on land and water. Walking along the beach north to the Jupiter Lighthouse or south to Biscayne Bay was often the preferred way of getting to neighboring communities. The prevalent sea breeze offered a measure of protection from mosquito swarms. Proximity to the beach also provided easier access to shipwreck debris.

In contrast, the western shore offered additional challenges and was settled only after preferable land on the eastern shore was taken. The encroaching Everglades made land transportation next to impossible, flooding was an ever-present danger, and the mosquitoes swarmed so thickly that only those with the thickest of skin could tolerate them.

Zeroing in on the south end of Lake Worth, the population figures cited on early post office applications were amazingly low. The Figulus Post Office, located near the present Southern Boulevard Bridge, opened in January 1886 to serve 60 individuals. The count included year-round as well as winter residents for the southern portion of the lake, including both the eastern and western shores.

The southernmost section of the west shore, stretching from what is now West Palm Beach to Boynton Beach, remained a wilderness into the mid-1880s. Henshall picturesquely described the vacant Lake Worth-Lantana area during his visit there:

> We made our first camp about two miles from the south end of the lake, on the west shore, near a clump of cabbage palmettos, and near a small brook of water. It was a delightful camping spot, and we found plenty of game. One day Ed was picking up shells on the beach, walking with his head bent down nearly to his knees, when two deer approached within thirty yards of him, stamping and snorting at the strange object.... (He looked up) just in time to get a glimpse of their white tails as they disappeared into the brush. We often saw deer come down to the edge of the lake near our camp. (Henshall, 91)

Not surprisingly, the southernmost 10 miles on the west side of the lake were the last to be settled. The State of Florida had classified much of it as "swampland" not open to homesteaders until 1885. (James HA1, 20) Lantana Point was unoccupied until the Lymans arrived in 1888, and West Palm Beach would not be established until the advent of the Flagler railroad in 1894.

The 1885 Florida Census listed only two families living on the southwest shore of the lake. Benjamin Lanehart had a lone homestead across the water from Palm Beach in what now is West Palm Beach. The Edwin Bradley place was about seven miles south, across from Hypoluxo Island. The area in between was a playground for deer, wild turkey, and alligators. Such was the wilderness that the Jameses entered.

Chapter 4: Arrival of Samuel & Fannie

When Samuel James first came to the lake area around Christmastime 1884, the population was on the verge of mini- explosion. Within a year, Andrew Garnett, James Porter, Ed Hamilton, William Stephan, Harry Stites, and others would take up homesteads along the southwest shore of the lake in the area that now comprises Hypoluxo, Lantana, and Lake Worth.

James had the advantage of arriving several months before the others and got first pick at a homesite. The common practice was to claim two waterfront lots of about 40 acres each and the contiguous 80 acres to the west to round out the permitted 160-acre claim. Samuel wisely selected four waterfront lots, which proved to be much more valuable than interior land.

A firsthand account of the homestead surge comes from Charles Pierce's autobiography. He had lived across the lake on Hypoluxo Island for twelve years and was an eyewitness to the influx of new arrivals.

> **New settlers arrived in numbers in the fall of 1885. It seemed to us the outside world had just heard of what the lake had to offer to those who were willing to work. (PLSF, 196)**

Pierce makes three references to the Jameses. The information he provides is widely known and forms the basis for most of what has been published about them.

> Along the west shore south of the little hammock that marked the halfway point between Hypoluxo and Palm Beach.... [South of the hammock] at a point three miles north of Hypoluxo, Samuel James and his wife took up a homestead. (PLSF, 196)

> Another [post office] established at the James place was called Jewel. Mr. and Mrs. James were of rather dark complexion, so the boys nicknamed that office "Black Diamonds." (Pierce, *On Wings of the Wind.* Compare PLSF, 213, where the editor, Donald Curl, omits the reference to the Jameses' complexion.)

> About the first of June in 1886, the Brelsfords and George Charter asked me to go with them as a witness when they made the proof of their homestead claims at Gainesville in the United States Land Office.... The plan was for the party to go to Jacksonville on the *Bessie B.* and from there take a train to Gainesville.... Our party consisted of Captain Ed and "Doc" Brelsford; Squire Hoagland; a young man who was the nephew of Mrs. Samuel James; Conradson... and myself. (PLSF, 205)

In the above quote, Pierce locates the Jameses' homestead, and states that they were of dark complexion, implying that they were African American. He is our source for the nickname "Black Diamonds."

The description of the group of settlers traveling together to the Gainesville Land Office shows a sense of community. They stood as witnesses for each other's claims and helped each other through the bureaucratic paperwork. The inclusion of Fannie's nephew demonstrates that the neighbors welcomed the Jameses and supported their claim.

Who was this unnamed nephew? A reasonable guess would have been Alonzo T. Anderson, a son of Fannie's sister from Ohio. Alonzo would have been 22 years old at the time, a good age for a Florida adventure. Throughout his life, he was close to Fannie and was later named executor of her will. (More about Alonzo later on.)

Pierce places the trip to Gainesville in the first part of June. That timing implies that the nephew delivered Samuel's document stating his intention to make final proof on his claim. The preemption notice was filed June 10, 1886.

In any case, Charles Pierce was a good neighbor and took the nephew along on the trip. In those early homestead days, land travel was difficult or next to impossible. Roads were sandy, bumpy, flood-prone, and ill-maintained. The preferred method of travel was by boat, and Pierce often described one or another of the early settlers going to Titusville or Jacksonville in sailing vessels for lumber and supplies. The ships *Bessie B*, the *Illinois*, and the *Creole* are often mentioned. (PLSF, 177)

Samuel James's preemption form dated June, 1886, probably delivered to Gainesville Land Office by Fannie James's nephew.

Colored band gives an excursion to Lantana.
(*Gazette*, May 18, 1895, as quoted in *1896 Directory*, 32)

BLACK DIAMONDS

The phrase Black Diamonds means little today, but in the late 1800s, Black Diamond Minstrels was one of the most common names for "colored" entertainment companies that performed a variety of songs, skits, and jokes. One such group put on shows around the lake in 1895.

> Black Diamond Minstrels, a home talent, give good entertainment. (*Gazette*, July 13, 1895 as quoted in *1896 Directory*, 33)

Unfortunately, all back issues of *The Gazette*, along with any further details the article may have provided on the Minstrel show, were lost in a fire in West Palm Beach in 1896, but the Black Diamonds may have been the same band referred to two months earlier.

There is no evidence that either Fannie or Samuel was connected with the troupe, but its usage demonstrates that "Black Diamonds" was a known term in that era and carried racial connotations.

Chapter 5: Homesteading

The homestead application process was detailed and rigorous. To claim a homestead plot of 160 acres, the applicant was required to take up residence on the land, clear a portion of it, and cultivate it for five to seven years. An initial entry application at the beginning of settlement and a final proof of compliance with the legal criteria were required. Two witnesses had to file notarized statements supporting the truth of the application. Legal notice, published for six consecutive weeks, had to be given in an area newspaper, the nearest to Lake Worth being Titusville's *Florida Star* until the *Tropical Sun* began publication in March 1891. Only modest filing fees were charged. The application, was sent to Washington for final approval. Successful applicants would receive a patent as their proof of title to the land, bearing the endorsement of the president of the U.S.

A shortcut to the Homestead Act was called preemption. Its provisions for acquiring land from the U.S. government were similar to homesteading, requiring the applicant to reside on the land and cultivate it, as well as secure two witnesses and publish a notice. Its advantage was that it lacked the lengthy five- or seven-year residency requirement of the Homestead Act. After settling on the property, an applicant could purchase the land for $1.25 per acre within a few months.

Copies of original homestead and preemption applications have been digitized and are available on CD from the National Archives in Washington, DC. These CDs contain the entire homestead file, not just the application form filled out by the settler, but all correspondence, witness testimony, receipts for the payment of fees, and any other relevant information that officials may have placed in the file.

THE JAMESES' HOMESTEAD

The Jameses were the first to stake a claim and settle in the area that was to become the City of Lake Worth. Copies of their homestead application were obtained from the National Archives. The Jameses' file contains 86 pages rich with insights into their personal histories and experiences as new arrivals. In it are found descriptions of the land, their first home, their efforts to clear and farm the land, their friendships, as well as the untold story of a land dispute with a group of Pennsylvania settlers who challenged part of the Jameses' claim.

In his circuit court testimony defending his claim, Samuel revealed that he and Fannie had been living in Cocoa, Florida, about 150 miles north. During the winter of 1884, Samuel ventured south to Palm Beach to find work in his trade as a carpenter. Fannie stayed behind in Cocoa.

While in the lake area, Sam made friends with several local settlers, including Edwin R. Bradley and John C. Hoagland. Both were prominent in the emerging community. Bradley served as the first of the famous Barefoot Mailmen and Hoagland as justice of the peace.

In due course, their conversation turned to land open for homesteading. During January 1885, Bradley took James to see a vacant waterfront parcel of 186 acres on the west shore of the lake, just north of his own homestead. The parcel encompassed an area that is now part of the City of Lake Worth, along the waterfront south of the Lake Worth Bridge, from Lake Avenue down to 12th Avenue South and west to near M Street.

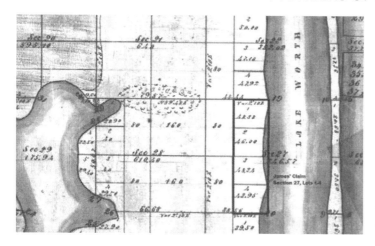

James Property, Section 27, Waterfront Lots 1, 2, 3, & 4.

In February 1885, Samuel took up residence on the property. He built a small palm-frond shanty, as was typical for early settlers, and began clearing the land. In March, he filed his entry homestead application with the U.S. Land Office in Gainesville.

Published sources, including the Lake Worth Post Office Monument, have dated the Jameses' arrival in 1883. (McCabe, "The Mystery of the Lost Grave".) However, the official records kept at the National Archives tell a different story.

George Potter sketch of typical palmetto shanty.

ZOOMING IN ON THE JAMESES' HOMESTEAD CLAIM

Within a few months, Samuel's palm shanty burned down and was replaced with an enlarged and more substantial structure. Edwin Bradley described Samuel's second home as "a frame house, painted, 14 or 15 x 23 or 25 feet." (James HA1, 37)

In response to questions on the homestead application, Samuel describes his land claim and his initial improvements in his own words. (James HA1, 24, 39)

Question: What is the character of the land embraced in the present claim?

Answer: It is farming land, high pine and scrub land. Ordinary agricultural land.

Question: If the land is timber land, state the kind, quality and amount of timber thereon at the date of your initiating your claim to it, the amount still standing, how much has been cut and removed, and by whom and how disposed of, and to whom?

Answer: It is small pine timber. Very little has been cut off and I did that myself. I do not know of any being cut by anyone else.

Question: How much real estate do you own? What was the actual value of all your personal property at the date of making original entry or filing? If living in a rented house just prior to original entry or filing, state monthly rental you paid.

Answer: I don't own any except my preemption claim now in question. My personal property at the date of entry of this land was about fifty dollars. I was living in a rented house just prior to making this entry and paid $5 per month.

Question: Are you now residing on the land in question?

Answer: I am.

Question: What is the value of your improvements on this land?

Answer: About $400.

Question: When did you first make settlement on the above-described land?

Answer: February 1885

Question: Were there any improvements on the land when settled?

Answer: No.

Question: What improvements have you made on the land since settlement?

Answer: I have built a house, cleared four acres of land, dug a well and planted out orange trees, pine apples, & vegetables with coconuts.

Samuel James soon realized that he would need funds to improve the land, finish his larger home, plant trees, etc. An opportunity arose for carpentry work back in Cocoa, building "a church for the colored people." (James HA1, 70) So, he left his homestead in charge of Harry Griswold and returned to Cocoa to earn some money and to be with Fannie. The record reports that he sailed to Cocoa "on April 23 with Captain Canova after a three day blow" and returned with him the following September 18.

Reproduced at the National Archives

[4—394]

Claimant—Cross-Examination.

HOMESTEAD, PRE-EMPTION, and COMMUTATION PROOF.

Not official.   Published by HENRY N. COPP, Washington, D. C.

NOTE.—The object of cross-examination is to ascertain the FACTS connected with claimant's alleged compliance with law.

Samuel James the claimant under *declaratory statement*
No 1610 Gainesville Land District *Ohio*, having been duly sworn, was cross-examined as follows:

Question 1.—Where and when were you born?

Answer *I was born in Halifax County Virginia, I was born August 182—*

Question 2.—What was your post-office address, where and by whom were you employed, or in what profession, trade, or business engaged just prior to making claim to this land now under consideration?

Answer *Lake Worth, I was employed at my trade as a carpenter by different people,*

Question 3.—Have you ever made a pre-emption filing for any other tract of land; or any other homestead entry; or any other land filing or entry of any kind?
[Answer each question separately, describe the land, and state what disposition you made of your claim to it.]

Answer *I have not, neither have I ever entered any land under any kind of land filing except my present claim.*

Question 4.—What is the character of the land embraced in the present claim? Is it timber, mountainous, prairie, grazing, or ordinary agricultural land? State its kind and quality, and for what purpose it is most valuable.

Answer *It is farming land, high pine and sand land. Ordinary agricultural land.*

Question 5.—Is the land valuable for coal, iron, or minerals of any kind? Has any coal or other minerals been discovered thereon, or is any coal or mineral known to be contained therein?

Answer *No, No,*

Question 6.—If the land is timber land, state the kind, quality, and amount of timber thereon at the date of initiating your claim to it, the amount still standing, how much has been cut and removed, and by whom and how disposed of, and to whom?

Answer *It is small pine timber, Very little has been cut off, and I did that myself I do not know of any being cut by anyone else,*

Question 7.—If the land is used for grazing purposes, state how and by whom it is so used, and whether it is within any stock range or fence or other enclosure, and who owns or controls the range or enclosure.

Answer *It is not,*

Question 8.—Does your claim control or include any water supply? If so, state the area of country dependent upon such water supply.

Answer *No,*

Question 9.—Has any other person or persons except yourself any interest in this land or in the timber thereon? If so, state who has any interest, and what interest.

Answer *No, neither in the timber,*

Question 10.—What arrangement, if any, have you made in regard to the cutting and disposal of the timber on this land?

Answer *I have made none,*

Question 11.—How much real estate do you own, where is it situated, and how was it acquired? What was the actual value of all your personal property at date of making original entry or filing? If living in a rented house just prior to original entry or filing, state monthly-rental you paid.

Answer *I don't own any except my pre-emption claim now in question, my personal property at date of entry of this land was about fifty dollars. I was living in a rented house just prior to making this entry, and paid $5.00 per month*

Image of page 1 of Samuel James's claimant form found in the National Archives

Samuel must have been disappointed when he received notice, while in Cocoa, that his Lake Worth homestead claim had been rejected. On September 5, 1885, the General Land Office in Washington, DC, wrote concerning the status of his claim, explaining the reasons for the rejection.

> In relation to the status of lots 1, 2, 3 & 4... I have to state that originally lots 1 & 2 were entered under the homestead law by James Murrin, but the entry has recently been canceled for expiration of the seven years and failure to make final proof. Lots 3 & 4 together with... [other adjacent land to the west]... were selected by the State of Florida as swamp and overflowed land under the Act of 1850, but the Swamp Claim was rejected by this office August 22, 1885. Therefore the whole section, including the lots in question, appears on the records of this office as vacant, unappropriated land subject to entry under the homestead and preemption laws.

The letter concluded by encouraging Samuel to reapply at Gainesville.

Following the advice of the Washington, DC, Land Office, James resubmitted his homestead application on September 14. He paid a $2 processing fee. This second application was likewise rejected, due to an error in the legal description of the property on the application form. He had put down Range 45E instead of 43E.

The Gainesville Land Office response explained the error and resulting confusion:

> The declaratory statement is lots 1-2, 3 & 4 Sec. 27, T. 44S – R. 45E. This paper was rejected on the date of its receipt for the reason that no such land exists being under the waters of the Atlantic Ocean.

Not to be dismayed by this further setback, James continued to pursue his claim. Knowing that the preemption and homestead laws prohibited absences of more than six months, he hurried back down south, in the middle of September, after an absence of a little more than five months. Further delay would have been considered as a legal abandonment of his claim.

At the bottom of the form, a curious fact emerges about Samuel James: Despite his expertise as a carpenter and despite his financial and business ability, he was illiterate, unable to sign his name. Instead of a signature, he affirmed the truth of his testimony with an "X" mark. Samuel consistently signed with an "X" on property sale contracts and other official documents of every sort. In contrast, Fannie was able to read and write and readily signed her full name as needed.

Chapter 6: The Land Dispute

En route south, back to his claim, James met a group of four friends from Pennsylvania with designs on settling along the lake. Dr. Harry Stites, Benjamin Himes, Orville Fulton, and William Hartzell were members of the Newport United Methodist Parish in Newport, Pennsylvania and had known each other for many years. Harry Stites was the leader of the group, a physician and a highly educated man. The foursome arrived together at Lake Worth on September 18, 1885.

Stites quickly established his claim on the west shore of the lake, a mile north of the Jameses' land. (This property now corresponds to the middle section of the Lake Worth Municipal Golf Course, between 7th and 13th Avenues North.) Himes selected a vacant parcel north of Stites. Hartzell, in turn, chose the parcel on Stites' south, abutting the Jameses' property.

AN AX AND A BLANKET

Here's where the story gets sticky. Fortuitously, the Jameses' homestead file contains a record of the claims and counterclaims, as well as a transcript of the resulting court hearing. These provide, as far as is known, the only preserved record of Samuel's and Fannie's spoken words. The transcript allows a peek at the events that led up to the land dispute and insight into the personality and temperament of Lake Worth's first citizens.

After Himes, Stites, and Hartzell had selected their homestead sites, their next step was to find a place for Fulton. Four days after their arrival, Stites led his friends on a walk down to have a chat with Samuel James and to inquire about vacant land farther south. They found Samuel at home but were told that he could not identify which lots might be open. He offered to take them down to Bradley, who might know.

Along the way, it started to rain. The men apparently never made it down to Bradley's.

According to the record, Stites pointed out to Fulton some land between the James and Bradley homes that he thought was vacant. He told Fulton to go back to his place, get an ax and a blanket, and "settle" on the land by sleeping there for the night.

Fulton later testified that James was present and overheard that conversation, but James denied having heard anything of the sort or of having any knowledge of Fulton's intent to stake a claim on his property.

At this point, Samuel James went home, apparently to get out of the rain, unaware that Fulton, ax and blanket in hand, was sleeping just a few hundred yards away, intending to stake a claim. It is not known exactly what Fulton did with his ax. Did he cut down a tree or two to justify his claim? Did James hear the chopping? In any event, Fulton slept under the stars that one night and the next morning headed north to Gainesville to file his claim at the U.S. Land Office.

It is hard to untangle the details or to determine if initially anyone was acting in bad faith. The lots were wild scrub and wooded without survey markers, hills, streams, or other distinguishing features. Adding to the confusion is the fact that there were two 40-acre parcels on the waterfront between James and Bradley claimed by Robert Stringfellow. But Stringfellow had never occupied the land, built a home, or otherwise improved it. Apparently, none of the settlers knew anything about Stringfellow, including Bradley, who had lived on the adjacent property for almost 10 years.

Going by steamer to Jacksonville and then by train to Gainesville, Fulton arrived on September 28, just ten days after first seeing Lake Worth and six days after spending one night on his "claim." In conversation with the officers at the Land Office, Fulton discovered that the Jameses' claim had been rejected due to confusion over the range designation. He then immediately filed his own claim.

Fulton must have known at that point that he was treading on dangerous turf. The Jameses' claim stated the identical township, section, and lot numbers that Fulton wanted. Determined, nevertheless, to take advantage of the legal confusion over the error in the range designation, he proceeded to file a claim for the southern half of the Jameses' land. Then, betraying his lack of interest in settling the land, Fulton returned to Pennsylvania for six months.

Thus, the lines were drawn for a battle that would split the tiny settlement. The Pennsylvania boys stood as one with Fulton. The rest of the neighbors sided with the Jameses, including John Hoagland, Edwin Bradley, Michael Merkel, William Stephan, Capt. Antonio Canova, and Elisha N. Dimick.

Fulton returned to Florida in March 1886 and quickly threw up a 12-by-14 foot palm-frond shanty on pine posts. The shanty consisted of two tiny rooms. One was for sleeping and contained a homemade bed, a board floor, and cheesecloth siding "to keep the mosquitoes out." The other half of the shanty was a small room with a dirt floor, a table, and 25 books. As required by the preemption law, Fulton made a nominal effort at cultivating the land. He set out "three fruit trees and planted some vegetables." (James HA1, 84)

The Pennsylvania colony's four sites were lined up along the lakefront, with Himes the northernmost, and Stites, Hartzell, and Fulton to the south. The Jameses' place was sandwiched between Hartzell and Fulton. Neither Himes nor Hartzell filed homestead claims.

A court date was set for August 2, 1886 to resolve the dispute. Stites and Hartzell filed sworn statements with the court on Fulton's behalf. Significantly, the statements were made and notarized in Perry County, Pennsylvania, in July. Apparently the two were not fully committed to taking up residence in Florida, especially during the hot, sticky summer months.

Stites's and Hartzell's statements essentially made two points in support of Fulton. First, they asserted that James was confused about the boundaries of his claim. Previously he had supposedly ordered Hartzell off the parcels to the north of his home and was now trying to get Fulton off the land to the south. They argued that James was confused about which land was his. Second, Stites and Hartzell asserted that James had not cleared or otherwise improved the land that Fulton was on and so had no valid claim to it.

Meanwhile, and in anticipation of the August 2 trial date, Michael Merkel and William Stephan filed sworn statements on James's behalf. The two men were James's neighbors and testified that James had been on his land, including the disputed lots, by February 1885, six months before the Pennsylvania friends arrived. Stephan went so far as to accuse Fulton's supporters, saying they were "engaged in a conspiracy to defraud Mr. James" with the goal of either getting the land or a monetary settlement. (James HA1, 9)

The two-day trial was held in Titusville, Brevard County. The venue required the Jameses, Fulton, and their string of witnesses to make the 150-mile journey by boat and stay overnight in a hotel or boardinghouse. Just making arrangements to attend the trial was an ordeal in those primitive times, not to mention any mental anxiety the parties might have felt at the prospect of losing the case and, more importantly, losing their claims.

Fannie accompanied Samuel on the trip to Titusville, along with John C. Hoagland and Edwin Bradley. All four took the stand at the trial on behalf of the Jameses' claim. All testified that Samuel had taken up residence on his claim in January or February of 1885. He had cleared four acres of land, built a frame house of approximately 15 feet by 25 feet, dug a well, and planted pineapples, orange trees, coconut trees, and vegetables. They confirmed that James had claimed the land that was in dispute from the beginning. Contradicting assertions to the contrary, he had cleared land at both the extreme north and south ends of his property.

Both Bradley and Hoagland proved to be effective witnesses.

Bradley was an enthusiastic recruiter of settlers for the lake, having induced Michael Merkel to move down. He also was instrumental in recruiting the Jameses. It was Bradley who brought Samuel over to the west shore and showed him the vacant land on the waterfront, north of his own place, which was the exact location of the land that Fulton was disputing. Consequently, Bradley was intimately familiar with the dispute as it unfolded and was in a position to be the perfect witness for the Jameses' interests.

Hoagland was a pillar in the lake community and justice of the peace. His credibility in support of Jameses' claim was unquestionable.

Fannie was called to testify on the second day of the trial. She supplied precise dates for the periods when she and Samuel were absent from their claim, as well as a doctor's note stating that at one point she was too ill to travel. She made the case that they never had abandoned their claim, or been away for more than the limit mandated by the homestead law. Her emotional side came out during her testimony when she commented that the dispute with their neighbors "wounded our feelings" and caused "heartache."

As the trial proceeded, Benjamin Himes testified in support of the Fulton counterclaim. He had little to add and essentially repeated the assertions of Stites and Hartzell.

Fulton next testified in his own behalf. Under cross-examination by the Jameses' attorney, his admissions about his negligible improvement are almost laughable and significantly weakened his case.

Question: Were you not informed that Mr. James claimed this land, Lots 3 & 4 at the time you applied to enter them?

Answer: No. There was a petition of James there but they did not understand it [apparently due to the aforementioned error in the range number on the Jameses' paperwork].).

Question: What do you mean by there and they?

Answer: I mean the Land Office at Gainesville and the officers connected therewith.

Question: Why were you in haste to go to Gainesville?

Answer: I was in haste to get to Cocoa to meet the boat to save delay.

Question: Where have you taken your meals since you have been on the place?

Answer: Hartzell, Himes, and I "bach" it together on Hartzell place.

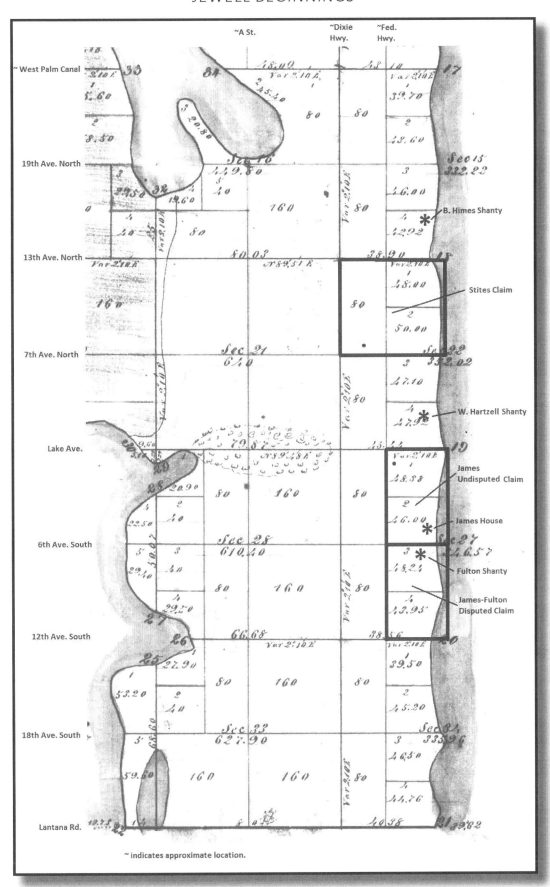

Homestead Map showing location of the members of the Pennsylvania colony
(in relation to the Jameses' land)

Question: How many living orange trees have you on your improvements?

Answer: I don't know. I have not examined them lately.

Question: How many did you plant?

Answer: I have only three trees and don't know which are limes or lemons.

Question: Why did you not make more improvements on your land?

Answer: Because I did not have the means to hire. It has been too warm, as I could not stand the heat and the mosquitoes.

There is no way to know which factors weighed on the judge's mind in rendering his decision, but he could hardly have been impressed by Fulton spending one night on the property and then rushing to Gainesville to challange the Jameses' long-standing but confusing claim. Judge Steward must have rolled his eyes at Fulton's comments about planting only three trees, his inability to tell a lime from a lemon, his cheesecloth shanty walls, hanging out with his buddies instead of working his land, and his disdain for Florida heat and mosquitoes.

A week later, on August 11, the judge ruled in the Jameses' favor and granted them title to the four waterfront lots. James paid the preemption fee of $1.25 per acre for 186.57 acres and received a U.S. government patent on his homestead.

In the wake of the court's decision, Fulton had to vacate the disputed property. Stites pursued his claim on the land a mile north of the Jameses and eventually received his patent. The other three Pennsylvania boys left the area, never to be heard from again. None chose to file for the land between Stites and James where Hartzell had his shanty. Four months later in December 1886, John Hoagland took possession, began building a substantial house with a long wharf, and making other improvements to the property.

With Bradley to the south and Hoagland to the north, the Jameses got along splendidly with their neighbors after Fulton left.

(Further detail on the land dispute and excerpts from the official court transcript can be found in Appendix C.)

Chapter 7: Zooming in on the Jameses' Neighbors

Of the men and families that tried their hand at homesteading on the lake in the 1880s and 1890s, many struggled in the tropical swelter for a few years and hightailed it back up North.

In contrast the Jameses, along with a small group of tough-minded pioneers, endured the primitive conditions, lack of roads, difficulty getting supplies, armies of mosquitoes, and heat and humidity. The successful settlers faced their challenges together and relied on each other. As a result they became close friends. A quick review of who came, who left, and who stayed demonstrates the transitory nature of the tiny Jewell community.

JAMES MURRIN

Murrin settled property on the west shore of Lake Worth near the current Lake Worth Bridge in 1878 and entered an initial claim with the Gainesville Land Office. The exact site is uncertain, as official records conflict, some indicating a location north of the current Lake Worth Bridge and others indicating south. It is not known how long he stayed or what improvements he might have made. Murrin never attempted to finalize his claim. In 1885, after the prescribed seven years, the land office declared the property vacant and open to any settler who would claim it.

Location: Waterfront near current Lake Worth Bridge

Acreage: Uncertain

Homestead legal description: Uncertain —variously described as Lots 3 & 4 of Section 22 or Lots 1 & 2 of Section 27

EDWIN RUTHVEN BRADLEY

Bradley was born in Chicago in March 1840, son of Asa F. Bradley. During the Civil War, he served in the Union Navy as a master's mate. (*Pioneer Days*, 18; *Tropical Frontier*, 67) He married Lydia J. Phillips in 1867. The 1870 census showed him living in Chicago's Ward 15, working as a "US Mail Agent." Bradley also had worked in Chicago as a newspaper reporter. Experience in both fields served him well as he found employment working for the U.S. Post Office Department and writing for the *Tropical Sun* after moving to Florida. (*Early Lantana*, 14, 20)

The Bradleys came to the lake about 1875. They moved from place to place for the first few years, often as caretakers for those away on business. (http://www.pbchistoryonline.org/page/desolation) In April 1878 (Bradley HA, 28), Bradley selected a homestead on the west shore, just across the lake from the Pierces on the north side of Lantana Point. The Bradleys were the first settlers to the Lantana area, several years before the arrival of Morris B. Lyman, Jacob T. Earnest, and other Lantana pioneers.

Location: Between 18th Avenue South and Lantana Road, on the lakefront east of Federal Highway

Acreage: 91

Homestead legal description: Section 34, Lots 3 & 4

On the 1880 U. S. Census. the Bradley family consisted of husband, wife and four children:

Edwin R., age 39, born in Illinois

Lydia, wife, age 39, born in England

Lewis E., son, age 12, born in Illinois

Guy M., son, age 10, born in Illinois

Flora M., daughter, age 5, born in Florida

Rose, daughter, age 2, born in Florida

The census form shows their immediate neighbors as Michael Merkel and Benjamin Lanehart. This demonstrates how sparse the population was at the time. Merkel lived two miles west on Lake Osborne, and Lanehart lived eight miles to the north, in what is now West Palm Beach.

In 1883, Bradley took a job as keeper of the New River House of Refuge, a government station on the beach for stranded sailors. The Pierces helped the Bradleys move in. Tragedy struck quickly. The family was afflicted with a mysterious illness that caused the body to "swell up as big as a barrel." Charles Pierce provides the heartbreaking details:

> Flora, who was 10 years old, died that afternoon only a few minutes after I got there. The workmen engaged in repairing the station made a coffin and she was buried the next day under a wide spreading sea grape tree in the hammock northwest of the house. Guy [who was also ill] swelled up so badly he could not walk; I carried him to the graveside. This sad incident took all the pleasure out of our lives for the time being. (PLSF, 164)

After a seven-month stint at New River, the Bradley family—Edwin, Lydia, and their three surviving children—moved back to Lake Worth.

Eager to promote settlement at the lake, Edwin befriended Samuel James in late 1884 and encouraged him to homestead on the west shore. He proved to be a good neighbor through the years and came to James's defense during "the fuss" with the Pennsylvania boys.

In July 1885, Bradley became the first Barefoot Mailman. Each week, he would sail to Palm Beach to pick up the mail, sail back to the south end of the lake, and then walk the 60 miles to Miami along the beach, sleeping either at the Houses of Refuge along the way or under the stars. It was a full-time job: three days down, three days back with Sundays off. At times, his eldest son, Louis, served as relief man. (PLSF, 195) The Bradleys kept the arduous route for a year and then passed the baton to the Pierces.

Edwin apparently was in no hurry to get title to his land. He lived on it for more than 10 years before filing a claim.

In his 1889 homestead application, he described his home as 16-by-20 foot, 1½-story frame building with a shingle roof, three doors, and six windows. He stated, "The old house has been removed." The land was said to be "scrub" level with "third rate pine," good only for firewood. He cultivated vegetables "more or less every season" and had planted 350 coconut trees, 125 guavas, and "a few limes, lemons and oranges." Bradley's occupation was "boating and farming." (Bradley HA, 29)

Lantana Point, December 1910—From Palm Beach Farms Company promotion pamphlet showing luxuriant coco palms. Lotus Cove is beyond the trees on the left. Courtesy of University of Florida Digital Collection: Miscellaneous Pamphlets and Brochures.

When the *Tropical Sun* began publication in Juno in 1891, Bradley wrote a neighborhood news column called "Lotus Cove," his nickname for the broad sweep of lakeshore north of Lantana Point. The column appeared weekly and related stories of the minor happenings on the west shore of Lake Worth "twixt Hypo & Jewell."

Bradley's writing style was cleverly whimsical, full of puns and offbeat literary allusions, and punctuated with Latin quotes that only the highly educated could understand. By contrast, the subject matter was mundane, covering everyday events. Out-of-town visitors, the weather, hunting and fishing exploits, and the doings of his children were standard fare. Bradley often reported on the progress of his vegetable-growing enterprise, particularly his eggplant and TOMS (tomatoes). The column customarily ended with an "R." or "Ruthven" sign-off.

Bradley was also quite fond of watercraft, often trading boats on a whim. He was one of the first to build a wharf on the lake, useful not only to send his tomatoes, eggplant, and other vegetables to market, but also for supply runs to Titusville or Jacksonville. Pierce describes Bradley's spontaneity on one such trip:

> **Bradley departed for Sand Point [Titusville] to renew their food supply. He returned home in a new boat, having traded his schooner for a twenty foot clinker-built sloop called Nautilus. (PLSF, 99)**

In another display of his diverse talents, Bradley served as Dade County Superintendent of Schools for two years starting in January 1893. Along with M. B. Lyman, he was instrumental in opening the first school in Lantana. The school was at the lakefront on the southern edge of the Bradley property. Edwin's youngest daughter, Rose, was 11 years old at the time and attended the first year of classes. *(Early Lantana, 50)*

COUNTY CORRESPONDENCE.

Interesting Items Gathered by Our Scribes Throughout The County.

LOTUS COVE.
(West Shore L. W. Twixt Hypo & Jewell.)

As the oldest settler on the West shore I propose arrogating to myself a local habitation and a name. That it is an appropriate name my past record fully justifies. For many years I carried the jack-knife, emblematic of the tired-est man on the coast, but—alas—I lost it some years ago—I think it was about the time Squre H. loomed up and located.

With the editor's permisson, I propose riding a free lance. With malice toward none and charity for all I shall take advantage of the license accorded by public consent, to the cartoonist—the spring poet and the would-like-to be funny man. There is no denying the fact now even that the S. P. is the funniest man of the three. From my coign of vantage I shall keep an eye on Hypo and if they ever let any news escape I will serve it up in my most inimical style. When my fleet-footed friend Burkhardt gives me a tib you shall all have some of the pie, and when Capt. Lyman slubhes down the the "Bessies" mast you shall be duly informed, and when that hotel is built at Jewell the fact shall be truly chronicled.

The days are made hideous by the ceaseless hammering all around and about—Mr. Lanbach and his new wharf to the north'rd, Capt. Lyman's new house to the south'rd and Will Moore's new kitchen over the way, all contribute their quota of confusion—and i wonder why it don't rain all the time.

Mr. Earnest and daughter are at Jewell. Miss Belle is contesting the Mc Donnell homestead. Now is the chance for Mack to do a gentlemanly act—let him relinquish to the fair contestant and everything will be lovely.

Guavas, melons and skeets are more than plentiful on this ranch.

Little Edgar Lyman had a very narrow escape from drowning last week, having fallen overboard from a skiff alongside the "Bessie B." He was rescued by Uncle Bob Fleming—cook on the "B."   RUTHVEN.

Bradley's first "Lotus Cove" column showcased his off-beat sense of humor, *Tropical Sun*, August 12, 1891.

After living on the lake for over 25 years, the Bradleys suddenly pulled up stakes and moved to the Keys. The announcement that a pillar of the community was leaving must have saddened the neighbors.

By 1910, the census shows they had moved for a second time, to Flamingo at the extreme southern tip of Florida. Edwin Bradley, once again, served as postmaster. Guy became the first warden in what is now Everglades National Park and was killed in the line of duty in 1905 while attempting to apprehend plume hunters. (*Early Lantana*, 14)

Edwin died May 18, 1915, in Homestead, Florida.

The first Lantana school house was located on the lakeshore at the east end of Lantana Road.

MICHAEL MERKEL (MERKLE, MERCKEL, MYRCKL)

Merkel was one of the earliest Lake Worth settlers. A German immigrant from Alsace-Lorraine, he was a bachelor and a close friend of Edwin Bradley. His name is spelled with many variants, including Merkle, Myrckel, and Myrckl.

Bradley recruited him to the lake area in November 1878. Charles Pierce described his arrival and settlement:

> Bradley [sailed] for Sand Point… and returned home in a new boat… A man named Michael Merkel returned with him. He was a German, but was French by birth because he was born in Alsace-Lorraine when it was French territory. He had lived in the United States since he was a small boy and had come to Florida from Chicago. He ate his meals with the Bradleys and slept on board the Nautilus for about two weeks. He was looking the country over and at last decided to locate on Lake Osborn, a large freshwater lake one and three-quarter miles west of Lake Worth.

> Merkel's first shack was of the most primitive type. It was made by placing pine and spruce poles on the ground and bringing them together at the top, tent fashion; these were covered with saw palmetto leaves for rain proofing. The shack was just large enough for his bed.

> Merkel contracted… for a fifteen-foot skiff to be delivered at his place on Lake Osborn… Up to this time no one from the settlements on Lake Worth had crossed this swamp to the woods beyond. (PLSF, 99–100)

Attracted to the solitary life, he created a Walden's Pond paradise for himself out at Lake Osborne. Like Thoreau, he lived off the land, mostly eating fish from the lake. Neighbors described him as a hermit who seldom spoke.

> Herr Merckel, our so-called hermit, has been on the sick list; a rash change of diet from fish to Japan beans was the cause.

Edwin Bradley's Lotus Cove column in the *Tropical Sun*, November 5, 1891.

Merkel is listed on the 1880 census as living next to Edwin Bradley. It's a bit of a mystery how the enumerator found him on the isolated shores of Lake Osborne, two miles west of Bradley. Others who lived inland, including the Jameses, were regularly missed by census takers as late as 1900 and 1910.

Rumor had it that Merkel was a defrocked priest. According to those who knew him well, he was highly educated, religious, and austere—traits that no doubt fed such rumors.

Mr. Merkle is a devote Catholic, and it used to be the delight of the children, myself included, to hide in the bushes as he passed, and listen to his chanting. Nowadays he works for other people and earns enough to buy some of the luxuries of life, of which, however, he is very sparing. His is a great reader and is exceedingly well informed on all subjects. He speaks several languages, but is very brief in conversation. (Voss, "Hypoluxo and Its History," *Lake Worth Historian*, 20.)

A friend and neighbor to Fannie and Samuel James, Merkel submitted a sworn statement on their behalf in their land dispute with Orville Fulton. His signature regularly appeared as a witness on the Jameses' legal documents with a Jewell, Florida, address.

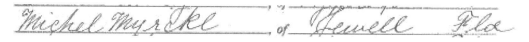

Mr. Merkel ended his days on Lake Osborne. One day he was found dead in his lean-to, with a pile of fish bones on one side of the cabin and coco plum pits on the other. (*Early Lantana*, 15)

ROBERT L. STRINGFELLOW AND WILLIAM N. WILSON— THE NEVER NEVER BOYS

Stringfellow and Wilson were land speculators who never lived on their Lake Worth property. Available records show their residence in Alachua County, Gainesville area. Bradley, who had been living on adjacent property since 1876, states that the land was empty and undeveloped. Under the preemption law, and without taking up residence on the land, they somehow managed to acquire a patent to the land between the Bradley and James properties.

The Stringfellow homestead application was stamped "swamp claim rejected" in August 1885 and then approved for settlement a month later.

County records do not sync with federal records, as they indicate that the Stringfellow property was auctioned off for unpaid 1884 taxes in March 1885, months before Stringfellow and Wilson gained legal title under the federal Homestead Act. H. B. Lum purchased the land at auction for $4.14.

T. B. Stringfellow, Robert's brother, also of Alachua County, repurchased the property from Mr. Lum in 1887, held it for some 27 years, and sold it to Palm Beach Farms Company (PBFC) in 1914 for a windfall price of $11,300.

Most of their homestead application has been lost, so it cannot be determined how Stringfellow and Wilson managed to acquire title without taking up residence on the land or shed any further light on the tax sale.

Location: 12th to 18th Avenues South, east of Federal

Acreage: 84.7

Legal description: Section 34, Lots 1 & 2

Settlement date: None

Claim filed: February 1884

Patent issued: December 10, 1885

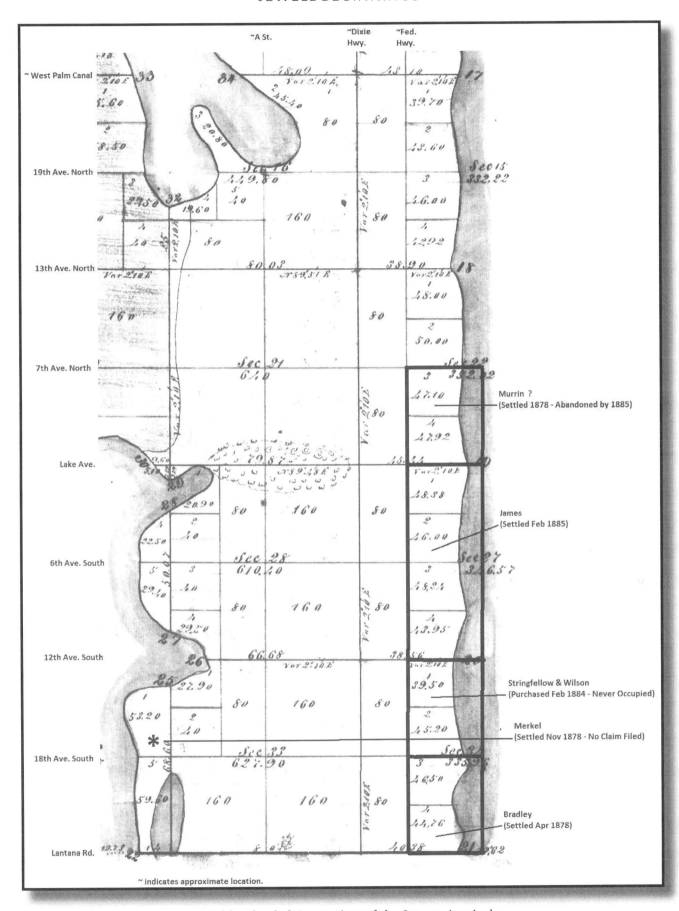

Neighbor land claims at time of the Jameses' arrival

OWEN LAUBACH

According to Charles Pierce, the German immigrant Owen Laubach built a home in 1885 on the water, north of Bradley and south of James. (PLSF, 196) Notices in the *Tropical Sun* provide confirmation of Laubach's presence on the waterfront by describing his construction of a wharf. Official records, however, describe Laubach's claim as the "west half of the southwest quarter of Section 34" which would have been inland, west of Bradley.

Pierce's placement of the Laubach home between the Jameses and Bradleys on the lakeshore raises the possibility that it may have been located on the Stringfellow property. Did Laubach communicate with Stringfellow and obtain his permission? With the lakeshore filling up, it would indeed seem strange for Laubach to build a frame home and a wharf as a squatter. Alternately, the Laubach place might have been on the northern end of the Bradley property. Perhaps Bradley's jestful complaint about hearing "ceaseless hammering" during the construction of Laubach's wharf was not much of an exaggeration.

> The days are made hideous by the ceaseless hammering all around and about—Mr. Laubach and his new wharf to the north'rd, Capt. Lyman's new house to the south'rd and Will Moore's new kitchen over the way, all contribute their quota of confusion—and i wonder why it don't rain all the time.

> Squire C. H. Hoagland, who may be seen daily skimming back and forth over the lake in the "Great Eastern," made us a short call and then went to inspect Mr. Laubach's new wharf which he pronounced good.

Tropical Sun, August 12 and August 19, 1891 – Laubach wharf

Regardless of the exact location of Laubach's home, the homestead claim he filed was for land to the west, within the current city limits of Lantana, not Lake Worth.

WILLIAM STEPHAN

Born in Germany about 1839 as a subject of King William, Stephan came to the lake at age 46 during the settler boomlet of 1885 and became a U.S. citizen in May 1891. While in Florida, Stephan lived as a bachelor and stated he was "single." Later it was learned that he had a wife and a married son back in Europe.

Homestead location: From 19th Avenue North to just north of the West Palm Beach C-51 canal (College Park).

Acreage: 163.3

Legal description: Lots 1 & 2 plus west half of northwest quarter Section 15

Settlement date: October 1885

Patent date: April 23, 1892

William Stephan's homestead on the west shore of Lake Worth transposed onto a 1931 map to show its location in relation to the future West Palm Beach canal and College Park neighborhood.

Stephan apparently had some cash to make substantial improvements to his homestead. He had a shingle-roofed house that was 12-by-16 feet, a packinghouse that was 10-by-15 feet, a well, a 200-foot-long wharf, and three acres in pineapples, fruit trees, and vegetables. After shipping crops for four consecutive seasons, his land was valued at $500. (Stephan HA, 11–13)

Stephan proved to be a good friend and neighbor to the Jameses. He filed a strong statement on their behalf during the land fuss, going so far as to accuse Dr. Stites and friends of "conspiring" to "defraud" the Jameses in July 1886. (James HA1, 9–10) Paradoxically, just a month prior, Stephan had served as a witness in support of Stites's homestead claim.

One can only guess at the nature of Stephan's relationship with Stites. Perhaps he wanted to be evenhanded in his relations with his neighbors, truthfully testifying to the presence of Stites on his land, despite his belief that Stites was not dealing honestly with James. Or, perhaps his opinion of Stites changed between June and July.

In any case, Stephan remained close to the Jameses. On August 3, 1891, William and Samuel, along with Michael Merkel, traveled together to the county clerk's office in Juno to give final proof on preemption claims for Stephan and James (James's second such claim). On that date, Merkel and Stephan gave testimony on James's behalf, and James and Merkel gave testimony on Stephan's behalf. In harmony with his preference for the simple life, Merkel never filed a claim of his own. All three give their place of residence as Jewell, Florida.

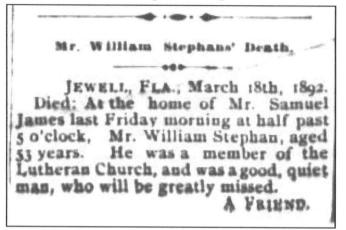

Tropical Sun, July 7, 1892—William Stephan obituary.

Stephan died in 1897. Apparently Fannie nursed him in his final days, as he passed away in the Jameses' home.

Another sign of the bonds of friendship between James and Stephan is evident in that James was named executor of Stephan's estate. In view of Samuel's inability to read, the appointment was a remarkable display of trust. James would be responsible to sell Stephan's land and distribute the proceeds to his heirs. Accordingly, notices were printed in the Juno paper, showing Samuel James as administrator for Stephan.

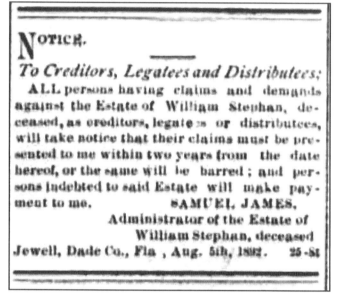

Tropical Sun, August 11, 1892—Samuel James gives notice to Stephan's creditors.

Almost five years later, the Stephan estate was not settled. Finally in the spring of 1897, Samuel listed the land to be sold at public auction.

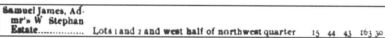

Tropical Sun, May 27, 1897—Legal notice of public auction.

Stephan denied having a family. Nevertheless, he named his wife, Marie Stephan, living in Eberswalde, Tudenstrasse, Germany, and a son, August Stephan, living in Bucharest, Romania, as his heirs. Apparently, the family instructed Samuel to auction the property, which took place in July 1897. Fannie must have been the winning bidder. County land sales records show she acquired the 163 waterfront acres for $500. Samuel forwarded the proceeds to Marie Stephan through the U.S. consulate in Berlin.

After gaining title, Fannie sold parcels to Charles C. Chillingworth, H. P. Bartholomew, Elizabeth J. Moore, Louis. W. Burkardt, and Mary L. Majewski, while retaining about 40 acres for her pineapple farm.

Chapter 8: Zooming in on the Pennsylvania Colony

> A colony from Pennsylvania settled along the west shore south of the little hammock that marked the halfway point between Hypoluxo and Palm Beach. There were four homesteads taken up by this group. (PLSF, 196)

The men Pierce refers to as "a colony from Pennsylvania" were Dr. Harry Stites, William Hartzell, Benjamin Himes, and Orville Fulton, the same men who were involved in the land dispute with the Jameses. Diplomatically, Pierce makes no mention of the controversy.

The arrival of new settlers was generally welcomed in the lake community. Everyone was supportive of growth and development. Nevertheless, the arrival of the four Pennsylvania boys and the subsequent land fuss with the Jameses was a notable exception. Despite any racial overtones that the dispute may have had, the neighbors, without exception, took the Jameses' side in the controversy. The newcomers were accused of fraud and ultimately thwarted in their attempted land grab.

The controversy is puzzling in several ways. First off, Dr. Stites was a man of excellent reputation, as were his companions. Secondly, their sworn testimony appears to have been truthful, even admitting to limited improvements on the disputed land, such as planting only three trees, which hindered their claim. Nevertheless, they did show bad faith at a number of points during "the fuss," such as Fulton filing a counterclaim when he knew Samuel James's earlier claim had been rejected for a simple clerical error, as well as lying to Samuel James's hired man about James having abandoned his claim and encouraging the man to file a claim of his own.

As it turned out, the Pennsylvania colony did not hold together. Three of the men were gone within a year. Stites proved to be the only one of the four to stay on his homestead, which he did with several prolonged absences until 1896.

DR. HARRY STITES

Stites was born in Dauphin County, Pennsylvania, on June 28, 1854, to Samuel Stites (1816–1882) and Catherine Matter Stites (1817–1885). The 1870 census showed him at 16 years old as a pharmacist's apprentice, his occupation described as "learning the drug business." Stites received his doctor of medicine degree from the University of Pennsylvania in 1876.

On July 4 of that same year, the exact date of the U.S. centennial, he married Mazie J. Singer at Newport United Methodist Parish. They had three children: Mabel (born 1878), Lillian (born 1881), and George (born 1886).

From 1876 to 1881, Dr. Stites practiced medicine in Newport, Pennsylvania.

In 1881 he moved to Sioux Falls, South Dakota. Shortly thereafter he was appointed government physician for the Indian Agency, serving first at the Black Foot Indian Agency in Montana and later at the Lower Bruley Sioux Reservation in South Dakota.

In July 1885, he resigned his position at the Indian Agency and took his wife and children to Pennsylvania to stay with his mother. (Kelke, *History of Dauphin County, Pa,* 83–84.)

In September 1885, leaving his family up North, he traveled to Florida with three long-time Pennsylvania friends. While there, he entered a preemption claim on the lake, built a palmetto house, and planted a citrus grove of more than 500 trees. Stites would have been 31 years old.

Homestead location: 13th Avenue North to 7th Avenue North, Dixie Highway to the Intracoastal

Acreage: 178

Legal description: Lots 1 & 2 and west half of the northwest quarter of Section 22

The portion of the Lake Worth Municipal Golf Course north of the clubhouse would have been the eastern part of the Stites property.

Stites's homestead application, on file at the National Archives, provides illuminating details of his life on the lake. While looking for additional land for his Pennsylvania friends, he orchestrated the land fuss, supporting Orville Fulton's challenge to the James claim.

In October 1885, Stites chartered the schooner *C. B. Smith*, sailing to Jacksonville to meet his family and purchase provisions for the improvement of his claim. Included in the shipment were "lumber, building materials, furniture and household supplies." Upon his return, Stites went to work building a wood frame home for his wife and two children, "1 ½ stories, 14 x 28 feet with a one story 12 x 12 foot addition," according to his homestead application. (Stites HA, 34)

Attached to his application was a photograph of the home. Unfortunately, the photo has severely deteriorated over time. The roofline, eves, shadows of the entry door, and window barely show. As poorly preserved as it is, this is the only photograph of any pre-1900 structure in the Jewell area.

Caption reads: Photograph of the Stites house at Lake Worth (Preemption Claim No 1521).
Courtesy of the National Archive.
The outlines of the house, entry door, and window have been retouched.

Like so many of his fellow South Florida preemptors, Dr. Stites did not remain on his homestead for long. By July 20, 1886, the Stiteses were back up north, as can be seen from the fact that Dr. Stites sent a notarized letter from Newport in behalf of Orville Fulton's land claim on that date. In his letter, he explained that he took his pregnant wife north "to be confined."

> **As his wife, not having been stout and having had one hemorrhage of the lungs, and as he is a Physician and had attended to her in her previous confinements, he does not feel it advisable to leave her in the hands of a strange Physician. (Stites HA, 52–53)**

The Stiteses' youngest child, George, was born in Pennsylvania in July 1886.

Testifying to Stites' stature in the Harrisburg community, the Notary Public wrote:

> Dr. Harry Stites, who has been well known to me for 15 years past, and who is a Physician in good standing and a man of good character and reputation and who is worthy of belief. (Stites HA, 51)

Stites continued to shuttle between Pennsylvania and Florida. From 1887 to 1893, he practiced medicine in Harrisburg, out of an office at Sixth and Reily streets. During that period, he also served as examining surgeon for the Harrisburg pension board.

While practicing in Harrisburg, Stites retained his foothold in Florida, continuing to hold title to his homestead and to arrange for fellow Pennsylvanians to farm it.

Mr. James F. Creamer and wife, of Harrisburg, Pa., arrived at Jewell on Sunday, and will live in Dr. Stite's house and start a pineapple plantation. Still they come.

Tropical Sun, **September 30, 1891.**

In August 1893, Stites was drawn to return south. He conceived a novel plan to travel from landlocked Harrisburg to Florida by water. After purchasing a sail boat in Havre de Grace, Maryland, he had it shipped to Harrisburg, where it was floated in the old Pennsylvania Canal at Maclay Street. With his wife and three children on board, the boat was towed down the canal until it reached the open sea. He, then, sailed it down the coast arriving in Florida nine weeks later.

The Stiteses moved back into their Jewell homestead, but once again got itchy feet. Within the year, they moved to West Palm Beach just as the city was beginning to form. Using his ever-present social skills, Stites was promptly elected president of the Village Improvement Association and became one of the signers of West Palm Beach's incorporation petition. ("Town's First Town Hall," *Palm Beach Post*, October 9, 1949.)

Once in the growing metropolis, Dr. Stites apparently cooled on the idea of being a farmer. In February 1894, he mortgaged his Jewell property to Elizabeth Moore for $2,000 and opened one of West Palm Beach's first medical offices.

Stites's ad appeared weekly in the *Tropical Sun* during 1894 and 1895.

HARRY STITES, B. E., M. D.

Graduate of the University of Pennsylvania

Offers his services to the citizens of Lake Worth and vicinity, as Physician and Surgeon. Office and Residence at West Palm Beach.   10-12-94

37

Stites continued to win one honor after another in his profession, serving as examining surgeon for the Florida East Coast Railway (FEC) under Henry M. Flagler and as a delegate to the National Medical Convention in Chicago in 1895, representing the Medical Society of Florida.

Within two years, Stites' restlessness cropped up yet again. In 1896, the family returned to Philadelphia and Dr. Stites went back to the university to pursue a postgraduate course at the Polyclinic College of Medicine. After graduation, he returned to his Harrisburg practice, being prominently associated with the Free and Accepted Masons, Knights Templar, and numerous other civic organizations.

Meanwhile, Stites's adventuring and interrupted medical career must have put a strain on family finances. His Florida mortgage loan was scheduled for repayment in 1897, but he defaulted and eventually lost the land to foreclosure after a circuit court proceeding in 1899. Court records show he owed $2,430 in unpaid principal and interest.

In 1900, to advance himself further in his profession, Stites took an extended trip abroad and visited the principal hospitals of Europe.

His passport, obtained for the trip, provided his physical description:

Age: 45 years	Mouth: Small
Stature: 5 feet, 4 ½ inches	Chin: Square
Forehead: High	Hair: Brown mixed with gray
Eyes: Light blue	Complexion: Light
Nose: Straight	Face: Round

Fortuitously, a photograph of Stites, in his later years, has survived. Similar to the photo of his house, this is the only known picture of a Jewell settler.

Dr. Harry Stites with wife, Mazie, at unspecified ceremony, *circa* 1903. Courtesy of his grandniece, Kathy Quin.

In January 1906, he left Harrisburg for a tour of the south. Two days after arriving in Cuba, he died suddenly of pernicious anemia.

Stites's life shows him to have been an intelligent man, sociable, and quick at making friends while rebuilding his career through a series of impulsive moves across the county. His conspiracy against the Jameses seems out of character and did not ingratiate him with his Jewell neighbors. What happened to his fine house and extensive orange groves is unknown.

ORVILLE H. FULTON

Orville H. Fulton was born *circa* 1861. Like the other members of the Pennsylvania colony, Fulton's family belonged to the Newport United Methodist Parish. The 1870 census shows him at age nine living in Newport with his mother, "Cath Fulton." No father is listed.

Arrival at the lake: September 1885

Homesite: Waterfront at Sixth Avenue South

Legal description of claim: Lots 3 & 4, Section 27

Claim rejected: August 1886

Fulton would have been 24 years old at the time of his Florida adventure. Apparently, the Florida climate and rough pioneer life did not agree with him. After losing his land dispute with Sam James, he did not attempt another claim, although plenty of land was still available in the area. Thereafter, Fulton disappeared from the South Florida scene.

WILLIAM E. HARTZELL

Hartzell (sometimes spelled Hartzwell) was born around 1852 to John and Augusta Hartzell. He was the least heard-from member of the Pennsylvania colony. He did not testify or witness any of his Pennsylvania friends' homestead claims.

Church records from 1869 show that he, too, was a member of the Newport United Methodist Parish. The 1880 census records list him living at home, still single in Newport Borough, Perry County, Pennsylvania. His name next shows up in the 1910 census, living in Harrisburg, age 58, having been married to "Katie E." for 30 years. The couple had two older children still at home, Frank, 27, and Ada, 20. Hartzell's occupation is listed as "Keeping Oil House" for "Rail Road."

Piecing together the above data, it appears that Hartzell got married shortly after the 1880 census at age 18 and had a child (Frank) three years later. He would have been about 23 years old when he came to Florida in 1885 while his wife and child remained up north. Perhaps he, like many others of that early Homestead Era, could not convince his wife to join him in harsh, swampy, buggy South Florida. After a few months of adventuring, he returned to Pennsylvania.

BENJAMIN J. HIMES

Himes was born in 1861 to Benjamin F. and Rachel Himes. His father is listed as a member of the Newport United Methodist Parish in 1865 when he was only 4 years old and Ben's name shows up on the Sunday School register four years later when he was 8.

Himes came to South Florida as a young man, age 24, presumably single. What little information exists on his brief stay in Lake Country comes from his August 1886 circuit court testimony on Fulton's behalf. Himes gave his residence as "Lake Worth, Dade County, Florida" and stated he lived on property adjoining Stites. (Stites HA, 26) Himes had known Stites for 15 years and Orville Fulton for over 20 years. (James HA1, 83) There is no record of Himes having filed a preemption or homestead claim on his own behalf.

Chapter 9: The Founding of Jewell

After living on Lake Worth for four years, Fannie took the step she is most famous for: opening the Jewell Post Office. It was to become the focus of the small rural community that tried and failed to get a footing between 1889 and 1903.

The process for creating a post office required significant paperwork. There were lengthy forms to fill out, an official survey of the proposed post office site to secure, and the need to obtain approval of a neighboring postmaster.

Fannie recruited George Potter to do her survey and Hannibal Pierce, then Hypoluxo postmaster, to sign off on her application.

Imagine the scene: Samuel rowing across the lake in his small boat, four miles north to the Potter home and then three miles south to the Pierce home, Fannie seated proudly in the stern, her precious paperwork tucked under her arm.

At that time, there were five post offices on the lake. North to south, east to west they were: Oak Lawn (now Riviera Beach), Lake Worth (at the northern end of Palm Beach), Palm Beach, Figulus, and Hypoluxo.

CHOOSING A NAME FOR THE POST OFFICE

A curious discovery on Fannie's post office application is that two other names were under consideration and rejected before Jewell was finally settled on. Selection of the name was important, as it would not only become the address for U.S. mail but also would be the name of the community.

The first name to appear on the application was "La Paz," meaning "peace" in Spanish. The name captures the natural tranquility and beauty of the place's isolated location. It also may allude to Fannie's comfort at having distanced herself from the racial chaos of their former homes in Tallahassee and Cocoa.

However, La Paz did not stick. Even before the application was filed, it was replaced with "Deer Park," which likewise suggests a place of quietude where gentle animals could browse in a restful, park-like environment. Early descriptions of the area attest to the appropriateness of such a name. Both the Pierce and Henshall journals report a prolific deer population. Large bucks grazed within a few yards of the waterline.

The southwest shore of the lake was especially well-known as a good place for deer hunting. Pierce reports numerous successful trips across the water in his small rowboat. Even the Seminoles were said to have gone out of their way to hunt there.

Despite whatever attractiveness Deer Park had, that name did not stick either. On page one of the post office application, Fannie wrote but then crossed it out.

The name finally submitted to and approved by the U.S. Post Office Department was Jewell, spelled with two *l*'s. The reason for the choice is a matter of speculation, but wordplay on the Jameses' nickname, "Black Diamonds," is an obvious possibility.

EXAMINING THE JEWELL POST OFFICE APPLICATION

There were several pages to the post office application form. The first page was called the Location Page, as it identified where the new proposed post office was to be located in relation to existing post offices and carrier routes. The Diagram Page or Map Page provides a visual aid to both post office officials and the mail-carrier as to where the new post office would be in relation to other nearby stops on the postal route.

ZOOMING IN ON THE LOCATION PAGE

Evidently, the form was not filled out at one sitting but gradually over a number of weeks. The application date at the top of the form is given as June 15, 1889, but the signature date at the bottom was July 9, 1889. During this time, Fannie was apparently gathering the necessary supporting documents and debating the name of the post office.

The post office received and stamped the form on July 15.

The proposed post office was to be located on route 16235, which ran from Jupiter to Hypoluxo, three times per week. The Figulus Post Office was nearest to the north at 4 miles away. Hypoluxo was nearest to the south at 3¼ miles away. Adding Jewell to the route was said not to increase the mail carrier's travel, since the new post office would be on the route between the two existing offices.

Fannie's mailing address was given as "care of the postmaster of Hypoluxo," who was Hannibal Pierce. Pierce also signed the application, verifying its accuracy.

A careful inspection of the handwriting shows that in all likelihood two different people filled out parts of the form, as two distinct styles are evident. Note the different forms of the capital *Hs* and *Fs*. (See next page.) Our best guess is that Fannie filled out most of the form and Hannibal Pierce added in items that Fannie may not have known, such as the name "Henry E Roop," the mail-carrier. Compare the ornate and simpler forms of the capital *Hs* in "Henry," "Hannibal," and "Hypoluxo" as they appear in various places on the document.

Two other significant facts can be gleaned from this historical document. First, the location of the first Jewell Post Office is given, not on the land to the west where Samuel would later be buried but on the waterfront in Lot 2, Section 27, Township 44, which was the Jameses' first homestead.

The other significant fact was that when asked about the number of people to be served by the proposed post office, Fannie's diminutive answer was "13."

As small as that number is, it is difficult to come up with names of 13 people who are known to have lived in Jewell in 1889. (Later, while reviewing the roster of nearby homesteaders, an attempt will be made to reproduce Fannie's count.)

(No. 1011—New Series—January 1, 1884.) (LOCATION PAPER.)

Post Office Department,

OFFICE OF THE FIRST ASSISTANT P. M. GENERAL.

WASHINGTON, D.C., June 15, 188 9.

Sir: Before the Postmaster General decides upon the application for the establishment of a post office at La Paz Deer Park, County of Dade, State of Fla., it will be necessary for you to carefully answer the subjoined questions, get a neighboring postmaster to certify to the correctness of the answers, and return the location paper to the Department, addressed to me. If the site selected for the proposed office should not be on any mail route now under contract, only a "Special Office" can be established there, to be supplied with mail from some convenient point on the nearest mail route by a special carrier, for which service a sum equal to two-thirds of the amount of the salary of the postmaster at such office will be paid.

You should inform the contractor, or person performing service for him, of this application, and require him to execute the inclosed certificate as to the practicability of supplying the proposed office with mail, and return the same to the Department.

Very respectfully,

J. S. ⟨signature⟩
First Assistant Postmaster General.

To Mr. Fannie A. James

care of the Postmaster of Hypoluxo O. , who will please forward to him.

STATEMENT.

The proposed office to be called Deer Park Jewell.

Select a short name for the proposed office, which, when written, will not resemble the name of any other post office in the State.

It will be situated in the Lot 2 quarter of Section 27, Township 44 (North or South), Range 43 (East or West), in the County of Dade, State of Florida.

It will be on or near route No. 16235, being the route from Jupiter to Hypoluxo, on which the mail is now carried three (3) times per week.

The contractor's name is Henry E. Roth.

Will it be directly on this route? — Ans. Yes

If not, how far from, and on which side of it? — Ans.

How much will it INCREASE the travel of the mail one way each trip? — Ans. Not any

Where will the mail leave the present route to supply the proposed office? — Ans.

Where intersect the route again? — Ans.

What post office will be left out by this change? — Ans. None

If not on any route, is a "Special Office" wanted? — Ans. To be supplied from

The name of the nearest office to the proposed one, on the same route, is Figulus

its distance is seven (7) miles in a Northerly direction from the proposed office.

The name of the nearest office on the same route, on the other side, is Hypoluxo

its distance is 3 ¼ miles in a Southerly direction from the proposed office.

The name of the nearest office to the proposed one, not on this route, is

distance by the most direct road .... miles in a .... direction from the proposed office.

The name of the most prominent river near it is

The name of the nearest creek is

The proposed office will be .... miles from said river, on the

side of it, and will be .... miles from said nearest creek, on the .... side of it.

The name of the nearest railroad is

If on the line of or near a railroad, on which side will the office be located; how far from the track; and what is, or will be, the name of the station? — Ans.

What will be the distance from the proposed site to the nearest flag station? — Ans.

State name of station:

What will be the distance from the proposed site to the nearest station at which mail trains make regular stops? — Ans.

State name of station:

If the proposed office is located where it can be supplied from a crane or flag station, or located over ½ mile from the station where mail trains make regular stops, will the mail be carried to and from the proposed office without expense to the Department? — Ans.

If it be a village, state the number of inhabitants. — Ans.

Also, the population to be supplied by the proposed office. — Ans. 15

A diagram, or sketch from a map, showing the position of the proposed new office, with neighboring river or creek, roads, and other post offices, towns, or villages near it, will be useful, and is therefore desired.

A correct map of the locality might be furnished by the county surveyor, but this must be without expense to the Post Office Department.

ALL WHICH I CERTIFY to be correct and true, according to the best of my knowledge and belief, this 9th day of July, 188 9.

(Sign full name.) Mrs. Fannie A. James Proposed P. M.

I CERTIFY that I have examined the foregoing statement, and that it is correct and true to the best of my knowledge and belief.

Hannibal D. Pierce ⟨signature⟩
Postmaster at Hypoluxo.

(OVER.)

ZOOMING IN ON THE DIAGRAM PAGE

County surveyor, George Potter, drew the survey map on the Diagram Page at Fannie's request. At that time, he lived at Figulus, on the opposite side of the lake from the Jameses and 4 miles north.

The map identifies the location of the proposed post office in relation to the then-existing postal stops on the lake. This document, once again, shows the series of proposed names for Fannie's post office. Although difficult to read, "La Paz" can be seen in the center of the page to the right of an arrow. Potter also refers to the site as "La Paz" in his written certification below the map. Yet in the heading at the top of the page, the proposed PO is called "Deer Park." A nearly illegible note on the map, perhaps in Fannie's handwriting, replaces "La Paz" with "Deer Park."

Vertically, on the upper right, the final approved name, "Jewell, Fla," appears.

DIAGRAM PAGE

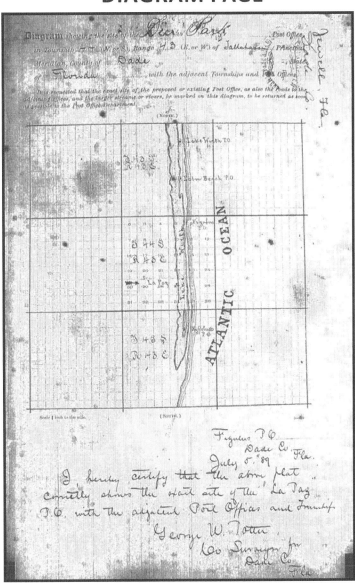

Survey map, prepared by George W. Potter, dated July 5, 1889. The heading calls the site "Deer Park" while the map and note at the bottom use the name "La Paz."

LA PAZ

Although the name "La Paz" was never officially submitted to the Post Office Department, there is other evidence that it was in common use for at least a brief period. A map of the lake on the back of the stationery of the Cocoanut Grove Hotel in Palm Beach shows La Paz at the appropriate spot on the southwest shore.

The map was updated frequently as the lake population grew. La Paz, as well as Oak Lawn and Cocoanut Groves were handwritten, indicating frequent updates to an older typeset map. A later version of the stationery map replaced La Paz with Jewell.

The sales blurb on the stationery illustrates the promotional attitudes and expectations of the early homestead community. The advantages of the lake's unique location are touted in superlative terms.

> The Lake lies parallel with the Ocean Beach; it is about 22 miles long and averages a mile wide; is connected to the Ocean by an inlet… The Gulf Stream comes nearer the land here than at any other point, making it the

> MOST TROPICAL PART OF THE STATE, AND INSURING THE MOST EVEN TEMPERATURE…

> This is probably the best point in Florida for hunting Deer, Turkey, etc., and Fishing in both salt and fresh water. Game and Fish in abundance.

> THERE ARE GOOD HOTELS, STORES, ETC.

In this promotional context, every bit of progress, even the establishment of a tiny post office to serve 13 people, was worthy of announcement.

DEER PARK

The name "Deer Park" appears on both pages of Fannie's post office application and apparently was under serious consideration, at least for a brief time, although the name appears in no other historical records or documents.

Deer Park would have been an appropriate name. Charles Pierce, who lived across the lake, paints a vivid picture of the abundance of wildlife on both sides of the lake, but the deer appear to have been especially abundant on the west shore. Among his many hunting stories, Charles describes an outing across the lake with his father, Hannibal, about a mile south of Fannie's would-be Deer Park.

> One afternoon about a week later, father proposed we go deer hunting along the west shore. Walking south along the lake, I stayed close to his heels. As we reached the top of a ridge near a deer trail he brought his gun to aim and fired both barrels. When the smoke of his gun cleared away I had a clear view and saw two deer running gaily away to the west with their white flags flying…. As I went out through the trees I saw right before me, not a hundred feet away, a great big buck, quietly feeding along the shore…. The ground was fairly cut up with deer tracks. (PLSF, 139–140)

Consideration of the name Deer Park, however, appears to have been short-lived. George Potter, as county surveyor, signed off on his map on July 5, when La Paz was still in the running. On July 9, when Fannie signed her application, she apparently crossed out "Deer Park" and replaced it with "Jewell." The only conclusion that can be drawn is that the favored choice for a name changed from La Paz to Deer Park to Jewell in a matter of four days.

Palm Beach, Dade County, Florida,

Is situated on the east shore of LAKE WORTH, lying between the Lake and Atlantic Ocean. The Lake lies parallel with the Ocean Beach; it is about 22 miles long and averages about a mile wide; is connected with the Ocean by an inlet, and is not over three-quarters of a mile at any point from the Ocean. It is the most eastern point of Florida, being 100 miles farther east than Jacksonville, and nearly 300 miles farther south. The Gulf Stream comes nearer the land here than at any other point, making it the

Most Tropical Part of the State, and insuring the most Even Temperature.

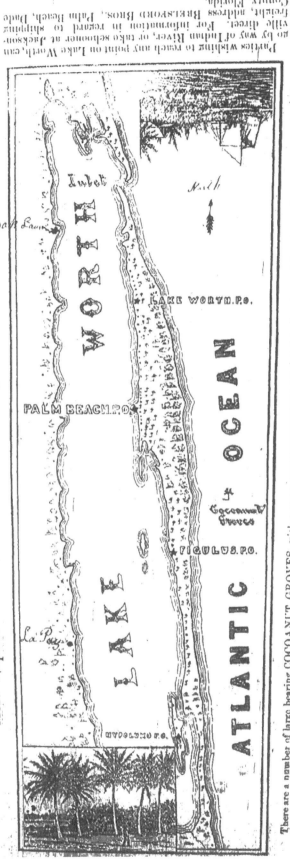

Parties wishing to reach any point on Lake Worth, can go by way of Indian River, or take schooner at Jacksonville direct. For information in regard to shipping freight, address Brelsword Bros., Palm Beach, Dade County, Florida.

There are a number of large bearing COCOANUT GROVES, with a great many young groves coming into bearing. Also, all other Tropical Fruits, such as Mangoes, Guava, Sapadillos, Sugar Apples, Alligator Pears, Almonds, Figs, Dates, Pineapples, Bananas, Mammee Apples, Limes, Oranges, Lemons, Citrons, and a great many other Tropical Fruit and Flowering Trees and Plants. A large business is done in Garden Truck each winter.

This is, probably, the best point in Florida for hunting Deer, Turkey, etc., and Fishing in both salt and fresh water. Game and Fish in abundance.

THERE ARE GOOD HOTELS, STORES, ETC.

(OVER.)

45

JEWELL

Surprisingly, the post official application was a working document that was revised and submitted with crossed-out words and corrections. In some cases, the new name simply was written next to the older one without crossing the replaced name out. The resulting ambiguity must have caused some confusion when the application was reviewed by the Post Office Department. The vertical notation "Jewell, Fla" in the upper right-hand margin of the Location Page was likely a note by an official clarifying the final approved name.

When it was all said and done, the Jewell Post Office officially opened on August 22, 1889.

Updated Cocoanut Grove stationery map showing Jewel Post Office with "PO" handwritten. Note the handwritten entry "Lantana PO," indicating this revision of the map was made sometime after the Lantana office opened in 1892.

Chapter 10:
Samuel James Subdivides His Land

Land speculation in South Florida is not a new phenomenon. In the 1880s, when the population of the entire county stood at a few hundred, landowners were already creating subdivisions and selling lots for winter homes and parcels for speculative investors. On Palm Beach, the Brelsford brothers were among the first to become real estate developers and to actively market a subdivision, which they named "Atlantic City."

Samuel and Fannie James were quick to see the profit potential in land sales. In May 1887, less than a year after the court had settled their land dispute with Fulton in their favor, they began selling off acreage in subdivided parcels.

The first two sales were 5 acres to Harry Griswold and 20 acres to Owen Porter at a standard $20 per acre.

Griswold was apparently a friend of the Jameses. Samuel had left him in charge of his place when he went to take care of Fannie in Cocoa two years earlier. It seems likely that Griswold lived on or near the Jameses' homestead. The location of the parcel, as identified by the old metes and bounds survey system, was situated south of the Jameses on Lot 4, an odd "3.16 chains" (208.5 feet) wide. The measurement might make sense if Griswold had already built a home and cleared land that the lot line was designed to encompass.

> The land from the inlet for some distance north is owned by Dr. J. H. Brelsford. He having had several applications for land there, has had it all laid off in lots of good width running through from the lake on the west to the ocean beach on the east, thus giving a frontage either way as desired, and has decided to put the lots on the market, hence he will sell one or more lots to any one who wishes them, and give perfect title, subject to no restrictions whatever. So any one can build or not, just as they please or merely purchase for speculation, its all one to the doctor. "Atlantic City" is the name.

Notice in *Florida Star*, Titusville, Florida, April 11, 1889.

Owen Porter was another personal friend of Samuel and Fannie. Even though he lived in Palm Beach at the time, he bought 20 acres from them, presumably for speculation. Later, Porter moved to Jewell and took up a 169-acre homestead claim. Samuel, using his carpentry skills, helped Porter build his house there, about a mile and a half north of the Jameses.

Interestingly, the Jameses sold a third parcel to Dorinda Brelsford the following November. Dorinda was the mother of Edmund and John. The Brelsford brothers were prominent in the Palm Beach community and were also active in selling real estate. They also operated a general store and a shipping company. Dorinda was as equally business minded as her sons, buying and selling property all around the lake.

In total, the Jameses sold eight parcels totaling over 180 acres between 1887 and 1890 for a substantial $5,000 in profits. They held on to one 6-acre waterfront lot.

By August 1889, when the Jewell Post Office opened, most of the property to the south of the Jameses' place had been sold.

The land to the north of the Jameses was sold as one 78-acre parcel to Josiah Sherman the following year. The Jameses got a fantastic price for this last parcel. Land sales were most generally priced at $20 per acre, with Edwin Dewey paying $25. But the Sherman purchase came to over $42 per acre for a whopping total of $3,300. It is natural to wonder what was behind such a large price difference.

Factors that may have contributed to Sherman's higher price include:

- Lot 1 was the last large acreage available of Jameses' lots on the waterfront, which naturally would have increased its value.

- Lot 1 contained the largest number of acres cleared. The Hoagland sketch in Samuel James's homestead application shows that most of Lot 1 had been cleared by 1886, four years previous to the sale. It is likely that this parcel was the field that James had been cultivating and was already generating income from pineapple, vegetable, or citris production.

- Another possibility is that there already existed a house, a barn, a wharf, or other improvements on the property.

In view of their financial success, the Jameses started to look for more land to acquire. In 1888, Samuel selected a 160-acre parcel to the west and began to improve it in preparation for making a second preemption claim.

In 1892, the Jameses sold off one additional lot on the water, a third of an acre lot measuring 50 by 300 feet, which they split off from their six acres. (Today this is the site of a well-known private residence at 5th Avenue South and Lakeside Drive, popularly called the "Birthday Cake Castle" for the stained glass window of cake and candles in its three-story tower.) The lot was initially sold to Amanda Malvina Moore of Pike County, Alabama, and was combined with 10 acres to the west on the Jameses' second preemption.

The purpose of this unique transaction is a matter of speculation. Apparently, Amanda Moore was a friend of Fannie's. Perhaps the two women wanted to be neighbors. (1870 census records show an Amanda Moore, age 11, of African American descent living in Pike County, Alabama. This would make her 33 at the time of the property sale.) Or, perhaps, in emulation of what was happening in Palm Beach and Lantana, the Jameses were considering forming a town of Jewell with smaller residential lots.

In any case, this lot was by far the smallest acreage of all the Jameses' land sales. Moore turned around and sold both properties to Dorinda Brelsford a year later.

The sale to Moore was the last of the sales of any portion of the Jameses' preemption claims. Nevertheless, then continued to deal in real estate by acquiring and later selling parcels bought from the William Stephan estate to their north and the Gudmundsen homestead to the south.

The accompanying map and chart show the locations and supplies details on the Jameses' first set of land dealings.

JAMES PROPERTY SALES
ABOUT 168 ACRES

On the Intracoastal, south of the Lake Worth Bridge
Lake Avenue to 12th Avenue South

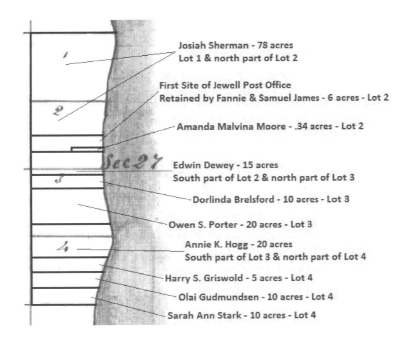

Josiah Sherman - 78 acres
Lot 1 & north part of Lot 2

First Site of Jewell Post Office
Retained by Fannie & Samuel James - 6 acres - Lot 2

Amanda Malvina Moore - .34 acres - Lot 2

Edwin Dewey - 15 acres
South part of Lot 2 & north part of Lot 3

Dorlinda Brelsford - 10 acres - Lot 3

Owen S. Porter - 20 acres - Lot 3

Annie K. Hogg - 20 acres
South part of Lot 3 & north part of Lot 4

Harry S. Griswold - 5 acres - Lot 4

Olai Gudmundsen - 10 acres - Lot 4

Sarah Ann Stark - 10 acres - Lot 4

Samuel and Fannie A. James Purchases and Sales of Homestead Property
in Sections 27-28, Township 44S, Range 43E

Purchases From:	Acres	Recorded	Location	Recorded Price
US Government	186.57	Nov 8, 1886	Section 27, Lots 1, 2, 3, 4	$ 233.21
US Government	160	Oct 19, 1891	Straddling Sections 27 - 28	$ 200.00
Totals	346.57			$ 433.21

Sales To:				
Henry S. Griswold	5	May 31, 1887	in Section 27, Lot 4	$ 100.00
Owen S. Porter	20	May 31. 1887	in Section 27, Lot 3	$ 400.00
Dorinda H. Brelsford	10	Nov 11, 1887	in Section 27, Lot 3	$ 200.00
Edwin D. Dewey	15	March 3, 1888	in Section 27, straddling Lots 2 - 3	$ 375.00
Annie K. Hogg	20	April 4, 1888	in Section 27, straddling Lots 3 - 4	$ 400.00
Sarah Ann Stark	10	March 15, 1889	in Section 27, Lot 4	$ 200.00
Olai Gudmusen	10	Nov 1, 1889	in Section 27, Lot 4	$ 200.00
Josiah Sherman	78.38	June 9. 1890	Section 27, Lots 1 -2	$ 3,300.00
Amanda Malvina Moore	10.34	Oct 25, 1892	in Section 27 (10 acres), plus Lot 2 parcel	$ 300.00
Palm Beach Farm Company	156	Dec 3, 1910	Straddling Sections 27 - 28, plus Lot 2 parcel	$ 1,124.00 (1)
Totals	334.72 (2)			$ 6,599.00
James' Net Profit				$ 6,165.79 (3)

(1) Fannie James received 2 notes from Palm Beach Farms Co of $562 each, payable at the close of one and two years, respectively.

(2) Acreage figures do not reconcile as some contracts use exact acreage following intracoastal shoreline, others use squared-off approximations.

(3) Equivalent to over $150,000 in 2012 dollars.

Chapter 11: Zooming in on the Site of the First James Homestead

With the information available online and in digitized governmental records, the site of the Jameses' first Lake Worth home, which doubled as the 1889 Jewell Post Office can be accurately identified. Previous published accounts have placed the site west on L Street or otherwise made a vague reference to the waterfront without naming a specific site.

Several independent pieces of evidence point to a site between 4th and 5th Avenues South on the Intracoastal.

Evidence #1

The Jewell Post Office application specifies Lot 2 of Section 27, which would be between 3rd and 6th Avenues South and east of Federal Highway.

It will be situated in the *Lot 2* quarter of Section ....*27*...., Township ...*44*...

Evidence #2

The surveyor's map from the Lantana Post Office application places Jewell on the waterfront in Section 27, in the SE corner of the NW quarter section, about equivalent to Lot 2.

Wavy north-south line represents the waterfront.

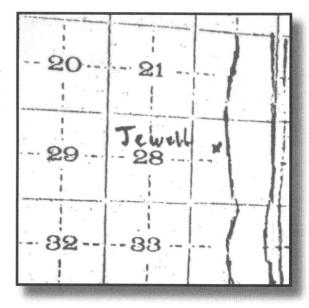

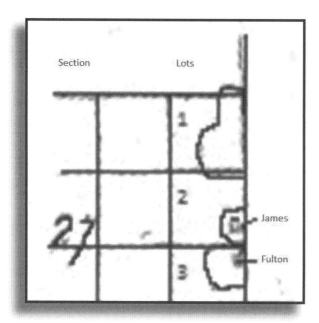

Evidence #3

John C. Hoagland's map shows the James home on the south end of the lot.

Evidence #4

The most precise description of the location of the first James home and Jewell Post Office is found in the sales contract between Fannie and the Palm Beach Farms Company. When Fannie sold her Lake Worth property, two parcels were included in the deal. The larger parcel was 150 acres from their second homestead. The other parcel was the location of the first post office, a 6-acre waterfront lot, the only portion of their first homestead that the Jameses did not sell.

18

FANNIE A. JAMES, Widow of
Samuel James,
to
THE PALM BEACH FARMS
COMPANY,
a Colorado Corporation

Warranty Deed.
Dated December 3, 1910.
Filed December 7, 1910.
Book 8, page 149.
Palm Beach County Records.
Consideration $10.00.

Conveys W½ of NW¼ of Section 27, except ten acres across the North end of the NW¼ of the NW¼ of said Section; E½ of NE¼ of Section 28, except a right of way 100 feet wide across said land in the Florida East Coast Railway Company; the South 3.16 chains of the North 14.59 chains of Lot 2, Section 27, together with all the riparian rights thereunto belonging, excepting from the above granted lands a parcel of land 50 feet North and South by 300 feet East and West in the SE corner thereof, and also excepting a parcel 10 feet by 10 feet upon which Samuel James is now buried.

Legal description of the site in the sales contract is given as "the South 3.16 chains of the North 14.59 chains of Lot 2, Section 27," *Lakeworth Abstract of Title* (See Appendix E for further details on how the parcel was identified using the metes and bounds method of surveying.) This corresponds to the area just north of the wall that currently separates South Bryant Park from the Birthday Cake Castle property. In other words, the first Jewell Post Office would have been within 100 feet of where the South Bryant Park picnic pavilion now stands.

Chapter 12: Who Were the Jewell Thirteen?

Jewell was never a large post office. As Fannie's 1889 post office application shows, the number of potential mail recipients was a scant 13. In subsequent years, the numbers did not grow much. Most of the Jameses' land sales were for speculative investment. Evidently, the land may have been rented out for agricultural purposes, as there is no evidence of homes on any of the parcels directly adjacent to the Jameses' place.

The *1896 Dade County Directory* gave the following description of the settlement pattern:

> Jewell is the only post-office and public stopping place between Lantana and West Palm Beach.... Mr. James and wife, the latter postmistress, are the only immediate residents, although there are several in the neighborhood. The Everglades are nearby. The country along the Lake shore has been taken up and is owned by someone. Quite a number of places are well improved and it is only a question of a short time when every foot of the land will be cultivated in fruits and vegetables. (*1896 Directory*, 59)

Reproducing Fannie's count is not an easy task, even though the number is a low one. Without a definitive list of who received their mail at Jewell, the best that can be done is to tally the homesteaders who lived in the area, looking for possible candidates. The effort is worthwhile in its own right, as it entails taking a closer look at the Jameses' neighbors and the nature of the Jewell community during that early stage of the Homestead Era. The following survey provides a snapshot of what is known about the population of Jewell in July 1889.

THE JAMESES' NEIGHBORS—SURVEY OF CANDIDATES

The count quickly starts with four. Besides Fannie and Samuel themselves, the two bachelors, William Stephan and Michel Merkel are known to have reported, Jewell, Florida, as their official address.

Fulton, Hartzell, and Himes can be quickly ruled out. By 1889, they had abandoned their claims and left the lake area. Dr. Stites, while holding title to his Florida land, was also back in Pennsylvania by that time.

Prior to the establishment of the Jewell Post Office, however, three other homesteaders took up nearby claims along the west shore, north and south of the Jameses: John Hoagland, the Porters and the Gudmundsens.

JOHN C. HOAGLAND

Born in 1832 in Somerset County, New Jersey, Hoagland moved to the Midwest before landing in South Florida, census data shows. Apparently, he had a stormy on-again, off-again relationship with his wife, Mary.

The 1870 census shows J. Calvin Hoagland living in Marshall County, Illinois, with Mary and a son, Irving, less than a year old. Ten years later, in 1880, John and Mary had apparently separated and she was living in Somerset, New Jersey, with her parents and two children, Irving, age ten, and Marie C, five. John C. was not at the New Jersey address.

Hoagland was on the lake as early as 1883, when he bought 64 acres of land for $500 from Charlie Moore. His 1885 census listing shows him in Palm Beach, single and a farmer.

By January 1887, John and Mary were back together. On his homestead application, he described himself as "head of a family." (Hoagland HA, 11) Later that same year, Mary signed a Release of Dower on September 8, 1887, dividing marital property. On March 10, 1893, during his final homestead proof, Hoagland testified to his once again "having no family." (Hoagland HA, 24)

Hoagland was a prominent member of the lake community, commonly honored with the title "Squire Hoagland." A public notary and justice of the peace, he was called upon to perform marriages when no resident minister was available and to serve as judge whenever legal matters arose.

A fellow pioneer, Ben Potter, said of him:

> **Squire Hoagland was the judge in the only legal court for miles around in those days. All the differences between the early settlers were settled in the Squire's court. We didn't have many cases for the Squire, but when the occasion arose he did a mighty fine job of presiding in his court of justice. (http://www.lwpa.org/pioneer_John_C_hoagland.html)**

No doubt his testimony carried considerable weight when he came to the Jameses' defense during the land fuss with the Pennsylvania boys.

Hoagland was known, not only for his legal skills, but also for his charity, donating half an acre of land for the construction of the first Palm Beach school, which was built in 1886.

During that same year, Squire Hoagland accompanied Charles Pierce, Fannie James's nephew, and others on their trip from LakeWorth to the Gainesville Land Office.

In January 1887, Hoagland made a homestead claim on the land directly to the north of the Jameses. This was the same land that William Hartzell had been living on just a year earlier.

Location: Seventh Avenue North to Lake Avenue, east of Dixie Highway (Lake Worth Municipal Golf Course south of the clubhouse)

Acreage: 175

Legal description: Lots 3 & 4 and the west half of the southwest quarter of Section 22

Land type: "Oak and spruce scrub with potential for farming," "5 acres in Pine Apples, Cocoanuts & Vegetables, Shipped Pine Apples 2 seasons"

Improvements: "Frame House, Shingle Roof 20 x 14, Well & Pump. Dock 300 ft. long, 5 ft. wide. Value $1,000."

Land claim witnesses: Owen S. Porter, James Porter, Samuel James, and Charles Pierce (Hoagland HA, 20)

Even after he moved to the west shore, Hoagland maintained strong ties with the Palm Beach community. Although his residence was at Jewell, he kept anchorage for his boat at Palm Beach and often went back and forth between the two locations, making good use of his 300-foot-long wharf. In 1889, two years after filing his Jewell homestead claim, he contributed to the first church building in Palm Beach, Bethesda-by-the-Sea Episcopal Church. On the final proof of his homestead claim, he states that he was from Palm Beach, but his approved patent was mailed to Jewell.

see Postmaster - Jewell. Fla. Feb. 10/94 M. J. G.

Hoagland died in Palm Beach on September 28, 1894. A few months later, a forest fire destroyed his house.

Hoagland's will revealed the state of his estranged marriage. He left $50 to his wife, Mary H. Hoagland, explaining: "She signed away her dower and all other rights to my property in Florida... in consideration that I should yield to her any and all rights I had... to her property in New Jersey, which said dower her relinquishment to me is upon the records at Juno, Dade County, Florida." (*Lakeworth Abstract of Title*, 6)

Hoagland's son, Irving, inherited the homestead, but he never lived on it or rebuilt the house. The 1900 census shows him living in New Jersey with his mother. Irving sold the property to the Palm Beach Farms Company in November 1910 for $3,750.

Despite his Palm Beach connections, John Hoagland is a good candidate for inclusion in the Jewell Thirteen. Unique among all the candidates, there is a record of his having, received at least one piece of mail at Jewell.

On the other hand, Hoagland's wife and son cannot be included in the count. Although, they were with him when he first settled on his claim in 1887, the family had split up by the time of the Jewell Post Office application in 1889.

> Tuesday night the homestead house of the late J. C. Hoagland was destroyed by a forest fire that was burning back of Jewell at that time. It was feared for a time that Dr. Stite's residence would be burned too, but it escaped destruction.

Tropical Sun, **January 3, 1895**—Hoagland house fire.

OWEN & SARAH PORTER

Owen, born around 1835, was married to Sarah McFarland, born 1840. The couple had one son, Archibald (born 1869).

Like so many others of the second wave of Lake Worth-area pioneers, the Porters moved to Palm Beach in 1885. From the moment of his arrival, Owen was active in buying and selling real estate.

Included among his many holdings was a 20-acre parcel that he bought from Samuel James in May 1887. Two years later, Porter made a homestead claim through preemption for a parcel about a mile and a half farther north. Owen was 54, his wife 49, and his son twenty at the time of his move to the west shore.

Settlement date: "The 26th day of March 1889... and moved family thereon."

Location: 19th Avenue North to 13th Avenue North, east of Dixie Highway.

Acreage: 168.92

Legal description: Lots 3 & 4 and west half of southwest quarter of Section 14, Township 44S, Range 43E.

Land type: "Ordinary agricultural land. Scrub oak and palmetto. Think it will be good for pineapples."

Residence: "Only absent to... procure supplies and to church."

Neighbors: John C. Hoagland testified that he lived a half mile from Owen Porter. "Being a close neighbor, have been on [his claim] frequently... every few days." "Only Wm. Stephan lives nearer."

Improvements: "House, 16 x 20, value $250. Outside kitchen, 12 x 12, value $75. Shed, 12 x 16, value $25. 300 foot long wharf, value $123. Well. Road." Owen states that his house was built by "Samuel James and myself." Logically, James made use of his carpentry skills. In view of Porter's many land dealings, James may very well have worked for Porter on other construction projects.

Crops: 350 coconut trees, 80 orange trees, 30 other tropical trees, 3,500 pineapples. Total value of improvements and plantings was $893.

Witnesses:

Charles C. Haight, Lake Worth, Florida

J. W. Porter, Palm Beach, Florida

J. C. Hoagland, Palm Beach, Florida

Sam'l James, Palm Beach [sic], Florida

(Porter HA, 11-14, 31)

In 1890, Porter briefly went into the real estate business with George Potter, his neighbor to the north. In perhaps his most profitable land deal, Porter sold 50 acres to Henry Flagler for $35,000, property that became part of the original plat of West Palm Beach. The Porter & Potter partnership dissolved a few years later.

Two years after receiving his land patent in February 1891, he sold his homestead to Dorinda Brelsford for the handsome sum of $7,000.

The three Porters are possible candidates for the Jewell Thirteen, having moved onto the land a few months prior to Fannie's post office application and owning land both north and south of the Jameses. However, Owen had ongoing business connections in Palm Beach and may well have continued receiving his mail there.

In 1893, the Porters left the lake area and moved to Daytona Beach, where Owen was elected mayor in 1896.

OLAI & SARAH GUDMUNDSEN

Olai was born around 1854, "a subject of Oscar King of Sweden." He married Sarah Ann around the time of settlement on their homestead property.

Settlement date: July 1889 with family, which "consists of myself and wife."

Location: Sixth Avenue South to 12th Avenue South, Dixie to Federal highways.

Acreage: 80.

Legal description: West half of southwest quarter, Section 27, Township 44S, Range 43E.

Land description: "Spruce and Oak Scrub Farming Land."

Improvements: "Frame House, 20 x 14, Well, Pump, 2½ acres cleared."

Crops: "Pine Apples" and trees valued at $1,500. "Shipped Pine Apples Four Seasons."

Gudmundsen took up residence on the lake in the same month Fannie was filling out her post office application. In his entry claim, Gudmundsen listed Hypoluxo as his address. However, once the Jewell Post Office began to function, he may have used it for convenience, since it was closer and on the same side of the lake as his homestead.

According to the *Tropical Sun,* the Gudmundsens did not live full-time on their homestead. Most likely they were "snowbirds" who came to Florida in the winter. Nevertheless, they were zealous about improving their property.

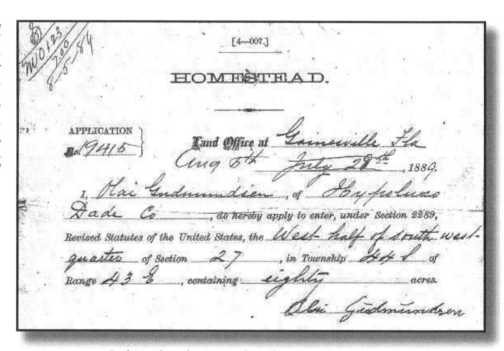

Gudmundsen homestead application, Aug 5, 1889.

MR. AND MRS. GUDMANSON own the next Lake front property, and though non-residents, are making continued improvements upon their place, which they homesteaded and have set to pines.

Tropical Sun, **September 1, 1891**
—Pines are pineapples.

Olai became a U.S. citizen on December 4, 1894. He and Sarah had one daughter, born around 1895.

By the mid-1890s, Lantana had grown into a small town with its own post office. When Olai made his final proof on his homestead claim, he put down Lantana rather than Jewell as his address, as did his witnesses. Even Michael Merkel, who had previously given his address as Jewell, now used Lantana.

Final proof witnesses with their addresses in 1895:

George R. Lyman, of Lantana, Florida

Andrew W. Garnett, of Lantana, Florida

Fred Myers, of Lantana, Florida

Michel Merkel, of Lantana, Florida

Land patent granted: October 16, 1895

County and homestead records show that Olai and Sarah acquired property in their individual names, not as a couple. Sarah Gudmundsen teamed up with Sarah A. Stark and filed a homestead claim for a contiguous parcel south of Olai's homestead. The two Sarahs received their patent in October 1893, two years before Olai. In 1897, they sold the north 30 acres to M. B. Lyman of Lantana. In 1903, they sold the remaining 130 acres to Fannie James's sister, Lucy Jones of Baltimore, Maryland, with Fannie acting as Lucy's power of attorney for the transaction.

Location: 12th Avenue South to 18th Avenue South, Dixie Highway to Federal

Acreage: 80

Legal Description: West half of northwest quarter, Section 34, recorded at County, March 31, 1893

Sarah Stark also owned an adjacent ten-acre waterfront tract that she had purchased from Samuel James in March 1889. In November 1889, Olai Gudmundsen purchased the ten acres north of Stark, which would have likewise been adjacent to his homestead. In the days before roads, ownership of these waterfront lots would have given Stark and Gudmundsen access to the water for shipping pineapples and other produce from their farms.

SUMMARY OF THE JEWELL THIRTEEN

A review of the known Jewell population in July 1889, when Fannie filled out her post office application, allows the ranking of the following possibilities (listed by name, number in household, given post office address, and likelihood of inclusion in Fannie's thirteen):

James Family – 2 – Jewel; certain

Michael Merkel – 1 – Jewel; certain

William Stephan – 1 – Jewel; certain

John Hoagland – 1 – Palm Beach and Jewel; certain

Counting the number of individuals specifically known from historical records to have used the Jewell Post Office yields a list with only the above five names. Who else might have been included among the initial Jewell population?

Harry Griswold – 1 – PO address unknown; probable

Porter Family – 3 – Palm Beach – possible

Gudmundsen Family – 2 – Hypoluxo; possible

Sarah A. Stark – 1 – PO address unknown; possible

Harry Griswold can be added as a good possibility. He worked as a hired hand on the James farm and also purchased a five-acre parcel just south of the Jameses. Likely he lived on the property and could accordingly have been counted among Fannie's 13.

Owen Porter had a prosperous real estate business in Palm Beach and evidently acquired his Jewell area homestead for its investment value. As soon as he acquired his patent, his sold the property. Most likely, he and his family actually lived in Palm Beach. Whenever he signed legal documents, he gave his address as Palm Beach. Nevertheless, it is possible that the Porters were on their homestead part time and might have received mail at Jewell.

Likewise the Gudmundsens did not claim to be Jewell residents but gave their address as Hypoluxo. Nevertheless, the proximity of their land to the Jewell Post Office would have made it convenient and Olai is associated with Jewell in at least one newspaper notice. Consequently, his family's inclusion in Fannie's list is rated as possible.

Sarah Stark's name is known only as co-owner of property with Sarah Gudmundsen. No newspaper or homestead records confirm Stark's physical presence in the lake region.

Several other individuals are associated with Jewell in newspaper notices, although nothing else is known about them. They may have been renters, workers, visitors, or squatters. Although their presence at Jewell is recorded after Fannie filed her Post office application, the possibility exists that one or more of them were living at Jewell before the notices were published.

Mr. Caswell – 1 – PO address unknown; possible

A. J. and James Huskey – 2 – PO address unknown; possible

Mr. P. Kitching – 1 – PO address unknown; possible

Tropical Sun, April 29, 1891—Caswell of Jewell.

Tropical Sun, August 18, 1889 – Huskey brothers.

If all the above individuals were at Jewell in August of 1889, that would bring our count of prospects to fifteen, yet several names on the list are suspect. Counting Mr. Kitching as a Jewell resident in 1889 is dubious, as the *Tropical Sun* announcement seems to cast him as a new arrival to Jewell in 1892. Likewise, the Huskey brothers appear to have been visiting the Gudmundsens.

Tropical Sun, September 1, 1892— Kitching plans to farm at Jewell.

One other candidate can be mentioned. Edwin Bradley customarily used a Hypoluxo address, due to his long association with the Pierces. Nevertheless, when he advertised several agricultural lots for sale in early 1892, he gave a Jewell address. This was about six months before the Lantana Post Office opened, so if prospective customers were to write, Jewell would have been the closest post office, rather than Hypoluxo. However, the ad encourages customers to visit and see the "adjoining lots," so it seems that Jewell appeared in the ad because of its proximity to Bradley's place, rather than for use as a mailing address.

Bradley Family – 5 – Hypoluxo – unlikely

To the above population inventory, the following open categories can be added:

1) Unnamed members of the James or other families. There are indications (to be discussed later) that Fannie was close to her sisters as well as her many nieces and nephews from out of state. Any of these may have briefly lived with Fannie during the summer of 1889. For example, Charles Pierce reported that one of Fannie's nephews accompanied him on a trip to the Land Office in Gainesville in 1886, indicating a prolonged visit. Likewise, it is conceivable that Griswold had a family.

2) Unnamed hired hands. From his early descriptions of his farming operation, it is clear that Samuel had associates and hired help. He specifically named Thomas Jones, who looked after his homestead during his absences. Workers on any of the operating farms (along with their families) may have been counted as Jewell residents.

3) Unnamed squatters. There was open land, especially inland off the water that was not claimed until after 1889. Michael Merkel, for example, built a shanty and lived on Lake Osborne without having filled out a claim. He used Jewell as his mailing address. There may have been others who did likewise.

HOE! FOR PINEAPPLES & COCOANUTS,
—OR—
Any other tropical fruits you may wish to grow.

Four ten-acre lots fronting on Lake Worth (West Side) for sale in Lotus Cove. Only forty rods from Benson Lyman's store and boat ways.

Three quarters of a mile across the Lake to Farrell's trail; only one hundred yards over to the sea beach.

$50.00 per acre and up.

Call and see samples of tropical growth on adjoining lots.

E. R. BRADLEY,
5-39   Jewell, Dade Co., Fla.

Tropical Sun, February 4, 1892—
Bradley uses Jewell address.

Part 2

Jameses in Historical Context

===

THE CIVIL WAR & ITS AFTERMATH

"Those who cannot remember the past are condemned to repeat it." - George Santayana

"Learn from the mistakes of others. You can't live long enough to make them all yourself."
- Anonymous

After the Civil War, the 15th Amendment granted voting rights to blacks. Federal troops occupied state capitols of the former Confederacy. As a result, during the Reconstruction Period, blacks were elected to a wide range of public offices including the Florida State Legislature and the U.S. Congress.

Chapter 13: Reconstruction & Backlash

After Confederate General Robert E. Lee surrendered to General Ulysses Grant on April 9, 1865, Union generals were dispersed to the various rebel states to reestablish federal governance. Union General Edward McCook was assigned to southwest Georgia and Florida.

In Georgia, McCook accepted the surrenders of Generals Albany, Thomasville, and Bainbridge, and then with just 300 cavalrymen, moved on to Florida, entering the state capital of Tallahassee on May 13.

> In Tallahassee Ellen Call Long, the forty-year-old daughter of Richard Keith Call, wrote, "I was startled on yesterday by a cry from our little 'black boy' of 'Yankees!' 'Yankees!' and I found myself running with the 'rest of the children' to the front to see Gen. McCook and staff enter to take command of our little city." She appreciated McCook's diplomacy in keeping his main force on the town's outskirts, adding, "The General was very properly received by representative men of the place, and the courtesies due him were gracefully extended."

(Ellis and Rogers, *Tallahassee & Leon County*, 16.)

Florida secessionist Governor John Milton shot himself in the head rather than submit to Union occupation. Col. George Washington Scott surrendered the last active Confederate troops in the capital.

The end of the Civil War, coupled with federal occupation, ushered in a short-lived golden age for African Americans.

On May 20, McCook organized a ceremony to mark the Union victory, attended mostly by his soldiers and black freedmen. Jubilant troops raised the U.S. flag over the state capitol and publicly read Abraham Lincoln's Emancipation Proclamation, freeing the slaves and sending a message that the Union victory signaled an end to chattel slavery. (http://www.museumoffloridahistory.com/exhibits/permanent/civilwar/19.cfm)

On May 22, the city was put under martial law, and the occupying force was beefed up to include five federal companies, including some black soldiers.

The military, the Freedman's Bureau, and a series of northern-born "carpetbag" governors assisted and protected the former slaves. A new state constitution adopted in 1868 guaranteed blacks the right to vote, provided for free public education, and restructured the court system to promote equal treatment. (Ellis and Rogers, *Tallahassee & Leon County*, 13-17.)

The so-called Radical Republicans, in control in Washington, DC, after the Lincoln assassination, passed the Thirteenth and Fourteenth Amendments to the U.S. Constitution. Their provisions:

- Outlawed slavery and involuntary servitude.

- Granted full citizenship to those born in the United States, including former slaves (but excluded Indians living on reservations "not taxed").

- Denied the vote to certain leaders of the "rebellion."

- Granted equal protection under the law for all citizens.

The net result of these federal mandates was to empower Republicans and blacks. For twelve years, from 1865 to 1877, federal troops kept the peace and secured the equal rights promised by the new constitutional amendments. Forty-four percent of Florida's population was black. With the aid of a minority of whites, equal-rights Republicans were able to maintain control of the governor's seat and the legislature. The election of 1868 saw blacks win three seats in the Florida Senate and 17 seats in the Florida House of Representatives. With a Republican majority in both houses, Florida easily ratified the Thirteenth and Fourteenth amendments.

The Fifteenth Amendment specifically challenged the political power of white supremacists. Ratified in 1870, it stipulated:

The right of citizens of the United States to vote shall not be denied or abridged by the United States or by any State on account of race, color, or previous condition of servitude.

Advances in civil rights began to unravel with the contested presidential election of 1876 between Democrat Samuel J. Tilden and Republican Rutherford B. Hayes. Nationwide, Tilden won the popular vote, while Rutherford won the Electoral College. The results in three southern states —Louisiana, South Carolina, and Florida—were in dispute.

The Compromise of 1877 settled the controversy. It granted the election to Hayes over Tilden in exchange for concessions to Southern Democrats.

The deal was struck behind closed doors, but the following elements are generally said to be the major points of the compromise:

- The removal of all federal troops from former Confederate States, particularly the three states with the largest percentage of black population, which not coincidentally were the disputed states: Louisiana, South Carolina, and Florida.

- The appointment of at least one Southern Democrat to Hayes's cabinet. (David M. Key of Tennessee became Postmaster General).

- The construction of another transcontinental railroad in the South to promote economic development.

- Legislation to help industrialize the South and get the former Confederate States back on their feet after the decimation of the Civil War.

In exchange, Democrats would:

- Peacefully accept Hayes' s presidency.

- Respect blacks' rights.

(Woodward, *Reunion and Reaction*, 77-91.)

The backlash against Reconstruction intensified as soon as the federal troops departed. Oppressive laws aimed at undermining black political power were enacted, at first subtly and later with greater boldness, rescinding the freedoms that emancipation had promised.

During the decade of the 1880s, black Floridians struggled to hold onto the ballot. Their adversaries were formidable. White supremacists terrorized would-be black voters with both threats and physical violence, while conservatives used growing legislative majorities to rig the electoral system.

A Republican activist testified that the 1880 election in Leon County was plagued by "the use of tissue tickets, violence, fraud in counting returns made the showing for the Democrats.... Our honest Republican majority of 5,000 reversed."

Terror endured well beyond Election Day. Black Floridians, who testified about election fraud in Jacksonville district court, often paid with their lives. John Byrd was lynched by white vigilantes, on his way back home to Madison County from after testifying in a contested election case.

> While Republican leader Malachi Martin... serving as a Republican poll watcher... attempted to count ballots inside the polling place, white "men stripped in their shirt sleeves brandishing their knives... frequently came to the window of the polling place, shook their fists and knives at me, and calling me by the most vile names it is possible to utter, told me they would kill me as soon as I came out." (Ortiz, *Emancipation Betrayed*, 37–38)

Such reports numbered into the hundreds while many other incidents went unreported. As a result of wide-spread intimidation, black voting dropped off as white supremacists consolidated power.

ROLLING BACK BLACK VOTING RIGHTS—THE POLL TAX

A major step toward curtailing the voting power of blacks was the passage of a new Florida State Constitution in 1885. While professing to promote equal rights, it found indirect ways of accomplishing the opposite. Among its provisions was a poll tax, which was prohibitive for the poor, both black and white, but with a disproportionate impact on blacks. Exceptions to the poll tax were made in the case of those whose grandfathers had voted. The net effect was to grant the right to vote too many poor whites while denying it to blacks. This legalism was the origin of the term "grandfather clause."

> Grandfather clauses, a peculiarly irksome impediment to achieving voting rights for African Americans, were enacted by seven Southern states between 1895 and 1910. These laws provided that those who had enjoyed the right to vote prior to 1866 or 1867 or their lineal descendants would be exempt from educational, property, or tax requirements for voting. Because former slaves had not been granted the right to vote until the Fifteenth Amendment was ratified in 1870, these clauses effectively excluded blacks from the vote. At the same time, grandfather clauses assured the right to vote to many impoverished, ignorant, and illiterate whites. In 1915, the U.S. Supreme Court finally declared the grandfather clause unconstitutional because it violated equal voting rights guaranteed by the Fifteenth Amendment. (http://civilrights.uslegal.com/voting-rights/grandfather-clauses-literacy-tests-and-the-white-primary/)

EXCERPTS FROM 1885 FLORIDA STATE CONSTITUTION

As can be seen in the excerpts below, the revised constitution paid lip service to the basic America precept that "all men are created equal" while providing the legal basis for a society that was inherently unequal, divided by class and race.

DECLARATION OF RIGHTS

Preamble

Section 1. All men are equal before the law, and have certain inalienable rights, among which are those enjoying and defending life and liberty, acquiring, possessing and protecting property, and pursuing happiness and obtaining safety.

Article VI – Suffrage and Eligibility (Poll Tax)

Section 8. The Legislature shall have power to make the payment of the capitation tax a prerequisite for voting, and all such taxes received shall go into the school fund.

Article XII – Education

Section 12. White and colored children shall not be taught in the same school, but impartial provision shall be made for both.

Article – XVI – Miscellaneous Provisions

Section 24. All marriages between a white person and a negro, or between a white person and a person of negro descent to the fourth generation, inclusive, are hereby forever prohibited.

(http://www.law.fsu.edu/crc/conhist/1885con.html)

In addition to the poll tax, other legal strategies were employed to further limit black suffrage, including hindrances to black registration, contrived literacy tests, and white-only primaries.

From 1885 to 1889, Democrat majorities in the Florida Legislature passed statutes aimed at reducing black voting in an effort to consolidate white control of the state government. Out-of-state carpetbaggers also were targeted. As Republican constituencies were stripped from voter rolls, white Democrats established a virtual one-party state, as happened in state after state across the South. By 1900 African Americans had been effectively disfranchised, although they made up 44% of the state's population, the same percentage as before the Civil War.

The charter of the Town of Lake Worth, like most communities in the South, provided for a poll tax.

The poll tax was repealed by the Florida legislature in 1937.

The Twenty-fourth Amendment to the U.S. Constitution outlawed poll taxes nationwide in 1964. The aim of the poll tax to disenfranchise African Americans can be seen in the language used in political debates over adoption of the amendment.

Mississippi Senator Theodore Bilbo declared, "If the poll tax bill passes, the next step will be an effort to remove the registration qualification, the educational qualification of Negroes. If that is done we will have no way of preventing the Negroes from voting." (Lawson, *Black Ballots,* 70.)

WHITE PRIMARIES

Another tactic used by Southern whites was the so-called white primary. The Democratic Party had become the dominant political party. Whoever won the Democrat primary was virtually assured of winning the general election. By declaring itself to be a private organization, the Party could exclude whomever it pleased. State party rules or state laws that excluded blacks from the Democratic primary essentially disenfranchised them. In 1944, the white primary was ruled unconstitutional in the U.S. Supreme Court case of Smith vs. Allwright.

RIGGED LITERACY TESTS

There were many uneducated African Americans in the post-Civil War era. Literacy tests were used to help exclude them from the polls. However, whites found that literacy tests also would exclude large numbers of whites from becoming eligible voters since many whites could not read or write either. As a remedy, some jurisdictions adopted a "reasonable interpretation" clause; these laws gave voting registrars discretion to evaluate applicants' performance on literacy tests. In many cases, blacks were given extraordinarily difficult tests while uneducated whites were given simpler tests. The effect was predictable: Most whites passed and most blacks did not. By the beginning of the twentieth century, almost every black had been disfranchised in the South.

WERE CONDITIONS BETTER FOR BLACKS IN SOUTH FLORIDA?

As seen above, there is good evidence that white supremacist attitudes had not yet penetrated fully into South Florida during the Homestead Era. To summarize, Samuel and Fannie were accepted as equals within the otherwise white settler community, establishing friendships, going into business, testifying in court in support of each other, being entrusted with executorship of William Stephan's estate, and including Samuel as a founding member of the Fleming committee (what today would be called a Political Action Committee and implying community support for his right to vote).

Another evidence was the editorial policy of the *Tropical Sun*, as shown in the article on the next page. When reporting on a debate over establishing separate posts for whites and blacks in a Union veterans' organization, the G.A.R. (Glorious Army of the Republic), the paper showed its sympathy for race mixing and its discomfort with segregation efforts in a variety of subtle ways, Consider:

- The headline "He Drew the Color Line" In South Florida, even as late as 1891, the existence of a strict color line of separation between the races was not a *fait accompli.*
- The use of the word "comrades" for black veterans.
- In its expression of surprise that the organization's leader would "so openly favor the separation of the races."
- In the prediction that those favoring race mixing would prevail.

HE DREW THE COLOR LINE

COMMANDER-IN-CHIEF VEAZEY SIDES WITH THE WHITES.

His Course Causes a Sensation—He Recommends That a Colored Department of the G. A. R. be Established in the Gulf States—A Contrary Opinion by the Judge-Advocate.

DETROIT, MICH., August 9.—The twenty-fifth annual encampment of the G. A. R. met in formal session this morning in the mammoth hall set apart for the business deliberations of the veterans. All that art could do to make the building attractive had been done in decorations, which adorned the interior in emblematic order. Despite the immensity of the hall, it was crowded by a multitude of veterans, attracted by the momentous questions to be settled. It was fully understood that the race question might be precipitated in the deliberations at any moment and become a subject of acrimonious discussion, and this impending problem, together with the projected revision of the constitution, combined to heighten the interest in the proceedings.

When General Veazey and staff entered the hall and were escorted to the grand stand they were greeted with applause. A minute later two bands burst forth with an inspiring military air in harmony with the martial scene. The commander-in-chief rapped the assembly to order and announced the formal opening of the 25th annual encampment of the G. A. R., directed the adjutant-general to call the roll of departments, and every State and Territory was represented. The opening address of the commander-in-chief was listened to with close attention by the assembled veterans.

The declaration of the commander-in-chief in favor of the establishment of departments of the G. A. R. for negro veterans created a decided sensation. It was hardly to be expected that he would so openly favor the separation of the races, and the whites of Louisiana and Mississippi were overjoyed at his decisive recommendations.

Commander Veazey went at some length into the question of negro posts. The pith of his remarks is embodied in the following extract:

"The present administration encounters the same disturbance in the department of Louisiana and Mississippi that had troubled my predecessors. From the various sources of information that have been accessible to me, I believe that the large majority of both white and colored comrades in the department of Louisiana and Mississippi is strong in the conviction that it would be for the best interests of all, individually and of their posts and of the order, to have a separate department in Louisiana and some of the other Gulf States, made up of such posts as may apply to come into it, and having concurrent jurisdiction with the departments already established in such States—concurrent in respect to the chartering and mustering of posts, but each department having exclusive jurisdiction over the posts which it may receive. My best judgment, after a year of painstaking investigation, is that it would be wise to confer upon my successor authority to create such department. He may neither find it necessary nor think it best to exercise the power if conferred. I have no policy to urge other than such as will be for the best interests of the order, and at the same time protect the rights of all the comrades. It cannot be expected that any plan will meet the approval of all comrades directly interested. I regard the subject as one of the first importance and invoke your deliberate consideration and best judgment in its disposition." The report of the judge advocate-general derives its chief interest from his decision on the vexed race question. As his conclusions differ from the recommendations of the commander-in-chief, the dispute is only further complicated. The decision is as follows: "The question proposed is 'wheth-er there can lawfully be two departments covering the same territory at the same time, for instance, one department made up of white posts and the other of black posts, or one of foreign-born and the other of native-born.' The judge-advocate thinks the question must be answered in the negative, because the proposition is contrary to the usage and understanding of the order, and because the rules and regulations governing the organization are against it."

The adjutant-general's report shows that there are in the order forty-five departments, with 7,409 posts, and 398,607 comrades in good standing. The sum expended in charities during the year was $333,699, against $317,957 in the previous year. There have been 5,530 deaths this year, against 5,479 in 1890. The total apparent membership is 447,-307. Suspensions, delinquencies and transfers bring the number down to 398,607.

Surgeon-General Stevenson read a letter from Commissioner Raum giving the number of pensioners now on the rolls and the amount paid by the government for pensions during the present fiscal year. Summarized it is:

Pensioners on the rolls May 31, 1891—Army invalids, 415,615; widows, 105,-759; navy invalids, 5,439; widows, 233.

Act of June 27, 1891—Army invalids, 55,417; widows, 8,114; navy invalids,

5,888; widows, 1,118.

Mexican war survivors, 16,350; widows, 7,753; total, 830,894.

To pay these pensioners will cost during the present fiscal year about $130,-000,000.

The women's relief corps reported general and relief funds on hand, $160,836.

Washington was selected on the first ballot as the location of next year's encampment.

The race question still remains unsettled but will be settled by the encampment to-morrow. The whole matter is temporarily in the hands of a special committee appointed to-day and it is understood to-night that a majority of this committee will oppose the relegation of the colored comrades to separate departments. The leading G. A. R. men of Louisiana and Mississippi still insist that the G. A. R., so far as the whites are concerned, will go to pieces in the South unless this is done; while, on the other hand, ex-Congressmen Smalls of South Carolina, Colonel Lewis of Louisiana and other leading colored men vow they will tear off their badges and forever renounce the G. A. R., unless colored comrades in every state are admitted to full fellowship without race distinction. The recommendation of General Veazey's annual address were unfavorable to colored comrades, but the sentiment of the encampment seems to be against separate departments.

Tropical Sun, August 19, 1891.

Chapter 14: Race and the U.S. Post Office

The history of race relations and the USPS provides background on the role of the federal government in countering Jim Crow laws in the South and specifically to Fannie James's appointment as Jewell postmaster in 1889.

Despite ups and downs of race relations in the United States, the U.S. Post Office has a history of being more accommodating to African Americans than many other governmental institutions. Fannie James's position as Jewell postmaster is a smallpiece of a much broader picture. By 1900, blacks were employed in substantial numbers as postmasters and letter carriers.

The earliest known African Americans employed in the United States mail service were slaves who carried the mail in the South prior to 1802.

Timothy Pickering was an ardent abolitionist who held the post of Postmaster General from 1791 to 1795 during George Washington's presidency. He was instrumental in the passage of the Northwest Ordinance of 1787, which specifically forbade slavery in the territory north of the Ohio River.

During his tenure as postmaster, he defended the hiring of blacks regarding a mail route in Maryland:

> If the Inhabitants… should deem their letters safe with a faithful black, I should not refuse him…. I suppose the planters entrust more valuable things to some of their blacks…. If you admitted a negro to be a man, the difficulty would cease. (Pickering to John Hargrove, August 8, 1794, National Archives Microfilm Publication 601, Letters Sent by the Postmaster General, 1789–1836, Roll 3, 372–373.)

After Pickering's tenure, the U.S. Congress closed the door on black mail carriers. An act of May 3, 1802, declared that "after the 1st day of November next, no other than a free white person shall be employed in carrying the mail of the United States, on any of the post-roads, either as a postrider or driver of a carriage carrying the mail." (http://about.usps.com/who-we-are/postal-history/star-routes.pdf)

From 1802 to 1865, postal laws required mail-carriers to be free white persons. This prohibition endured until March 3, 1865, when Congress reversed itself and directed that "no person, by reason of color, shall be disqualified from employment in carrying the mails." (13 Stat. 515)

In a letter to Booker T. Washington, First Assistant Postmaster General James S. Clarkson claimed to have appointed "over eleven hundred" African Americans to various positions. [Letter of February 7, 1896, in The Booker T. Washington Papers, Volume 4 (Chicago, Illinois: University of Illinois Press, 1975), 111, as found at http://www.historycooperative.org/btw/Vol.4/html/111.html, 1/12/2007.

The U.S. Postal Service (USPS) has compiled a partial list of 142 African Americans who served as post-masters in the later part of the nineteenth century. (http://webpmt.usps.gov/pmt003.cfm) The next page shows those the 12 women and five Floridians, including William G. Stewart, who are on the USPS list. (More on Stewart later.) Fannie James is not listed, but her name has been submitted and approved for future updates.

AFRICAN AMERICAN POSTMASTERS IN FLORIDA, 1865–1899

Postmaster	Post Office	State	Date Appointed	Served until approximately
Harris, Thomas S.	Liveoak	FL	9/17/1898	3/2/1905
Meacham, Robert	Monticello	FL	2/19/1869	3/22/1871
Lewey, Matthew M.	Newnansville	FL	2/19/1874	2/8/1875
Elijah, Zebulon	Pensacola	FL	1/30/1874	2/14/1878
Stewart, William G.	Tallahassee	FL	3/26/1873	7/20/1885

AFRICAN AMERICAN WOMEN POSTMASTERS IN UNITED STATES, 1865–1899

Postmaster	Post Office	State	Date Appointed	Served until approximately
Fletcher, Frances Jennie/Jenny	Nicodemus	KS	12/9/1889	1/5/1894
Dumas, Mrs. Anna M.	Covington	LA	11/15/1872	6/18/1885
Cox, Mrs. Minnie M.	ndianola	MS	1/16/1891 5/22/1897	4/17/1893 2/2/1904
Montgomery, Mary V.	Mound Bayou	MS	5/2/1895	9/27/1902
Baker, Mary A.	Dudley	NC	11/26/1897	8/22/1911
Dickens, Ada	Lawrence	NC	8/9/1897	11/22/1899
Commander, Harriet "Hattie" R.	Chesterfield	SC	6/11/1889	12/11/1893
Reed, Laura	Edisto Island	SC	4/30/1898 9/21/1908	3/12/1901 1/12/1910
Sperry, Mrs. Frances J.M.	Georgetown	SC	9/27/1890	6/19/1893
Middleton, Mary S.	Midway	SC	12/16/1872	8/30/1875
Jones, Louisa C.	Ridgeland	SC	9/30/1897	1/7/1910
Davis, Mrs. Eliza H.	Summerville	SC	7/23/1873	9/10/1884

In the early twentieth century, Republican President Theodore Roosevelt began to test the power of the federal government—through the Post Office Department—to "interfere in the race problem" when he refused to allow a community to drive out an African American postmaster, Minnie M. Cox of Indianola, Mississippi.

In the fall of 1902, some white citizens of Indianola drew up a petition demanding that Minnie Cox resign as postmaster. Following veiled threats to her safety, Cox decided to resign. However, President Roosevelt refused to accept her resignation. According to a report in The *New York Times* on January 3, 1903, "The case was discussed by the Cabinet and the President decided that this was the best possible time to test the question whether a community could force out an office holder appointed by the Executive, and also the question whether the Federal government was powerless to interfere in the race problem."

That same day the President ordered that the Indianola Post Office be closed until the townspeople accepted Minnie Cox as postmaster. In the interim, their mail was sent to Greenville, 25 miles away. The situation resolved itself in January 1904 at the expiration of Cox's term. Minnie Cox adamantly refused to be reappointed postmaster. (http://about.usps.com/who-we-are/postal-history/african-american-workers-19thc-2011.pdf)

Chapter 15: The Jameses in Tallahassee

Fannie and Samuel James were not youngsters when they moved into the untamed wilds of South Florida. Samuel was 57. Fannie was 42. Where had they been and what had they done with their lives in the years before homesteading at Jewell?

Much conflicting information on the Jameses' origins has been published, including reports that they came from Pennsylvania, Ohio, Georgia, or were Black Seminoles native to Florida. The first census listing available for either of the Jameses is from 1880. It located Samuel and "Fanny" James in Leon County, Tallahassee. (See lines 28 and 29.)

Partial page from 1880 U.S. Census, Leon County (Tallahassee), Florida, showing Samuel and Fannie Jones, lines 28–29, their roommates the Robinsons, lines 25–27, Fannie's sister, Lucy Jones, line 24, and the lawyer family that Lucy was working for, lines 17–24. The numbers in the left hand column group residents by household.

An examination of each item found in the census record provides valuable insights into the Jameses' background.

Our first surprise is to find the Jameses living with a much younger family, consisting of Joseph Robinson, age 24, his 18-year-old wife, Rosana, and his 10-year-old brother, John. Who were the Robinsons, and how did the two families come to share a household? All that is known is that the family was African American, and Joseph worked as a porter in a store. No family tie is shown. The Robinsons and Jameses simply may have been housemates of convenience.

Samuel's profession is shown as "carpenter," which was also his trade as described in his homestead application. "Fanny," here spelled with a "y" rather than the usual "ie," was "keeping house."

Samuel's ethnic background has been questioned by some authorities who claim he was either

71

white or so light-skinned he could pass for white. However, this federal census reports both Fannie and Samuel as "mulatto" or mixed race. In Florida at the time, anyone with one-eighth or more of African blood was legally considered a "negro," but the federal census made a distinction between blacks and mulattos with varying consistency.

The fact that the Robinsons are listed as black and the Jameses as mulatto is an indication that Fannie and Samuel were noticeably lighter-skinned than the Robinsons and their other African American neighbors.

Information on census forms is generally reliable but not completely so. Census takers usually talked to one person per household who sometimes gave incorrect information. Here, for example, Fannie's given age, at 35, is too young. She was born in 1842 or 1843 and would have been at least 37 in 1880. Also, Fannie's birth state (not shown in the inset) is given as Virginia, same as Samuel's. Yet other sources provide strong evidence that she was born in North Carolina.

A comparison with the nearby households reveals that the Jameses lived within a small cluster of black families in a larger racially mixed, middle-class neighborhood. Occupations ranged from physicians and nurses to lawyers, school teachers, silversmiths, and shopkeepers. There were also a postmaster, a tax collector, and a census enumerator. Heads of households were white, black, and mulatto. Some of the whites were affluent enough to have black cooks and servants. (1880 Federal Census, Leon County, 12–16.)

Significantly, Fannie's sister, Lucy Jones, lived next door. Her race was shown as "black," and she was working as a "house servant" for the family of a white lawyer. The two sisters remained close to each other through various moves around the county. Later in life, they collaborated on numerous real estate deals but then had a falling out. Lucy was excluded from Fannie's will and contested it in probate court claiming the Fannie was not in her right mind when the will was written. More details on their collaborations and disputes will be given later.

Another interesting neighbor of the Jameses in Tallahassee was William G. Stewart. During the Reconstruction era, Stewart was a prominent man, a black member of the Florida Legislature (1873) who had also served as Gadsden County commissioner (1870–1872), Tallahassee clerk and treasurer (1872), and "postmaster" of Tallahassee from 1873 to 1886. The Tallahassee *Weekly True Democrat* also described Stewart's church role in his June 1911 obituary:

> [Stewart] began to assist in the organization of the A. M. E. Church in the State in 1865.... He was the presiding elder twenty-seven years. He was an exceptional and progressive pastor and an able preacher for fifty years. He was of unusual high moral character. He died at his post of duty. (Brown, *Florida Black Public Officials,* 128–9.)

It is natural to wonder what influence living in close proximity to a man of such prominence as Stewart might have had on the Jameses. His public service-oriented life and his example as a postmaster may well have contributed to Fannie's later decision to open the Jewell Post Office.

The record does not indicate how long the Jameses lived in Tallahassee, when they arrived, or when they left. In any event, 1880 was a significant year, marking the first presidential election after the departure of Union-occupation troops.

White backlash against the progress blacks had made during Reconstruction brought threats, intimidation, and violence intended to suppress the black vote. Tallahassee proved to be a turbulent place and 1880 a violent time. Especially if the Jameses were associated with black leaders of Reconstruction, as appears to have been the case, it should come as no surprise that they might have sought a quieter, safer life for themselves. In any case, they did not stick around Leon County.

Chapter 16: The Jameses in Cocoa

By 1885, Samuel and Fannie James had left Tallahassee and were living on the southeast coast of Florida in Cocoa, Brevard County, Florida. The state conducted a census that year, which supplemented the federal census and provides another timely snapshot of the Jameses.

"Sam" and "Fannie" James are listed on lines 41 and 42 of the Florida census page. Fannie's age is once again off, but in this case the record shows her as older than she really was by a few years, 45 instead of 42.

The 1885 Florida Census confirms data found in the 1880 Federal Census. In both, Samuel is a carpenter and Fannie is a housekeeper. Their race is listed as mulatto. Samuel's age matches precisely. The presence of Fannie's sister in Tallahassee provides strong evidence that the data resemblances are more than coincidence. Despite the differences in the spelling of Fannie's first name and the deviation in her given age, both censuses evidently refer to the same Fannie and Samuel James.

During the "land fuss" hearing, Samuel testified that he'd gone south to the lake alone, leaving Fannie behind in Cocoa. While in Lake Worth, he established his homestead claim in February 1885. Then in April, he returned to Cocoa, where he found Fannie ill and under Dr. Hughlett's care. Samuel remained in Cocoa for five months, helping to care for his sick wife and to "build a church for the colored people."

What infirmity could have caused Fannie to have been ill for so long and later return to a vigorous life? One possibility is that she had a troubled pregnancy. Fannie would have been 43 years old. Pregnant women, in those days, often stayed in bed for weeks or months at a time in an effort to avoid a miscarriage. The nature of their "illness" was spoken of ambiguously, if at all. Dr. Stites refers to his wife as being "confined", a euphemism for pregnancy. At such an anxious time it would be natural for Samuel to arrange to be Fannie's side to provide needed care and emotional support.

The heading on the census page shows that the census taker made his rounds in July, confirming Samuel's court testimony that he was in Cocoa that summer.

In Cocoa, as in Tallahassee, the Jameses are found living in a middle-class, racially mixed neighborhood. Their neighbors were mostly tradespeople—carpenters, printers, and a cooper. Perhaps not coincidentally, Walter Speed, an African American man, is shown living next door (line 46). On the earlier 1880 census, this same Walter Speed was listed in Palm Beach, working for the Spencer family. Sometime between 1880 and 1885, he got married, had a daughter and moved to Cocoa. The Speeds and the Jameses undoubtedly knew each other and perhaps Walter precipitated the Jameses' interest in relocating to the lake community.

Another of the Jameses' Cocoa neighbors was an African American preacher by the name of Butler Reed (Line 49). Like their neighbor William G. Stewart in Tallahassee, Reverend Reed was a popular community leader. Although fragmentary, the record of Reed's activities provided insight into the political and racial climate that prevailed at that time and the likelihood of ties to the Jameses.

Excerpt from 1885 Florida Census, Cocoa, Brevard County, Florida
Columns are household number, name, race, gender, relationship, and occupation.

REVEREND BUTLER REED

In 1885, Reverend Reed lived in Cocoa, Florida, with his wife, Emma, and 10-year-old son, Willie, three doors down from the Jameses. Five years earlier, he established a small church in Tallahassee and served as its first minister.

> The place was Tallahassee, Florida. The year was 1880. The event was the organization of Zion Orthodox Primitive Baptist Church of Jesus Christ. The founder was the late Reverend Butler Reed. Its membership consisted of nine persons, five of whom were Reverend Butler's sisters. (http://www.zionorthodoxpbchurch.org/about_us/church_history.htm)

Sometime between 1880 and 1885, the church moved to Cocoa. It is entirely possible that the Jameses were members of the church and followed Reverend Reed from Tallahassee to Cocoa. Zion Orthodox Primitive Baptist Church (ZOPBC) is still functioning at 715 S. Fiske Boulevard in Cocoa.

Circumstantial evidence convincingly points to a connection between the Jameses and the Reeds. In his homestead application, Samuel described helping build a "church for the colored people" in Cocoa. The only other black church in Cocoa at the time, Mount Moriah AME, was not built until the following year. (http://www.mtmoriah.net/A.M.E%20History.html) Therefore, there is a distinct possibility that the church Samuel James helped build in 1885 was Reverend Reed's church.

In short order after his arrival in Cocoa, Reed became a leading figure in the black community. In the run-up to the 1888 presidential elections, Reed was elected president of the Harrison and Morton Club, a group of "colored" Republicans campaigning on behalf of Benjamin Harrison for president and Levi Morton for vice president. The club was formed after white Republicans left blacks out of the Brevard County Republican Convention.

A letter to the editor that appeared in the August 25 issue of the *Florida Star* sheds light on how racial segregation was settling in, even within the party of Lincoln, as the light of Reconstruction faded. Reverend Reed's role in fighting for equal rights was highlighted in the letter.

Reed, like William Stewart, the Jameses' neighbor in Tallahassee, was an educated black man who had experienced brief relief from racial oppression during Reconstruction. By the 1880s, they saw the doors to freedom closing in their faces as white supremacists found new ways to disempower blacks.

The Jameses lived through these turbulent times and surely would have been disheartened, disillusioned, and eager to find a way to carve out a better life for themselves. Homesteading in South Florida offered both economopportunity and a chance to get away from the increasingly oppressive environment of emerging "Jim Crow."

Other evidence of Reverend Reed's leadership position in the Cocoa black community can be seen in his involvement in the Prohibition movement. Many church leaders of that era time saw the dangers of alcohol and were working toward the passage of the Eighteenth Amendment, which eventually succeeded in outlawing intoxicating beverages in 1919.

It is noteworthy that the two speakers who joined Reverend Butler on the program show up in other places in the story. Dr. Hughlett was the same physician who attended to Fannie during her illness in Cocoa during the summer of 1885. This provides some confirmation of the ties between the "Colored Baptist Church" and the Jameses. Guy Metcalf published the *Indian River News* (Melbourne) at that time and later moved to the lake area to publish the *Tropical Sun.*

There was a mass-meeting in Cocoa last Saturday night in the interest of the prohibition cause at the Colored Baptist Church. Dr. Hughlett and Guy Metcalf opened the meeting, and Butler Reed (col.), addressed the colored brethern.

Florida Star, Titusville, Florida, September 25, 1889.

We Cannot Hold Our Peace.

COCOA, BREVARD CO., FLA.,
Aug. 27th, 1888.

Editor of the Florida Star:

MR. EDITOR—Please allow space in your most valuable paper to say a word in regard to the politics of this place. So far as the Republicans are concerned we met here on Saturday night, August 25th, when Butler Read was elected chairman of the meeting and E. B. Stidum was chosen secretary.

The object of the meeting being stated to the vast multitude assembled, considerable confusion was manifested, as we felt much aggrieved from the past actions of the chairman of Republican executive committee, viz., in calling together the white Republicans of this county at Melbourne, and electing delegates to the district and State convention without notifying even a colored man of the county of such meeting, and we, the colored Republicans of Brevard county, and especially this district, desire all interested to understand that we are legal voters, and that we are also Republicans, and that our votes count as strong as theirs so far as they go. Where we have been wrongly dealt with, we have got nerve and manhood to contend for recognition especially when we are thought to be ignorant by those of our leaders, we must be recognized if we are looked upon as a part that make up the Republican party, however we abbreviate. After some discussion we organized a club, numbering about twenty-five, styled as the Harrison and Morton Club. We are pledged to support those men at the head of our ticket, to be voted for November next, leaving ourselves unpledged, so far as the county matter is concerned; for, as we claim we have been wrongly treated, as true men of our party in regard to our committee, we shall, in future, be controlled by our own option. We shall be heard, and we here announce that with Butler Reed as president of our club, and E. B. Stidum as secretary, we expect to swell the number of our club to forty-five or fifty ere the day of business. I now submit.

Yours for right,

B. S. E.

Chapter 17: Racial Attitudes on the Lake

If their choice of neighborhoods was any indication, the Jameses were people who believed in racial integration. They mixed well with both blacks and whites while living in Tallahassee and Cocoa. This same pattern held true for their neighbors in Lake Worth. Their friends included affluent Palm Beachers, such as the Potters, Porters, Hoaglands, and Brelsfords, as well as people of more modest means on the west side of the lake, the Bradleys, Pierces, Stephan, and Merkel.

The Jameses' hospitality was their hallmark. No barriers of class, education, or race interfered with their capacity to build friendships with people of all sorts. Fannie no doubt was an excellent cook. Illustrative of their cordiality, the *Tropical Sun* recounted the following story. While sailing around the lake one Sunday, a visitor stopped at the Jewell wharf and was spontaneously treated to a banquet.

> Our Cocoa ex-editor is down on Lake Worth and writes glowing things home about that famed region. Sunday last the 17th, was the anniversary of his birthday, which he celebrated in most becoming style near the foot of the Lake at Jewell In making the tour of the Lake he, with his friends, stopped about mid-way at the residence of Samuel James and were induced to stay till dinner, which he declares was the most generous and agreeable spread he had enjoyed for years. The gratifying feature of the meal was that it was almost entirely home-made. The milk, butter, eggs, chickens, fruits, jellies, etc., were all from the home garden and home resources.

Tropical Sun, July 21, 1892—
James hospitality.

The members of this small pioneer community supported each other, serving as witnesses for each other's homestead claims. As a carpenter, Samuel James helped his neighbors build homes and barns. The fact that the Jameses were black and their neighbors white does not seem to have affected their relationships. Only the four Pennsylvania friends protested the Jameses' homestead claim. All the other neighbors stood up for Fannie and Samuel in court.

In fact, the Jameses got along so well with their white neighbors that some have wondered whether they were so light-skinned that they could pass as white or if their neighbors knew about their African American roots. However, the evidence indicates that they made no attempt to hide their background.

- Census records show they listed themselves as "mulatto."

- The Jameses lived with a "black" family in Tallahassee.

- Samuel publicly testified about his association with the "colored" church in Cocoa.

- Charles Pierce and the "boys" came up with the nickname "Black Diamonds," due to the Jameses' dark complexion.

- Members of Fannie's "mulatto" family came to visit her in Jewell, some of whom were dark-skinned enough to be labeled "black" on the census. Fannie publicly acknowledged these family relationships. (See Chapter 43-Fannie's Genealogy particularly with references to Alonzo Anderson and Lucy Jones.)

There can be little doubt that the Jameses were what they claimed to be, namely people of mixed African and European ancestry.

On the whole, race appears to have been much less of a contentious issue in South Florida than it was in other parts of the state. For one thing, pioneer life was so hard in the early days that the few scattered inhabitants were eager to welcome any new settler who was willing to work. Unlike the northern part of the state, which had been steeped in prejudicial attitudes by the institution of slavery and the bloodshed of the Civil War, most South Florida settlers came from the north, sympathized with the Union cause during the War, and carried racial attitudes more in line with the spirit of the Emancipation Proclamation and equal rights promoted by the Thirteenth through Fifteenth amendments. Several settlers are known to have been Union veterans including Edwin Bradley and Harvey Geer. This divergence of backgrounds helps explain why the racial climate on the lake was decidedly different from the white supremacist attitudes prevalent in the Panhandle and Central Florida.

Lemuel Livingston, an African American writer from Key West, reported that blacks living in coastal South Florida and in the Keys retained many of the benefits of Reconstruction into the 1880s and 1890s, including the right to vote.

> There are no attempts at bulldozing and intimidation during campaigns and at elections here. No negroes are murdered here in cold blood, and there are no gross miscarriages of justice against them as is so frequently seen throughout the South, to her everlasting shame and disgrace.... A (race equality) vigilance committee here would meet with the warmest kind of reception and a klu klux clan would be unceremoniously run into the Gulf of Mexico or the Atlantic Ocean. (Rivers and Brown, "African Americans in South Florida: A Home and a Haven for Reconstruction-era Leaders," 9.)

A prominent Lake Worth example is the viewpoint of the *Tropical Sun*, and its editor, Guy I. Metcalf. Metcalf was a man who personally mixed with blacks. (His father, William I. Metcalf, was Fannie James's personal attorney.) The editorial policy of the *Tropical Sun*, while low-key, leaned toward egalitarian rather than segregationist views.

- Metcalf spoke at the black Baptist Church in Cocoa, alongside the African American minister. (*Florida Star*, September 25, 1889)

- Metcalf published an article covering a debate over separate divisions for whites and blacks in the G.A.R. (Glorious Army of the Republic, an organization for Union veterans of the Civil War.) Throughout the article, black veterans are referred to as "comrades." editorializing comments are found such as "It was hardly to be expected that he would so openly favor the separation of the races." How could such a statement be made if segregation were already considered the norm by the *Sun's* readership? The article went on to conclude that "the sentiment of the encampment [convention] seems to be against separate posts." Such pro-egalitarian statements are made without hesitation or any sense that readers would find the advocacy of race mixing to be offensive. (*Tropical Sun*, August 19, 1891. See Appendix A for a copy of the full article.)

- In its coverage of events on the lake, Metcalf's paper gave equal treatment to the Jameses, despite the common knowledge of their ethnic background. At a time when "a single drop of negro blood" degraded a person in the eyes of segregationists and white supremacists, the Jameses were spoken of with respect and dignity.

In confirmation of the democratic attitudes found in the Homestead Era community, the following statement of principle was printed in the *Tropical Sun*. As the column was customarily dedicated to local happenings, parties, visitors, boat launchings, and gardening, the comment was, in all likelihood, a veiled reference to a specific incident, although the writer provided no details.

> Mr. and Mrs. Samuel James, of Jewell, were at the County Seat Wednesday, on legal business. THE SUN acknowledges a pleasant call.

Tropical Sun, August 11, 1892—The Jameses are welcomed at the *Sun* office.

> **HYPOLUXO HAPPENINGS.**
>
> We believe in equal rights to all, special privileges to none.

Tropical Sun, March 3, 1898—Equal Rights.

POLITICS AND RACE

After the departure of Union troops, the State of Florida introduced measures designed to reduce black political power in small, subtly crafted but relentless steps. The 1885 revision to the state constitution put in place a poll tax. Segregated schools were established with a pretense at "separate but equal." Literacy tests and white-only primaries soon followed. Poor and illiterate whites were immunized from disenfranchisement by the grandfather clause, which granted voting rights to those whose grandfathers had voted (whites) but denied them to blacks.

In view of the systematic harassment of black voters during this period, it is remarkable to see the courage of people like Reverend Butler Reed who stood against the incoming flood of intimidation. Black leaders began to talk of deserting the Republican Party, which had deserted them.

> Embitterment of Negro voters over.... Republican policies since 1877 led conservative leaders of the Southern Democrats to attempt a concerted drive to attract them away from their traditional party. The Negro voters were therefore courted, flattered, 'mistered', and honored by Southern white politicians in the 'eighties as never before. (Woodward, *The Strange Career of Jim Crow*, 59)

In this context, it is odd to see Samuel James as a member in a political club organized to support Democratic candidate Francis Fleming for Florida governor along with most of his neighbors. Being a registered voter was a qualification for membership. Apparently, neither Samuel's illiteracy nor his race was a hindrance to his membership.

However, James's support of Fleming is doubly ironic. Fleming had been a Captain in the Confederate Army and was an ardent segregationist. As governor, he outlawed mixed marriages, such as apparently those of his and Fannie's parents, and he put in place literacy tests designed to restrict black voting rights. (Bessette and Warren, "From Our Past," *Florida Times-Union*, May 13, 2006.) In view of Samuel's inability to read and write, he likely lost his right to vote under the Fleming administration.

DADE COUNTY FLEMING CLUB MINUTES AND RESOLUTION

A meeting of the voters of Lake Worth Dade Co. Florida was held at the Cocoanut Grove House on the afternoon of July 14, 1888 for the purpose of organizing a political club to take various actions the coming campaign. The meeting was called to order by Fred. S. Dewey and the following Preamble and Resolution were unanimously adopted.

Whereas, the election of Francis P. Fleming of Duval Co. Florida as Governor of the state will guarantee by his high character and finer abilities, a notable and honest administration of State affairs – and

Whereas, there has been a co-called Democratic Club organized on Lake Worth, Dade Co, Florida composed mainly of newcomers, of unknown antecedents, politically and personally, who having no property or interest in the County, and which by combining with similar elements in other parts of the County, by misrepresentation and slander, has gained an influence in County affairs, far beyond that due to it.

Be it resolved, that a Fleming Club be organized on Lake Worth, Dade Co. Florida, for the purpose of working for the election of Francis P. Fleming as Governor; to obtain for taxpayers and old residents the influence in the County's affairs to which they are entitled thereby ensuring an honest and economical County administration, and last but not least, that the election this fall may be untainted by the fraudulent practices which prevailed at the Miami and Elliot's Key precincts in the last election, and which, by the negligence or connivance of those in authority remain unpunished to this day.

For these purposes, we the undersigned hereby organize ourselves under the name of the Dade County Fleming Club and adopt the following by-laws for our guidance.

The officers of this Club shall consist of a President and a Secretary, whose duties shall be such as are usual for similar organizations.

Any voter of Dade County who pledges himself to support and vote for Francis P. Fleming for Governor and the Democratic State Ticket may become a member of the Club upon receiving a majority of ballots cast on the question of such membership.

(Original Members)	Wm Stephan		(Admitted later)
Fred S. Dewey	Sam'l James	July 29	A. F. Quimby
James W. Potter	N. W. Pitts	July 28	E. B. Plunket
E. N. Dimick	Geo. W. Potter	Aug 4	J. C. Hoagland
L. D. Hillhouse	Wm H. Wade	Aug 11	O. S. Porter
J. F. Highsmith	J. S. Jenkins		
M. W. Dimick	J. N. Parker		
George W. Lainhart	A. F. Quimby		
A. W. Garnett	E. B. Plunket		
Fred Mayer	J. C. Hoagland		
M. K. Lyman	O. S. Porter		
Allen E. Heyser	James McFarland		

DID THE JAMESES' DECISION TO HOMESTEAD HAVE A POLITICAL ASPECT?

The 1880s marked the turn of the tide. On the political front, the backlash against equal rights saw voter intimidation and black officials hounded from office. On the economic front, ex-slave owners were reestablishing their supremacy as well, denying blacks economic opportunity and forcing former slaves into sharecropping where the bulk of the profits went to the ex-plantation owners.

Black intellectuals fought back against the onrushing tide, but they were facing a losing battle. Various ideas were floated on how blacks could escape the enclosing net of Jim Crow. The federal government offered fairer treatment, resulting in blacks seeking employment by the U.S. Post Office Department or as U.S. customs agents.

Another federal haven was found in the Homestead Act, which offered an opportunity for black landownership and a way to escape the poverty of the sharecropper. In the environment of increasing oppression, homesteading took on political as well as economic significance.

> The vision of a new land that would welcome the oppressed was part of the core ideology of the black freedom struggle in Florida. African-Americans based their hope on Florida's large public domain—Florida had more than twice as much public land (available for settlement) than any other southern state.... Wrote Rev. John R. Scott; "here they may secure beautiful and happy homes, and the means of educating their children." Enhanced opportunities for land ownership offered an alternative to white domination....

> African American ministers used the language of emancipation to exhort black Floridians to purchase their own homes and farms. Reverend Robert Brookens told his people... "A man without a home is a slave to the man that he rents from... Now while our people are following up these lordly farmers they could all get settled on some Government land that is near them and build Good houses, and let their families stay there and improve them." (Ortiz, *Emancipation Betrayed*, 18–22)

The Jameses had lived in close proximity to educated black leaders, such as William G. Stewart and Butler Reed. Both men were astute and politically active. It would be surprising if Fannie and Samuel had not been exposed to the concept of economic freedom through landownership. The anti-black political tides would have made the prospect of homesteading on Lake Worth that much more appealing.

With that insight, Fannie James's first choice of La Paz as the name for her South Florida home may be seen as having special significance. More than just a reference to the physical isolation and tranquility of the place, it may have also represented a refuge from the political storms that were battering African American hopes.

Part 3

Jewell Progress

===

POPULATION GROWTH, 13 TO 308

"It is not hard to see the day will soon come when the entire lake front from West Palm Beach to Lake Worth will be built up as a fine residential district." – Lake Worth Herald, 1912

Bird's Eye View of Development Plans from around 1910.
Courtesy of University of Florida Digital Collection:
Miscellaneous Pamphlets and Brochures.

Chapter 18: Jameses' Second Homestead

In 1888, just three years after arriving in Lake Worth, the Jameses began to develop a second homestead parcel. These 160-acres lay directly west of their waterfront property. The square parcel covered the area from Lake Avenue to Sixth Avenue South, from M Street to F Street. The FEC right-of-way ran north to south across the Jameses' property.

Their new homesite was near what would become Fourth Avenue South and L Street. (The precise location of the house is known from the later application to move the Jewell Post Office.)

Samuel's improvements on this second homestead stand in dramatic contrast to the Jameses' first palmetto shanty. At 49 by 21 feet, the new house was over 1,000 square feet—three times the size of their earlier home on the waterfront and larger than many of the cottage homes in Lake Worth today. This one had a shingled, not a thatched, roof.

Samuel also built a barn for expanded farm operations. "Pine apples" and fruit trees on the second homestead were valued at $1,200 as compared with $400 on the earlier property.

The Jameses were prospering. Profits from the sale of waterfront lots allowed them to accumulate a little nest egg to build a nicer home and to increase agricultural production on this second homestead. By this time (and despite the fact that the new fruit trees and pineapples were not yet producing market crops), they had the resources to invest thousands of dollars in their farm, as compared with the $50 that Samuel had in his pocket when he first came to the lake.

> A fine looking watermelon, weighing some twenty-five pounds was one of the sights down the Lake, Saturday. It was grown by Mr. James of Jewell.

Tropical Sun, **May 18, 1893**—
25-pound watermelon.

Meanwhile, Samuel was gaining a reputation as a productive farmer.

In addition to their new home, the Jameses continued to use their original waterfront structure as the post office for a number of years. The two lots were a little over a quarter of a mile apart. As Samuel was over 60 years of age at this time, it seems likely that he had hired help who may have been living in one or the other of the houses.

A U.S. land patent to the Jameses' westward 160 acres was granted in April 1892. With title to this additional acreage, Samuel sold a ten-acre strip on the north end to Amanda Malvina Moore during the following October. They designated the Moore tract as Lot 1.

 The Moore deal also included a 50-by-300-foot waterfront lot, adjacent to and just south of the Jewell Post Office. At a third of an acre, this was by far the smallest piece of land that he had ever sold and stands out as unique in several ways. In contrast to previous sales of five- and ten-acre agricultural lots, the small lot was apparently intended as a homesite. Its location is still easy to identify, being the lot south of Bryant Park, where the private residence known as the "Birthday Cake Castle" stands. In fact, 5th Avenue South curves slightly as it nears the park to accommodate this exceptional tract.

 The idea to subdivide the land into smaller residential lots may have been the beginnings of a new business plan—that is, to develop Jewell into a residential community. Land speculation seems to have been on the rise. Moore paid $30 an acre, held on to the property for only six months, and then flipped it, selling both the waterfront lot and the ten-acre agricultural lot to Dorinda Brelsford for $43 an acre.

(4—369.)

HOMESTEAD PROOF—TESTIMONY OF CLAIMANT.

Samuel James, of Jewell Fla, being called as a witness in his own behalf in support of homestead entry, No. *21026*, for *W½ of NW¼ Sec 27 & E½ of NE¼ Sec 28 Tp 44 S R 43 E* testifies as follows:

Ques. 1.—What is your name, age, and post-office address?

Ans. *Samuel James, 65, Jewell, Dade Co, Fla.*

Ques. 2.—Are you a *native born* citizen of the United States, and if so, in what State or Territory were you born?*

Ans. *Native Born, Born in Virginia*

Ques. 3.—Are you the identical person who made homestead entry, No. *21026*, at the *Gainesville* land office on the *Seventh* day of *January*, 1891, and what is the true description of the land now claimed by you?

Ans. *Yes, W½ of NW¼ Sec 27 & E½ of NE¼ Sec 28 Tp 44 S R 43 E*

Ques. 4.—When was your house built on the land and when did you establish actual residence therein? (Describe said house and other improvements which you have placed on the land, giving total value thereof.)

Ans. *August 1888, established residence then. House 49x21 Shingle Roof, Packing House, 12x10, Well, 4½ acres planted in Pine Apples & Fruit Trees Valued at $1200.00*

Ques. 5.—Of whom does your family consist; and have you and your family resided continuously on the land since first establishing residence thereon? (If unmarried, state the fact.)

Ans. *Myself & Wife, we have resided continuously on the Claim*

Ques. 6.—For what period or periods have you been absent from the homestead since making settlement, and for what purpose; and if temporarily absent, did your family reside upon and cultivate the land during such absence?

Ans. *I have not been Absent*

Ques. 7.—How much of the land have you cultivated each season and for how many seasons have you raised crops thereon?

Ans. *4½ Acres in Fruit Trees & Pine Apples, no market Crops yet*

Ques. 8.—Is your present claim within the limits of an incorporated town or selected site of a city or town, or used in any way for trade and business?

Ans. *No to all*

Ques. 9.—What is the character of the land? Is it timber, mountainous, prairie, grazing, or ordinary agricultural land? State its kind and quality, and for what purpose it is most valuable.

Ans. *Pine & Oak Scrub, Agricultural land*

Ques. 10.—Are there any indications of coal, salines, or minerals, of any kind, on the land? (If so, describe what they are, and state whether the land is more valuable for agricultural than for mineral purposes.)

Ans. *No Minerals, fit only for farming purposes*

Ques. 11.—Have you ever made any other homestead entry? (If so, describe the same.)

Ans. *No*

Ques. 12.—Have you sold, conveyed, or mortgaged any portion of the land; and if so, to whom and for what purpose?

Ans. *No*

Ques. 13.—Have you any personal property of any kind elsewhere than on this claim? (If so, describe the same, and state where the same is kept.)

Ans. *No*

Richard B Potter
Fred S. Dewey

Samuel X James

I HEREBY CERTIFY that the foregoing testimony was read to the claimant before being subscribed, and was sworn to before me this *Third* day of *August*, 1891.

[SEE NOTE ON FOURTH PAGE.]

A H Quimby, Clk Ct Ct
June Dade Co Fla

* (In case the party is of foreign birth a certified transcript from the court records of his declaration of intention to become a citizen, or of his naturalization, or a copy thereof, certified by the officer taking this proof, must be filed with the case. Evidence of naturalization is only required in final (*five year*) homestead cases.)

Notice For Publication.

LAND OFFICE AT GAINESVILLE, FLA.,
June 8, 1891

Notice is hereby given that the following named settler yas filed notice of his intention to make final proof in support of his claim, and that said proof will be made before A. F. Quimby, Clerk Circuit Court at Juno on Aug 31, 1891, viz:

WILLIAM STEPHEN, OF JEWELL, FLA.

H. E. 10075, for the lots 1 and 2 and W. ½ of N. W. ¼ of Sec. 15, T 44 S R. 43 E.

He names the following witnesses to prove his continuous residence upon and cultivation of said land, viz:

E. R. Bradley and Louis S. Bradley of Hypoluxo, Fla., and Michel Myrckl and Samuel James, of Jewel, Fla.

17   ALEX LYNCH, Register.

LOTUS COVE.

West Shore L. W. Twixt Hypo & Jewell.)
when that hotel is built at Jewell the fact shall be truly chronicled,

Tropical Sun, August 12, 1891.

There are signs that Jewell was beginning to see itself as a community. The James-Moore deal was signed and notarized, not at Palm Beach or Juno but at "Jewell," the first time that had happened, with neighbor, John C. Hoagland serving as notary. Apparently, the closing took place either at the James or Hoagland residences. (See copy of sales contract in Appendix D.) Simultaneously, more and more settlers were identifying themselves as residents of Jewell.

When Edwin Bradley began to write his Lotus Cove column for the *Tropical Sun*, he likewise took a step toward raising Jewell's visibility, when he subtitled his column "West Shore L.W. Twixt Hypo and Jewell."

Bradley alludes to rumors about the possible construction of a hotel at Jewell, a development that had the potential to rapidly transform the community. He quipped in his column:

Apparently, there was a bit of a buzz about growth potential at Jewell in 1891 and 1892, but little came of it. The rumored hotel was never built and the Jameses, after the sale to Amanda Moore, discontinued subdividing and selling either residential or agricultural lots. Rather they held on to the remaining 150 acres of their second homestead until it was sold to PBFC in 1910. Jewell was destined to remain a cluster of farms. Any hopes for a town at the site were put on ice until the founding of the Town of Lake Worth, 20 years later.

Notice For Publication.

LAND OFFICE AT GAINESVILLE, FLA.,
June 6th, 1891.

Notice is hereby given that the following named settler has filed notice of his intention to make final proof in support of his claim and that said proof will be made before A. F. Quimby, Clerk Circuit Court, at Juno, Fla., on Aug. 31, 1891, viz:

SAMUEL JAMES, of JEWELL, FLA.,

H. E. 21025 for the W. ½ of the N. W. ¼ of Sec. 27 and the E. ½ of the N. E. ¼ of Sec. 28 T 44 S, R 43 E.

He names the following witnesses to prove his continuous residence upon and cultivation of said land, viz:

E. R. Bradley and Louis S Bradley of Hypoluxo, Fla and William Stephan and Michel Myrckel, of Jewell, Fla.

17   ALEX. LYNCH, Register.

Chapter 19: Mail Routes

BAREFOOT MAILMAN ROUTE TO BISCAYNE BAY

Mail service between the two population centers of Dade County, Lake Worth and Miami was intermittent until 1885, when a "Star Route" was established. Star Routes were serviced by third-party contractors, rather than USPS employees, and were marked in postal records with an asterisk or "star." Choice of route and delivery method was left to the contractor as long as delivery met a required schedule.

Route 16210. Lake Worth to Biscayne.

Leave Lake Worth Thursdays at 7 a. m.

Arrive at Biscayne Saturdays by 7 p. m.

Leave Biscayne Mondays at 7 a. m.

Arrive at Lake Worth Wednesdays by 7 p. m. [19 oct 85.

Daily Bulletin, Post Office Department, October 20, 1885.

At a time when there were no roads, the mail-carrier would sail from the Lake Worth Post Office to the southern end of the lake and then walk along the beach for the sixty-mile trek to Biscayne Bay. The beach-walk portion of the route is the origin of the name "Barefoot Mailman." The postal position was romanticized after the publication of Theodore Pratt's 1943 novel of that title.

Hypoluxo lays claim to being the "Home of the Barefoot Mailman" by virtue of the fact that the first and most of the Star Route mail-carriers lived there. In 1887, the Hypoluxo-based mail-carriers arranged to have the route shortened by having another carrier deliver the mail to Hypoluxo by boat, although the change was not made official with the USPS until the following year.

Route 16236. Hypoluxo to Miami.

Leave Hypoluxo Mondays at 6 a. m.

Arrive at Miami Wednesdays by 6 p. m.

Leave Miami Thursdays at 6 a. m.

Arrive at Hypoluxo Saturdays by 6 p. m. [19 sept 88

Daily Bulletin, Post Office Department, September 29, 1888.

The shortened route was still physically grueling, requiring six full days of walking each week under less than ideal conditions. Turnover was rapid. According to the Historical Society of Palm Beach County (HSPBC), 20 different carriers served the route in the nine years of its existence from 1885 to 1893, including Edwin Bradley, Andrew Garnett, and Charles Pierce. (http://www.pbchistoryonline.org/page/mail-routes) The most famous Barefoot Mailman was Ed Hamilton, who died in the line of duty, apparently swimming the shark- and alligator-infested Hillsborough River when his rowboat turned up missing.

BOAT MAIL ROUTES

Prior to 1880 the U.S. mail was delivered from Saint Lucie to Miami by ship. Service was irregular. The first deliveries to Palm Beach became stops on the ocean side. Edwin R. Bradley established the first mail route on Lake Worth with delivery once a week. He would sail to Palm Beach to pick up the mail, deliver it to the various POs on the lakeshore down to Hypoluxo at the south end, and then continue the barefoot-walking route to Miami.

In 1887, the U.S. Post Office Department established a separate sailing route from Jupiter to Hypoluxo with Henry E. Root as carrier. Service was upgraded to three times per week.

This hand-drawn carrier map, taken from the Juno Post Office application, shows the mail boat route in 1890 zigzagging across the lake from one post office to the next. The map is crowded with details and requires a bit of deciphering. Starting at the top, the mail route began at the "Jupiter P.O." and then traveled on the "Lake Worth & Jupiter R. R." (Informally called the Celestial Railroad) to the proposed new PO at Juno, as shown by the outline of a pointer-hand in the upper left of the map.

From there the "Mail Route by Boat" headed south to Oak Lawn PO (later called Riviera Beach) and then across the lake to Lake Worth PO, Palm Beach PO, and Figulus PO on the eastern shore, before finally crossing the lake and stopping at Jewell.

Also labeled are "Lake Worth Creek" to the left of the train tracks, the "inlet" from the Atlantic Ocean, and "Wagon Road passing Jewell, Oak Lawn and Juno." (Further discussion on the wagon road later.)

Not shown is the Lantana Post Office, which had not yet been established, and Hypoluxo, the final stop on the lake and link to Miami via the Barefoot Mailman Route.

Especially in the early years, a variety of vessels were used to carry mail to the Jewell Post Office, not always without mishap.

Map showing mail route by boat from Juno to Jewell.

When Uriah D. Hendrickson was awarded the contract to carry the mail from Jupiter to Hypoluxo, he used both his sailing schooner, the *Mary B.*, and a small custom-built steamer, the *Lake Worth.* The Mail Boat Route initially ran three times per week (PLSF, 209). By 1893, daily steamboats were scheduled to carry passengers, merchandise, and the mail from Juno to Hypoluxo, stopping at each post office along the way.

> Last Monday as the "Arthur B." made the Jewell wharf with the mail she capsized. Everything in the boat was soaking wet except the mail, which reached its destination in good order.

Tropical Sun, January 14, 1892—
Mail boat capsizes at Jewell wharf.

Handwritten caption at top reads, "The first Steamer ever on Lake Worth, February 1883".
Courtesy of Historical Society of Palm Beach County.

RAILWAY MAIL ROUTES

With the completion of Flagler's FEC Railway, the train became the faster and more convenient means of moving the mail. Train delivery was scheduled to start for post offices on the west side of the lake on July 1, 1896. The service actually started two weeks ahead of time.

> **RAILROAD SERVICE ESTABLISHED.**
>
> FLORIDA.
> Route 123054. West Palm Beach, by Jewell, Lantana, Hypoluxo, Linton, Fort Lauderdale, Biscayne, Lemon City, and Buena Vista, to Miami, Fla. Florida East Coast Rwy. Co., 67.53 ms. and back, six times a week, or as much oftener as trains may run. From July 1, 1896. [25 may 96

Daily Bulletin, Post Office Department,
May 26, 1896.

Chapter 20: Relocating the Jewell Post Office

From 1889 to 1896, Fannie James ran the post office from her home on the shore of the lake. Mail was delivered by boat three days a week. But with the advent of the railroad, times were changing and the Jameses kept pace.

In 1894, the Flagler Railroad reached West Palm Beach. The City of West Palm Beach was established, and population on the west shore began to grow exponentially. During the week of September 25, 1895, the FEC commenced its extension south to Miami (*1896 Directory*, 34). Within a year, the extension was complete.

The new track ran across the western end of the Jameses' second homestead property. The abstract of title, recorded in Dade County records, shows the circuit court granting the FEC title to the right-of-way on February 15, 1896, several months after the track had been laid. Apparently, rather than squabbling with each landowner between West Palm Beach and Miami, the FEC was determined to push ahead, without explicit permission, and deal with the legal fallout later.

Samuel James, along with several of his neighbors, ended up suing the FEC. According to county records, the net result was that the railroad got its right-of-way and the landowners received an undisclosed amount of cash as compensation.

> Reciting condemnation of a right of way 100 feet wide through the property of the defendant, to wit: A strip of land 100 feet in width, being 50 feet in width on either side of the center of the track of petitioner's railroad as it is now located and constructed.... Clerk's certificate of payment of money into court therefor is shown. (Florida East Coast Railway Company v. Samuel James, Dade County Deed Book "O," page 180.)

In June 1896, with the railroad already built and operating, Fannie determined to keep pace with modernization. She applied to the Post Office Department to shift delivery from the boat route to the train and to move the Jewell Office closer to the tracks. The application included a map showing the new post office site, directly west of the earlier location.

Laying track in South Florida, about 1894.
Courtesy of Lake Worth Historical Museum.

Post Office Department,

TOPOGRAPHER'S OFFICE,

Washington, D.C., June 4, 1896.

Sir:

　To enable the Topographer of this Department to determine, with as much accuracy as possible, the relative positions of Post Offices, so that they may be correctly delineated on its maps, the Postmaster General requests you carefully to answer the questions below, and furnish the diagram on the other side, returning the same as soon as possible, verified by your signature and dated, under cover to the Topographer's Office, Post Office Department.

　　　　　Respectfully, &c.,

　　　　　　　　　　TOPOGRAPHER P. O. DEPT.

　　　　　　　　　　　　Topographer P. O. Dept.

To Postmaster at *Jewell* 　　NEW SITE

Dade Co.

Fla.

The (P. O. Dept.) name of my Office is *Jewell*

If the town, village, or site of the Post Office be known by *another name than that of the Post Office,* state that other name here:

The P. O. is situated in the *Lat 2 in N 1/2* quarter of *Section No. 27*, in *Township* *44* (north or south), Range *South 43 East* (east or west), County of *Dade*, State of *Florida*

The name of the most prominent *river* near it is *Lake Worth*

The name of the nearest *creek* is *Lake Osborn*

This Office is *1750* miles from said *river*, on the *W* side of it, and is *one* miles from said nearest *creek*, on the *E* side of it. *Lake Osborn*

My Office is on Mail Route No. *12305.7*

My Office is a Special Office supplied from *Railway 1680* miles distant.

The name of the nearest Office on my route is *Lantana*, and its distance is *2 1/4* miles, by the traveled road, in a *Southern* direction from this, my Office.

The name of the nearest Office, *on the same route,* on the other side, is *West palm beach* and its distance is *7* miles in a *Northern* ly direction from this, my Office.

The name of the nearest Office *off the route* is *Lake Worth*, and its distance by the most direct road is *12* miles in a *North E.* direction from this, my Office.

The name of the nearest railroad is *Florida East Coast*

If on the line of or near the railroad, on which side and how far from the track is your Office located? *1680 ft west from West door to the track*

　　　　　(Signature of Postmaster.) *Fannie A. James*

　　　　　　　　　　(Date.) *June 15 1896*

5-2342

The nearest POs on the new train route would be West Palm Beach, seven miles to the north, and Lantana, 2½ miles to the south.

The location of the new post office is given with impressive precision. It was situated 1,750 feet west of the lake and 1,680 feet east of the FEC tracks. Information about its north and south position is shown on the post office application's Diagram Page, pinpointing the location of the site.

The diagram represents one square mile. The handwritten notes on the right indicate that this area is bounded by what is now Lake Avenue on the north, F Street on the west, 12th Avenue South, and M Street. The double horizontal line down the center of the grid is the approximate location of Dixie Highway with the FEC tracks to the west.

The dot represents the new site of the Jewell Post Office, which would have been near K Street at 5th Avenue South. The spot also represents the location of the Jameses' second house, which would have been about a third of a mile due west of their first house and former post office site on the lakefront.

There is no way of knowing which house the Jameses occupied or if and when they moved. One or the other may have been used to house hired farmhands.

MAIL MESSENGER SERVICE ESTABLISHED.

FLORIDA.

Route 223044. Jewell, Dade Co., from Florida East Coast Rwy. Route 123054, .61 m., often as required. From September 21, 1896. [14 sept 96

Daily Bulletin, Post Office Department, September 16, 1896.

Since the Jewell Post Office was located some distance from the track, a mail messenger service would ferry the mailbag between the train and the post office. The route number 223044 is identified both on the postal application and in the USPS *Bulletin* with the round-trip distance from the track to the post office site being .61 miles. Such special delivery was not unusual. Lantana and Linton also required mail messenger service.

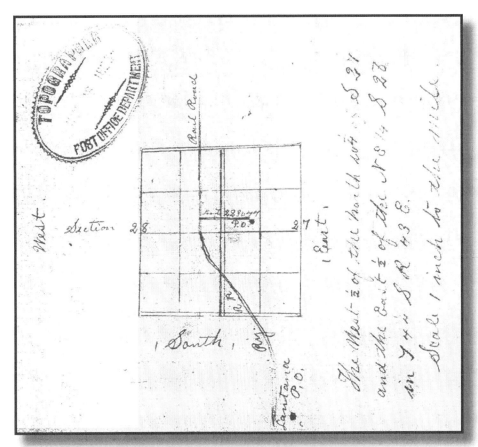

Chapter 21: A New Batch of Neighbors

Another change brought about by the arrival of the railroad was increased interest in nonwaterfront property. The years between 1895 and 1903 saw the establishment of four new homesteads in Jewell, west of the current Dixie Highway.

ELLA DIMICK-POTTER

Ella Dimick was born March 1870 in Illinois to Frank Dimick and Anna Geer. The family moved to Palm Beach around 1876 and built a home south of the present site of the Flagler Museum. Ella, along with her two siblings, was among the eight students to enroll when the first schoolhouse opened in 1886.

Ella married George Wells Potter in 1893. The newlyweds traveled to Illinois on their honeymoon to see the Chicago World's Fair, as well as visit with family. The young couple paid for the trip by selling George's homestead at Figulus. After their return, George and Ella moved to the west side of the lake in the area that within a year would become West Palm Beach and built a house on the waterfront on Hibiscus Street.

George and his brother, Richard Potter, were prominent people in the pioneer community. George was county surveyor and an artist. Many of the hand-drawn maps and illustrations of early pioneer life were his work. Richard was a medical doctor and was often on call throughout the region. He was twice elected to the Florida Legislature, served as U.S. Customs Collector, and was, for a time, the official surgeon of Flagler's FEC railroad.

In February 1895, Ella purchased 160 acres near Jewell from the Florida Board of Education, which had, in turn, received the land from the U.S. Government as one of the public provisions of the Homestead Act. Thus, unlike her Jewell neighbors, she acquired the property by direct purchase rather than through homestead or preemption. As a result, there are no records of the buildings and farm production, if any, that were typically provided on homestead applications. In view of the Potters' many real estate dealings, it seems likely that the property was acquired for speculation, either leased out or unused. Most certainly, the Potters never lived there.

Location: 13th Avenue North and Lake Avenue, A Street and F Street

Legal description: West half of the northeast quarter and the west half of the southeast quarter of Section 21

The property was sold to Palm Beach Farms Company in 1911 for $1,200.

Ella died in 1964. She was 19 years younger than her husband and outlived him by 40 years.

The two Potter brothers and their wives are buried alongside each other in the Potter family plot at Woodlawn Cemetery in West Palm Beach.

HARVEY GEER

Geer was born around 1845 in Lyons, Wayne County, New York, to Harvey Sr. and Angeline Roys. A Civil War veteran, Harvey served as a private under Capt. John F. Stewart in Company D of the 9th Regiment of New York Heavy Artillery Volunteers from August 18, 1862, until July 6, 1865. His military records state that he was a farmer, 16 years of age at the time of enlistment, and 5 feet 8 inches tall with dark complexion, hazel eyes, and dark hair.

After the war, Harvey married Helen in 1868. The couple moved from New York State to Wheatland, Michigan, in the early 1870s.

Harvey's older brother, Albert, was one of the first settlers in Palm Beach. He arrived in 1876 with longtime Illinois friends, the Dimicks. Albert built a home in the heart of Palm Beach. After spending ten years in the tropics, he sold his place for $10,000, an outrageous sum at the time, and moved to Michigan. The old Geer property later became the site of Flagler's famous Royal Poinciana Hotel.

About six years later, brother Harvey tried his hand at Florida homesteading, arriving from Michigan in November 1892. The lake area was by now more populous and prosperous than when Albert lived here. Waterfront property was no longer available for homesteading. So Harvey filed his claim on vacant land west of the Jewell Post Office.

As a Civil War vet, Harvey made use of the GI Bill of his day, filing his land claim under the Congressional Act of June 8, 1872, which expedited homestead grants "to honorably discharged soldiers."

Location: Lake Avenue to 6th Avenue South, A Street to F Street.

Acreage: 80.

Land description: "spruce pine agricultural land."

Legal description: West half of North east quarter Section 28, Township 44 South, Range 43 East.

Improvements: "House built June 1893, Frame, 12 x 14, Well & Pump."

Land Use: "3 Acres Grubbed and Planted in Pine Apple, Fruit Trees and Vegetable garden."

During the years that Harvey was in the lake area, he lived alone, although he had a wife and six daughters back in Michigan. According to comments on his homestead application, his "family would not come here." It appears that he may have been estranged from his wife, since he states that his residence on his claim was continuous "except 80 days Visiting World's Fair at Chicago." Apparently, he chose to go to the Fair, yet never found occasion to visit his family in Michigan. (Geer HA, 7)

Even though his property was close to the Jewell Post Office, Geer gave his address as Lantana, rather than Jewell, on his Homestead Final Proof, submitted April 17, 1895.

When Geer finally did return to Michigan sometime before 1900 (per census), he held on to his Florida land until he sold it to the Palm Beach Farms Company in 1910.

Harvey Geer died March 15, 1925, in Berrien County, Michigan.

THURZA BELLE EARNEST

"Belle" was born in Woodstock, Ohio, *circa* 1869, to Jacob T. and Annie Earnest. Her parents moved to the lake with their six children (three girls and three boys) in 1886 when Belle was 17.

Upon their arrival, the family first settled at the northern end of the lake, near Mangonia, and then moved to Lantana. Their new home was a large two-story structure to accommodate their large family. Noted for its flourishes, the house had "lots of hips and hurrahs on top." (*Tropical Sun*, February 1, 1894) The house was situated on the lakefront, north of Lantana Point and just south of the Bradleys.

The camaraderie of the pioneer community can be sensed from gossip-column-like articles in the *Tropical Sun*. On one occasion, the paper described a carefree sail outing of young singles from Lantana, including Belle and her sister, Maude. Guy Bradley had a talent for showing the "fair ladies a good time." (*Tropical Sun*, February 8, 1894)

At the other end of the emotional spectrum, relations between neighbors could be strained at times. An oft-repeated story tells of Belle's father's role in pacifying a raucous Democratic Party meeting, held at Juno in 1892.

> Bitter taunts were exchanged and violent language used. I believe it is a fact that practically every man in the convention had either one or two guns upon his person. Our beloved clerk of the court, Albert F. Quimby, what was a man of most peaceable disposition, sat with his six-shooter over his knees covered with a handkerchief. (**McGoun**, *Southeast Florida Pioneers*, 46.)

> The opposing factions were very bitter and come armed and ready to fight. At the critical moment when one shot would have precipitated a bloody battle, an old gentleman from Lantana, Mr. Jacob Ernest, arose and in an easy, kind voice, entreated them to be calm. His long white beard and patriarchal appearance, plus his serene attitude, brought reason to the caucus. They came to their senses and arranged a compromise which if it didn't suit everyone, at least it precluded the possibility of bloodshed." (*History of Juno Beach*, 8)

Jacob Earnest was an industrious man. He built and operated a sawmill on Lake Osborne and also served as Lantana's postmaster between 1903 and 1906.

At age 23, Belle took up a homestead claim in her own name, although according to the newspaper report, her father had a hand in the affair.

> Mr. Earnest and daughter are at Jewell. Miss Belle is contesting the McDonnell homestead. Now is the chance for Mack to do a gentlemanly act—let him relinquish to the fair contestant and everything will be lovely.

Tropical Sun—August 12, 1891.

In May 1892, she filed her claim on a property 2 miles northwest of her parents' home, planting pineapples and fruit trees. As a single woman, it is uncertain how much time she actually spent on her claim, especially with her fine family home nearby. Most likely, her homestead was acquired for business purposes.

Location: 13th Avenue North to Lake Avenue, west of Dixie Highway to F Street.

Land description: 160 acres, "Spruce Pine Palmetoe Scrub."

Legal description: East half of southeast quarter and east half of northeast quarter Section 21.

Improvements: First house built May 1892—10 by 12 feet; Second house built July 1894—12 by 20 feet. Well & Pump. Three acres cleared.

Residence: "Continuous" except "Absent 4 months. Went North visiting. My improvements were kept up whilst I was away."

The Earnests could not have been counted among Fannie's Jewell Thirteen, as they were living in the Mangonia area when the Jewell Post Office opened.

Thurza Belle Earnest's Final Homestead Proof was submitted July 23, 1897, when she was age 28. She listed her address at Lantana.

Witnesses:

E. H. Dimick of Palm Beach

J. Willis Comstock of West Palm Beach

J. N. Parker of West Palm Beach

L. E. Bradley of Lantana

(Earnest HA, 6, 13)

There was a considerable lapse of time before Earnest received her land patent. The delay may have been related to a conflict with the FEC railroad, which crossed her land. The application was approved on March 11, 1901, the same date an FEC proceeding against her was dismissed. The railroad track had been laid at least six years previously, so the legal status of the FEC right-of-way was pending for quite some time.

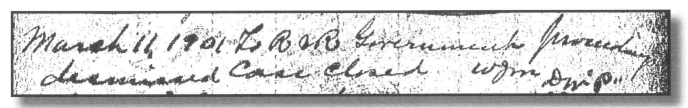

Handwritten note reads: "March 11, 1901. R&R Government proceeding dismissed case closed".
Source: Dade County Records.

Belle remained close to her family and moved with them in 1908 to Melbourne, Florida, where she married widower Charles T. McBride.

The McBrides sold their 160 acres to Palm Beach Farms Company on December 10, 1910 for $1,350.

ERNEST LINWOOD CRENSHAW

Ernest Crenshaw was born in Trigg County, Kentucky about 1868. He moved to Florida with his wife and three children in June 1903. He was the last to take up a homestead on what would become the original plat of the Town of Lake Worth and arrived in the Jewell area two months after Fannie had closed her post office.

Homestead location: A Street to Dixie, 6th Avenue South to 12th Avenue South.

Land description: 160 acres "high sandy land covered with scrub spruce pine."

Legal description: Southeast quarter of Section 28.

Crops: "planted mango and guava trees," "about 2½ acres of pineapple crop each season."

Residence: "Have resided continuaisly *[sic]* on land since June 1903 except when absent working at my trade, earning money to keep up improvements."

Family at time of settlement:

Anna May, wife, age 31

Sally Belle, daughter, age 8, born in Kentucky

Mary, daughter, age 5, born in Kentucky

Millimore William, age 4, born in Kentucky

Children born in Florida:

Charles, 1903

Earnest Jr., 1908

Improvements: "Began improvements in May 1903. Built frame house with shingle roof, 24 x 28 ft. worth $300 or more. Built barn worth $100 or more…." "Built chicken coop and yards and other improvements worth $50 to $100." (Crenshaw HA, 10)

Crenshaw's five-year homestead residence was fulfilled in 1908. He listed his post office as Lantana, Dade County, Florida.

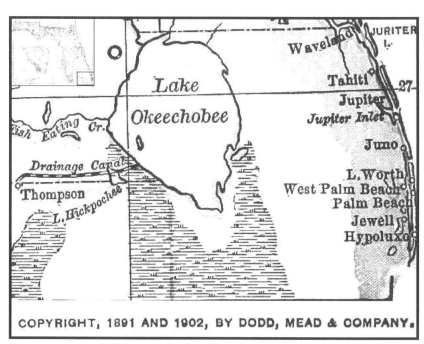

1902 map showing Jewell at its height.

Witnesses at Final Proof:

M. B. Lyman of Lantana, Florida

Dan. McCorley of Lantana, Florida

A. W. Garrett of Hypoluxo, Florida

James. L Garrett of Hypoluxo, Florida

The Crenshaw family left Florida and moved to Georgia sometime between October 1908 and April 1910.

Chapter 22: The Decline of Jewell

The year of 1903 was a turning point for the Jameses. They'd been living in the lake region for 18 years. Fannie had been postmistress for 14 of those years. According to undocumented sources, Samuel fell sick in that year. He would have been 75 years old.

Whatever the proximate cause, a rapid succession of events demonstrates that something significant had changed in their lives. In what would today be called an estate planning strategy, they legally transferred all their land assets to Fannie's name, supporting the idea that Samuel may have been in declining heath. That same year, Fannie closed the Jewell Post Office.

Meanwhile, Lantana, just two miles south, was steadily growing. M. B. Lyman opened an active trading post and would make frequent trips to Jacksonville in his schooner, the *Bessie B.*, carrying farm produce to the northern market and bringing goods back to sell in his store, including a wide variety of farm needs and consumer goods. He also ran a boatyard where other vessels could be dry-docked and repaired.

The Lantana Post Office opened in 1892. Commercial and residential lots were sold. A variety of shops and businesses moved in. A hotel was built. Individuals who had previously received their mail at Jewell, including Michel Merkel, began to use the Lantana Post Office as the most convenient alternative.

Perhaps contributing to the diminished importance of Jewell was the decision by the Dade County Commission not to build the wagon road along the western shore of the lake. Shortly after the county seat was moved to Juno in 1889, the Commission hired E. L. White to survey the route for a road between Juno and Biscayne Bay. This is likely the same as the "Wagon Road passing Jewell, Oak Lawn and Juno" depicted on the 1890 Juno Post Office application map.

In all likelihood, the illustrated road was White's proposed route, never built. In order to save expenses, the County Commission shortened the route by 26 miles when they let out bids for a road from Lantana to Arch Creek (just north of Miami) in September 1892. Travelers would have to get from Juno to Lantana by water. Guy Metcalf was awarded the roadway construction contract. The work was quickly accomplished with the grading of a bumpy but passable eight-foot-wide roadbed and the construction of eight wooden bridges. Thus the land route from Lantana to Biscayne Bay was completed by December. (Peters, "The First County Road: From Lantana to Lemon City," 3–5.)

To take advantage of the new transportation corridor, a hack line (a stagecoach pulled my mules) was then started by Metcalf for the two-day ride with an overnight stop at New River.

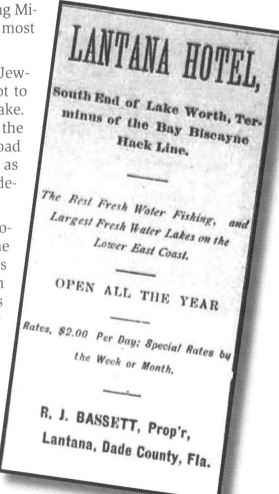

LANTANA HOTEL,

South End of Lake Worth, Terminus of the Bay Biscayne Hack Line.

The Best Fresh Water Fishing, and Largest Fresh Water Lakes on the Lower East Coast.

OPEN ALL THE YEAR

Rates, $2.00 Per Day; Special Rates by the Week or Month.

R. J. BASSETT, Prop'r,
Lantana, Dade County, Fla.

Tropical Sun, June 11, 1893

The net result of the shortened route was the bypassing of Jewell and the increased importance of Lantana.

Even at its height, Jewell had been a tiny community of farmers. While the Jameses tried their hand at running a small store, it could not compete with larger stores in Palm Beach and Lantana. No other commercial enterprises took root. The population peaked at less than 25. Jewell never flourished as a townsite. What little there had been of Jewell as a community hub disappeared when the post office closed.

Nevertheless, Jewell continued to appear on published maps for several decades. The 1907 Currie map of Palm Beach County identifies "Jewel" but erroneously places it farther north than it should have been, up near Lake Clarke.

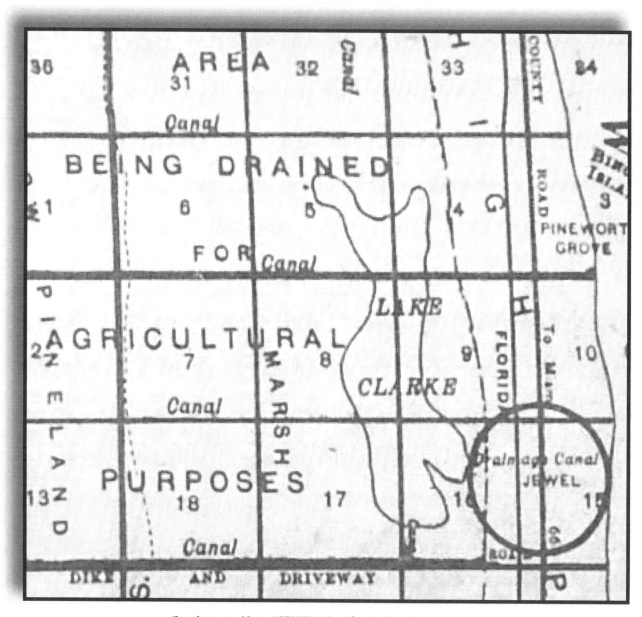

Currie map. Note "JEWEL" inside circle at lower right.

A 1920 state map shows Jewell tucked in between Lake Worth and Lantana. (Note the two hard-to-read "ll"s in Jewell in the shadow skewed up and to the right.)

Detail of 1920 Florida map. A copy hangs in the entry foyer of Old Key Lime House restaurant in Lantana.

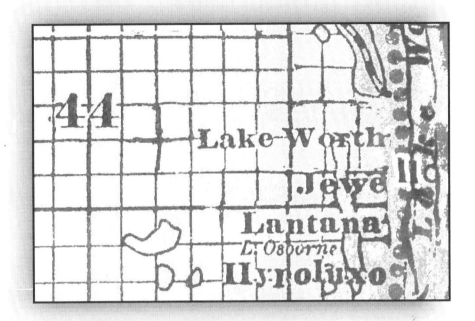

As late as 1952, "Jewel" could still be found on official state maps, tucked between Lake Worth and Lantana. These remnants, however, did not reflect the reality on the ground. With the founding of the Town of Lake Worth, virtually every trace of Jewell was obliterated.

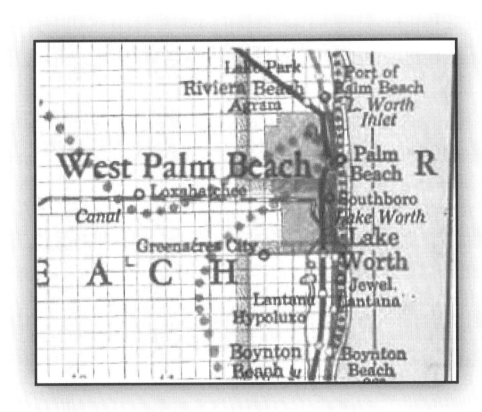

1952 Florida Department of Agriculture map.

Chapter 23:
Fannie after Closing of Jewell Post Office

In the years between 1903 and Samuel's death in 1909, Fannie spent much of her time attending to her sick husband. As a result of Samuel's illness, she was forced to take on greater responsibility as breadwinner. To provide income, she continued farming and selling real estate.

At age 64, Fannie was not capable of performing all of the fieldwork for both farms by herself. Rather she must have recruited and managed a sizeable crew of hired help. Fannie likewise continued to raise her beloved chickens until her death in 1915.

The June 9, 1906 *Tropical Sun* listed "Mrs. Fannie James" among the large pineapple growers in West Palm Beach. What land did Fannie own in West Palm Beach? The farm in question must have been the former Stephan property, which Fannie had acquired in her own name. That area was considered West Palm Beach at the time as shown on her property tax bill. The land was later annexed into Lake Worth as the College Park neighborhood.

Also in the income mix were profits from various real estate deals. Starting in 1897, with the acquisition of the Stephan Estate property, Fannie had taken on more and more responsibility. Whereas previously both Samuel and Fannie's names appeared as cosigners on all their dealings, from that time forward Fannie's name often appeared alone. After 1903, Samuel fell out of the picture entirely. Fannie continued to arrange deals on her own.

Samuel and Fannie A. James Buy and Sell Land from Stephan Estate - Fannie Begins to Take An Independent Role					
in Section 15, Township 44S, Range 43E (corresponding to area now in College Park)					
Seller:	Buyer:	Acres	Date	Location	Sale Price
Marie Stephan (widow)	Fannie	163.3 (3)	July 5, 1897	Section 15, Lots 1 & 2 and west	$500
Fannie & Samuel	Graham & Chillingworth	25	December 1, 1897	Section 15, Lot 1 and west	(1)
Fannie	H. P. Bartholomew	1.5 (3)	May 10, 1898	Section 15, Lot 1 and west	(1)
Fannie & Samuel	Elizabeth J. Moore	6	May 24, 1898	Section 15, Lot 1 and west	$100
Fannie & Samuel	L. W. Burkardt	74	November 29, 1902	Section 15, Lots 1 & 2 and west	$500
Fannie	Elizabeth J. Moore	10 (3)	January 13, 1913	Section 15, Lot 1 and west	(1)
Fannie's Estate	Edwin C. Davis	41	July 8, 1919	Section 15, West of Lots 1 & 2	$5,000
Totals		157.5 (2)			
(1) Received mortgage of undisclosed amount.					
(2) Acreage figures do not reconcile as some contracts use exact acreage following meandering shoreline. Others use square approximations.					
(3) Transactions where Fannie bought or sold property on her own.					

Note that of the six transactions involving the former Stephan property, Fannie handled three of them.

THE STRANGE CASE OF SISTER LUCY JONES

Lucy Jones was Fannie's sister. Born in 1860, she would have been 17 years Fannie's junior. The two sisters were close and stayed in contact with each other despite the fact that both of them moved from state to state a number of times.

The only record of them living near each other is the one previously referred to, 1880, in Tallahassee. Lucy Jones is listed living next door to Fannie and Samuel and working as a domestic. (1880 Federal Census, Leon County, Florida)

The next time Lucy is found in historical records is in Baltimore, Maryland, in 1903, although, she may have been there decades earlier. A cryptic quote in the local paper alludes to someone sending Samuel a "new pair of shoes built in Baltimore." Who else would have sent the shoes other than Lucy?

In early 1903, around the time that Samuel's health began to fade, Fannie brought Lucy into her Florida real estate ventures. No hints are given as to Fannie's motive for involving Lucy, who lived so far away. Perhaps she simply wanted to share her good fortune and help her sister make some easy money on speculation in the booming Florida real estate market.

Mrs. Fannie A. James has a hennery also a Samuel and a postoffice. Samuel has a new pair of shoes built in Baltimore.

Tropical Sun, September 16, 1891—Samuel's shoes.

When the Gudmundsen property went up for sale, Fannie had Lucy sign a power of attorney and put the property in Lucy's name. They got an incredible deal, paying only $250 for 130 acres. There would have been no need for a power of attorney if Lucy had been physically present in Florida, so it appears that this and subsequent transactions were done long-distance, with Lucy still in Maryland. Fannie certainly could have afforded to pay the $250 herself. With Fannie doing the leg work of arranging the transaction, the reason for Lucy's involvement is unclear.

Subsequently Fannie, still using Lucy's Power of Attorney, began subdividing the former Gudmundsen homestead and selling off smaller parcels, just as she and Samuel had done with their homestead years earlier.

On several occasions, Fannie mailed Florida forms to Lucy, which she signed and had notarized in Baltimore, showing conclusively that Fannie was the one on hand, arranging the sales for Lucy's benefit. Why Fannie would have needed Lucy's involvement at all is unclear.

Then in 1911 and 1912, Lucy and Fannie's real estate dealings became quite strange. For no apparent reason, they started trading properties back and forth, like a ping-pong ball. In December 1911, Lucy gifted or sold the remaining 100 acres of the Gudmundsen estate to Fannie. The following September, Fannie transferred the identical land back to Lucy.

A similar thing happened with the remnant of the Stephan estate, that Fannie still owned. In September 1912, Fannie transferred the remnant to Lucy. Lucy transferred it back in November, just two months later.

Financially speaking, Lucy was the big winner in these dealings. Fannie received the proceeds from just one outside sale, while Lucy benefited from five. County records do not reveal the sale prices on most of the transactions, but Lucy received over $6,000 from sales to Harold Bryant of the Palm Beach Farms Company in 1913 and 1914.

When Fannie passed away in 1915, Lucy was left out of the will. Fannie's estate went to her other sisters and their children. Perhaps Fannie felt that Lucy had already been well provided for.

Then in perhaps the strangest twist of all, Lucy contested Fannie's will in Palm Beach County Probate Court, arguing Fannie was not in her right mind. (More on the contested will later.)

Lucy Jones Land Transactions (Stephan Estate and Gudmundsen Homestead)
in Sections 15, 27-28

From:	To:	Acres	Date	Location	Recorded Price	
Lucy A. Jones	Fannie A. James		September 23, 1912	Power of Attorney Lucy to Fannie		
Fannie A. James	Lucy A. Jones	51	September 23, 1912	In section 15, west of Lots 1 & 2	$ 10	(1)
Lucy A. Jones	Fannie A. James	51	November 20, 1912	In section 15, west of Lots 1 & 2	$ 5	(1)
Fannie A. James	Elizabeth J. Moore	10	January 13, 1913	In section 15, west of Lots 1 & 2	$ 1	(2)
Lucy A. Jones	Fannie A. James	41	December 6, 1913	In section 15, west of Lots 1 & 2	$ 5	(1)
Lucy A. Jones	Fannie A. James		February 13, 1903	Power of Attorney Lucy to Fannie		
Sarah & Olai Gudmendsen	Lucy A. Jones	80	February 13, 1903	In Section 34, west of Lots 1 & 2	$ 150	(2)
Sarah & Olai Gudmendsen	Lucy A. Jones	50	February 13, 1903	In Section 27, west of Lots 3 & 4	$ 100	(2)
Lucy A. Jones	Eadley J & Kate Davis	10	June 24, 1903	In Section 34, west of Lot 1	$ 10	(2)
Lucy A. Jones	T. J. Brit	5	September 6, 1906	In Section 34, west of Lot 1	$ 10	(2)
Lucy A. Jones	W. D. Griffin	15	February 4, 1907	In Section 34, west of Lot 1	$ 1	(2)
Lucy A. Jones	Fannie A. James	100	December 26, 1911	Unsold former Gudmundsen land	$ 5	(2)
Fannie A. James	Lucy A. Jones	100	September 23, 1912	Unsold former Gudmundsen land	$ 1	(1)
Lucy A. Jones	Fannie A. James		December 19, 1912	Power of Attorney Lucy to Fannie		
Lucy A. Jones	Harold Bryant	50	February 15, 1913	In Section 27, west of Lots 3 & 4	$ 2,500	(3)
Lucy A. Jones	Fannie A. James	1.25	July 3, 1914	In Section 34, west of Lot 1	$ 5	(1)
Lucy A. Jones	Harold Bryant	48.75	July 11, 1914	In Section 34, west of Lots 1 & 2	$ 3,750	(3)
Estate of Fannie A. James	Erle J. Reed	1.25	March 30, 1925	In Section 34, west of Lot 1	$ 10	(2)

(1) Transaction details undisclosed
(2) Received mortgage of undisclosed amount
(3) Mortgage paid off July 11, 1914

Chapter 24: Samuel's Passing

Samuel died on November 11, 1909, after a prolonged illness. His death certificate explains his struggle with progressive dementia, which apparently started in 1903. "This man was in an advanced stage of senility and had been declining for long," adding "Would not have a doctor called, but took medicine sent by Dr. Charles M. Merrill."

The certificate reveals one important fact about Samuel: His father's name was "Joseph James." This unique piece of information is available from no other source.

Despite the fact that Fannie is listed as "informant," the death certificate contains a number of glaring errors and omissions that merit investigation and explanation.

The father's place of birth is left blank, although the 1880 and 1885 censuses both show his state as Virginia, a fact that Fannie must have known.

It is likewise puzzling that Samuel's mother's name is missing. Even if they had never met, it is hard to imagine that Fannie would not have learned her mother-in-law's name from Samuel.

At the same time, the mother's place of birth is given as Ireland. The 1885 Florida Census confirms Ireland as the place of Samuel's mother's birth, although the handwriting is difficult to read.

It is puzzling that Samuel's mother's birthplace is shown but not her name.

Most glaring is Samuel's place of birth, shown as "Fayette County, Ohio." It was Fannie, not Samuel, who had ties to Fayette County, Ohio. The evidence is clear that she was born in Granville County, North Carolina and probably fled to Ohio during the Civil War. Other sources, including Samuel's court testimony and census reports, confirm that Samuel was born in Virginia. Clearly, the death certificate form was not filled out with particular care.

Perhaps the most discussed anomaly on Samuel's death certificate is that his race is listed as "white," contrary to the weight of evidence that Samuel was black. To review the evidence previously discussed, their neighbors nicknamed the Jameses "Black Diamonds" due to the "dark complexion." The 1880 Federal Census and 1885 Florida Census both show Samuel's race as "mulatto." Perhaps he was light-skinned, but he was known in the community to be at least partially of African American blood.

What is the solution to this riddle?

Significantly, the death certificate was filled out by the undertaker, J. B. McGinley. Fannie is listed as the informant, although a comparison of the handwriting shows that McGinley signed the form in her behalf. There were several undertakers in West Palm Beach at the time, but the McGinley Brothers were one of the best known.

The distance between Lake Worth and West Palm Beach might help explain some of the misinformation and gaps on the Death Certificate. Samuel died at home in Lake Worth. It seems unlikely that Samuel's body was taken to West Palm Beach and then back to Lake Worth for burial. Fannie may have simply purchased a casket from McGinley without his having met Samuel or seen his body. The misinformation on the death certificate could have come from only him.

McGINLEY BROS. CO., UNDERTAKERS

Phone 7, Residence 64 and 43

PARLORS McGINLEY BPILDING

Opposite Court House   West Palm Beach

One possible explanation for this set of anomalies is a by-product of McGinley's background. His ancestry was Irish. Other facts may have been confused or omitted due to faulty memory. But perhaps their common Irish heritage was the one fact that stuck most clearly in McGinley's mind, with the false assumption that Samuel was white. This, of course, is speculation, an attempt to make sense of conflicting data. (Those so inclined may, of course, feel free to connect the dots in other ways, as they see fit.)

Chapter 25: Tracing Samuel's Family Background

In view of the scanty and questionable information, tracing Samuel James's genealogy is no easy task. The best data indicates his birth in Halifax County, Virginia, in 1827 or 1828 and his father's name as "Joseph James." However, a comprehensive search of the 1830–1860 federal censuses turned up no Joseph James in Halifax County, Virginia.

There are three possible explanations:

1. If the James family was enslaved at the time of Samuel's birth, census figures would not have included their first names. The 1830 and 1840 censuses give only the names of the head of household with a count by age, gender, and race of the other members of the household, slave or free. Not until 1850 did the census begin recording the first names of wives, children, and other household members for "free inhabitants" of the state. Slaves were reported on a separate census form, enumerated by their owner's name, and counted as three-fifths of a person according to the compromise provisions of the U.S. Constitution.

2. If a "free colored person," Joseph James may not have been the head of his household. As such, his name would not show up on the 1830 or 1840 census. By 1850, the Jameses may have moved to another county.

3. The census taker simply missed the Joseph James household.

Slave genealogy presents special challenges. In those few cases of large estates, where the slave owners kept and preserved records of their slaves' names and duties, some African Americans have been able to trace their family history back through slavery times. However, records for Joseph or Samuel James have not been located.

Most commonly, slaves were given the last name of their owners, and those names continued in use after emancipation.

Given the oral tradition that Samuel was an ex-slave, it makes sense to search for slaveholders surnamed "James" in Halifax County, Virginia, in 1830. Further, making use of the available breakdown by age and gender, there would have to be at least two male slaves in the household, one of childbearing age and one child. It turns out that there were two James households that meet the above requirements: those of Wiley James and James W. James.

Wiley James, Halifax County, Virginia, 1830.

Slaves—Males—Under 10: 1

Slaves—Males—10 thru 23: 3

Slaves—Males—24 thru 35: 1

Slaves—Females—Under 10: 1

Slaves—Females—10 thru 23: 5

Slaves—Female—36 thru 54: 1

Total Slaves: 12

James W. James, Halifax County, Virginia, 1830.

Slaves—Males—Under 10: 1

Slaves—Males—10 thru 23: 1

Slaves—Females—10 thru 23: 1

Total Slaves: 3

Perhaps further research will reveal better evidence on Samuel's slave background and life story. At the present time, there is a long gap in his biography between his birth in Virginia in the late 1820s and his appearance in Tallahassee on the 1880 census.

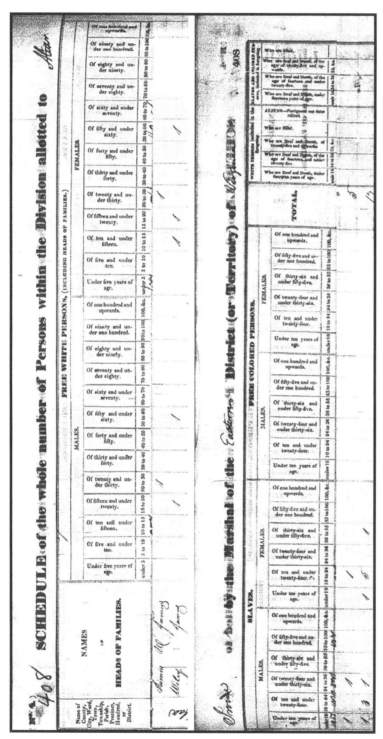

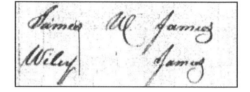

The 1830 Federal Census for Halifax County, Virginia, showing the James W. James and Wiley James households, number in household counted by age, gender, race, and slave/free status. Inset shows magnified view of heads of households.

Chapter 26: Zooming in on Palm Beach Farms Company

By the early 1900s, South Florida was opening up and was ready for mass development. Construction of drainage canals was turning swamplands into rich, muck-soil farmlands. The railroad provided the means for conveniently getting crops to market. Improvements were rushing ahead at a head-spinning pace, not only along the coastal areas but inland as well.

Experienced developers from the American West turned their attention to the Florida Atlantic Coast and the Everglades as their next potential hot spot. A number of new companies formed to exploit Florida's economic potential, including Richard Bole's Florida Fruit Lands Company and Thomas Will's Florida Everglades Land Company. Planned communities, from Lake Okeechobee to both coasts, dotted the South Florida map.

The business model followed the pattern that land development firms had used through the Midwest and West. They would buy a tract of undeveloped land, lay out streets and lots in the wilderness, and through vigorous promotion attract businesses and residences to relocate to their town.

Promotional materials enumerated Florida's distinct advantages over the West:

- Comfortable year-round warm climate

- An extended growing season

- Proximity to markets on the Atlantic Coast, including major cities from Washington, DC, to Philadelphia, New York, and Boston

- Potential to raise tropical fruits not available elsewhere

- Potential to raise vegetables in the winter

Whereas most western farmers and ranchers lived on their land, the Florida developers introduced a new angle, suited to the age of the automobile. They included both an agricultural lot and a town homesite in each sales contract. Good roads linked rural and urban areas.

In 1909, with similar goals and strategy, Percy Hagerman, William Greenwood, Harold Bryant, and Frederick Bryant got together to form the Palm Beach Farms Company (PBFC). The new firm incorporated in Colorado, an unlikely founding place for a business that would operate in Florida. But this move makes more sense when considering that the partners had connections with bankers and previous experience in town development out west.

Harold Bryant and William Greenwood ran the public relations and sales operation. To market property for PBFC, they formed a separate company, named, naturally enough, Bryant & Greenwood, with headquarters in Chicago. Their sales pitch was exuberant, a P. T. Barnum-like invitation to "live where the sun spends the winter," work "the richest soil on earth," grow three crops a year and live nearby in an exciting, growing, and prosperous community. A 16-page photograph-laden brochure hawked the land and its development potential. (*UF Digital Collection*, 64 – 79. See also 2 – 6, 118 – 121.)

Bryant & Greenwood and PBFC worked hand in glove. In 1909, they eagerly purchased thousands of acres of the Everglades to be subdivided into agricultural lots, ranging from 5 to 40 acres in size. In 1910, they accumulated a large coastal tract for their townsite. Their contracts routinely coupled a parcel of rural agricultural land with home sites in town.

PBFC's initial choice for a townsite was near the Linton (Delray Beach) stop on the FEC Railway. They built a Demonstration Farm there and began attracting winter visitors and sales prospects.

The Palm Beach Farms Company

OUR DEMONSTRATION FARM: "Nothing is convincing as an actual demonstration of what can be done. We may state that certain crops are suitable for this soil and climate, and can be raised at a handsome profit, but our statement will be immeasurably strengthened by a demonstration – by actually raising the crops... Our farm... [is] located on section 21 west of Delray." (Palm Beach Farms Company promotional brochure, 1911, *UF Digital Collection*, 21.)

Without warning, in the fall of 1910, Palm Beach Farms Company abandoned the Linton area and began buying property north of Lantana. No reason for the move was given, but it is likely that landowners in the Linton area had already bid up prices, making the Jewell area a less expensive alternative.

"Lucerne" was the original name choice for the new town, but after learning that another Florida community had a claim on the name, it was changed to "Lake Worth." (This bit of historical trivia is still evident in the names of two main downtown streets, Lake and Lucerne Avenues.)

The name Lake Worth was had several things going for it. The name was well known, having been used to refer to the beautiful 22 mile long lake since the end of the Second Seminole War when it was named after Colonel William Jenkins Worth. Further, the entire region surrounding the lake had been called Lake Worth for decades and was associated with the affluence of Palm Beach. (Modern sensitivities against naming the town after an "Indian Killer" were not a consideration in the 1910s. Colonel Worth was considered a hero.)

Col. William Jenkins Worth, "hero" of the Second Seminole War.

The original plat of the Town of Lake Worth represented a core area bounded by A Street, 13th Avenue North, and the Intracoastal Waterway. The city limit on the south consisted of a series of stair steps that began at 5th Avenue South and the water and then worked its way down to 12th Avenue South and Dixie. Later, the city expanded north to the West Palm Canal, west to Lake Osborne, and south to 18th Avenue South.

One of the folkloric aspects of the Fannie and Samuel James story is that they had been the owners of all the land in the original town. (*Lake Worth Herald*, March 11, 1915.) This overstated the case. What is true is that when the acreage of all their holdings are added up—their first homestead of 187 acres, the second homestead of 160 acres, the 130 acres they purchased from the Gudmundsens and the 163 acres from the Stephan estate—it becomes clear that at one time or another, the Jameses had owned a far larger proportion of city land than anyone else.

The Jameses were unique among the early settlers, not only in the number of acres that they owned but also in terms of the length of their residency. Of Jewell's Homestead Era settlers, only Fannie was still living in the area at the time of incorporation.

The following list of homesteaders who acquired property directly from the U.S. Government shows their whereabouts in 1910:

Robert L. Stringfellow & William N. Wilson—Gainesville, never Jewell residents

Samuel James—Deceased

William Stephan—Deceased, no heirs in area

Harry Stites—Deceased, no heirs in area

John C. Hoagland—Deceased, no heirs in area

Owen S. Porter—Moved to Daytona Beach, deceased

Olai and Sarah Gudmundsen—Moved to Mobile, Alabama

Thurza Belle Earnest—Married Charles McBride and moved to Melbourne, Florida

Harvey Geer—Moved to Berrien County, Michigan

Ella Dimick Potter—Living in Palm Beach, never a Jewell resident

Ernest L. Crenshaw—Moved to Ben Hill County, Georgia

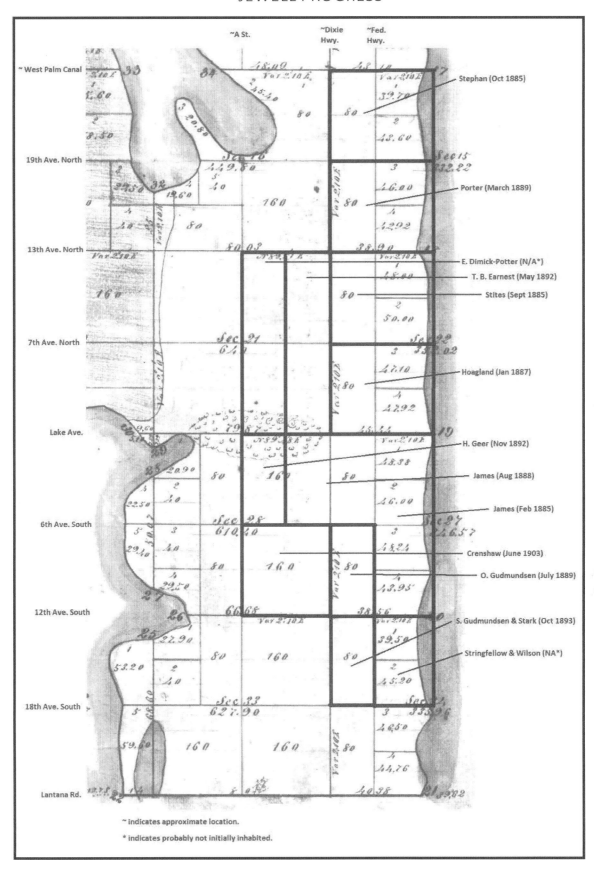

Map of original Lake Worth landowners
showing homestead land acquired from U.S. government with settlement dates.

Chapter 27: Palm Beach Farms Company's Acquisition Strategy

Anyone who wants to accumulate a large contiguous property from many landowners has to be concerned about keeping costs down. Holdouts are prone to dramatically raise their asking price or play a waiting game, hoping to get a better price later on. It is possible that PBFC's initial interest in Linton/Delray was a ruse, intended to prevent bidding up of asking prices. In any case, once it focused on territory to the north, PBFC went to work quickly. The majority of proprieties were bought in a matter of weeks, between November 28, 1910, and January 5, 1911.

It can be safely assumed that those who sold in late 1911 or 1912 had declined an earlier offer to purchase. PBFC used intermediaries or recorded sale prices as "$1 and other valuable considerations," presumably to be able to give some who demanded it a sweeter deal than others. All these measures were aimed at holding down PBFC's acquisition costs.

Below is a list of landowners who sold land to Palm Beach Farms Company. Note that Fannie was one of the first to sell and her sister Lucy one of the last, resulting in a huge difference in sale prices.

In most instances, properties were not purchased for cash but with mortgage notes that split the sale price into a series of balloon notes, payable in one, two, or three years at 8% interest.

SEQUENCE OF SALES TO PBFC

(Showing seller, sale date, acreage, and sale price, if available.)

Irving Hoagland (November 23, 1910)—160 waterfront acres—$3,750 as three notes.

Harvey Geer & wife (November 28, 1910)—80 inland acres—$900 as three notes payable in one, two, and three years.

Fannie A. James (December 3, 1910)—150 inland acres plus six waterfront acres—$1,124 as two notes.

Ella Dimick-Potter (December 7, 1910)—160 inland acres - $1,200 as one note.

Thurza Belle Earnest-McBride (December 10, 1910)—160 inland acres—$1,350 as one note.

Alice B. Smith (December 15, 1910)—80 waterfront acres—sale price undisclosed.

Sarah McFarland-Potter (January 5, 1911)—70 waterfront acres—$1,764 as three notes.

Heirs of Elizabeth Moore (Richard H., Medford J., John A. Wilder & wife, Elizabeth C. Moseley & husband, Eliza J. Russell & husband, Earl T. Wilder & wife) mortgage by Bank of Palm Beach (January 23, 1911)—80 waterfront acres—$1,173 as two notes.

Earnest L. Crenshaw (via William F. Greenwood et. al. (June 9, 1911)—160 inland acres—price undisclosed.

S. Fisk Worthington & wife; A. L. Haugh & wife (January 18, 1912)—40 inland acres—$1,000 cash sale.

M. B. Lyman & wife (January 20, 1912)—30 inland acres—$500 + undisclosed mortgage.

Dorinda H. Brelsford (January 24, 1912)—10 inland acres—sale price undisclosed.

Jeanie & Sidney Maddock (December 2, 1912)—87.05 waterfront acres—sale price undisclosed.

Lucy A. Jones—sister of Fannie James (via Harold Bryant) — (February 15, 1913)—50 inland acres—$2,000 mortgage.

T. B. Stringfellow (March 10, 1913)—70.64 waterfront acres—$11,302.40 mortgage.

Lucy A. Jones—sister of Fannie James (via Harold Bryant)—(July 11, 1914)—48.75 inland acres—$3,750 mortgage.

Estate of Fannie James, sold to Edwin C. Davis (July 8, 1919)—41 inland acres—$5,000 in cash.

Estate of Fannie James, sold to Erle J. Reed (March 30, 1925)—1.25 inland acres—mortgage of undisclosed value.

 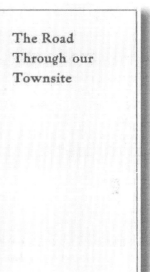

In December 1910, PBFC organized an auto tour of the future townsite of Lake Worth for prospective buyers. From the length of the shadows and the surrounding terrain, it appears this photo may have been taken looking north from what would become Dixie Highway. Note the pine ridge in the background, which could mark the future track of Lake Worth Road. Compare with pine ridge on George Potter's survey map. (Photo from *UF Digital Collection*, 120.)

PBFC concept map of Lake Worth townsite, *circa* 1911. West Palm Beach is on the right. Note square townsites, FEC tracks, numerous wharfs, Lake Osborne in the upper left. (*UF Digital Collection*, 76)

Chapter 28: The Pioneer Mystique

Since its inception, at the core of the American experience has been the drive to move west, push back the frontier, and establish Western "civilization" in the wilderness. Ideas about pioneer life were romanticized in literature and popular culture. By 1910, the United States had spread "from sea to shining sea." In 1912, Arizona and New Mexico, the last of the Lower 48, were admitted to the union. Under these circumstances, the harsh environment of South Florida became a last frontier.

When Palm Beach Farms Company began to develop Lake Worth as a planned community, it found it useful to give potential customers a sense of adventure. The townsite was promoted as virgin pioneer territory. It served no purpose to tell the stories of the homesteading families who had lived on and farmed the land during previous decades. Those who bought PBFC contracts were dubbed "pioneers."

> A year ago last April a solitary Indian mound surrounded by wild woods marked the spot where flourishing Lake Worth is now growing beyond the most vivid imagination. People are swarming to us.... Dame Nature is responsible for our splendid climate and the matchless beauty of our townsite. Then Palm Beach Farms company, the personifi cation of the Western spirit, has taken hold of it. (Promotional ad in the *Lake Worth Herald*, 1912, reprinted 1963.)

The developer's first step was to send in a survey crew to plat the new town. It laid out streets and created both commercial and residential lots that could be marketed to eager "pioneers" and investors.

Surveyors at James house near the future L Street in Lake Worth —Courtesy of Lake Worth Historical Museum.

The survey team worked from January to August 1912, living in tents and moving from place to place as their work progressed. During those eight months, they platted 7,000 town lots, 7,000 tracts of farmland, and 55 miles of streets and roads. The house on the left is reported to have been the Jameses' house, the one near L Street.

> When the survey team was sent to lay out the Town of Lake Worth in January 1912 they used the James house as their headquarters as it was the only building they had seen in the area. As they continued surveying, the team came upon several other widely scattered dwellings. (*Early Lantana*, 17.)

Despite the presence of homesteaders on the land for the previous 30 years, and despite the planting of thousands of trees and the erection of dozens of buildings, the truth was that much of the scrub still was in the same undeveloped condition as when it was acquired. A settler might have received a patent on 80 or 160 acres, but homestead applications uniformly report only three to five acres cleared. Over the following decades, only a small portion of the land was put into fruit or vegetable production. Additionally, several of the "homesteaders" could more properly be called land speculators who took possession of the land, cultivated the bare minimum to satisfy the legal requirements for obtaining title and then allowed the land to go back to nature. Therefore, it is no surprise that the Palm Beach Farm's survey team encountered much untamed wilderness.

Edward Utter, who was a member of the survey team that laid out the original street plat for the Town of Lake Worth, described his experience and the land they surveyed.

> We camped in a big tent during the work.... [The area] was a complete wilderness. We hacked our way through countryside dark as night because of custard apple trees that were tall and lush. It was a virtual jungle. (Powell, "City's Too Crowded for 1911 LW Pioneer.")

It would be interesting to know what happened to the buildings that lay within the boundaries of the new community, the homes, barns, sheds, and wharfs built by Stites, Porter, Hoagland, and the Jameses' other neighbors. Likewise, what happened to the pineapple fields, the guava orchards, and the thousands of citrus trees? Was previous development removed, leaving residential and commercial lots ready for new construction? Or did some of the first city residents benefit from the improvements of their forerunners?

Regardless of the answers to these questions, nothing remains of the Jewell era. From day one, Lake Worth developed at a feverish pace, clearing away anything that remained of the earlier settlement. Amenities sprung up one right after the other, transforming the former farm community into an attractive town, decorated with parks, a waterfront golf course, a ferry to the beach, a recreation hall called the Club House, free lots for churches and civic groups, and a host of other goodies. Prices were kept low to accommodate average incomes. Agricultural lots, west of town, were bundled with a residential lot in town. The combined parcels went for $250 with only $10 down.

The first Lake Worth lots were sold in May 1912. Even before the survey team had finished its initial work platting the townsite, Bryant & Greenwood was successfully attracting "pioneer" residents and the town was on the move. The *Lucerne Herald* began publication that same month. The Public Library opened in November. Businesses, churches, and hundreds of settlers quickly followed.

The first town pioneers, not unlike their homesteading predecessors, encountered harsh living conditions. They often lived in the same style of palm frond shanties, while braving the same heat, humidity, snakes and mosquitoes.

Photo of early Lake Worth resident on his town lot in 1912. Most lived in shanties for a few months while building more substantial homes. Note the outdoor cook-stove and coffeepot on the right. Courtesy of Lake Worth Historical Museum.

Despite their hardships, town pioneers had distinct advantages over the previous generation. They were aided by an already existing transportation system of trains, steamboats, canals, and inlets. Settlement was aided by a nationwide publicity campaign run by a well-financed corporation. Within a few short months, they were joined by hundreds of fellow "pioneers" who banded together to help one another. All benefited from a planned cityscape of streets, an array of stores, and an embryonic government.

Town pioneers, however, had a large and rapidly developing community around them. By the end of 1912, the Town of Lake Worth had 308 residents, 125 houses, 10 wagons, 7 automobiles, 36 bicycles, and 876 fowl.

Wood-frame house, *circa* 1913. Note raised floor of house, wooden barrels in horse-drawn wagon, outhouse in the background, and touches of landscaping in the front yard.

Development charged ahead without a backward glance. Within three years of the town's founding, the new community had a bank, several good hotels, a dance hall, police and fire departments, a ferry to the beach, and a city band. As far as many of the town pioneers were concerned, their history had begun with the labors of Bryant & Greenwood. They knew little to nothing of the Homestead Era settlers who had hacked their way into the tangled native scrub and paved the way for future success.

Chapter 29: Fannie James after 1910

Samuel died in November 1909. After 30 years of marriage, it would not be surprising if Fannie went through an extended period of grief. There is no direct record of where she went or what she did. Curiously, the 1910 Federal Census lists a "James, Fannie A." in Richmond County, Washington District, Virginia (a rural area in the eastern part of the state, not to be confused with the state capital). She is shown to be a "Boarder" living with the Brockenbough family. Curiously, no gender, race, or marital status is shown. Her age, at 68, would have been correct for our Fannie.

If this is the same Fannie James from Lake Worth, what was she doing in rural Virginia?

One possible hint lies in that the next-door neighbor also had a boarder. His name was Frank James, white, male, age 40, and single. Since Samuel was from Virginia, Fannie may have gone north after Samuel's death to spend time with a relative of her husband, perhaps a nephew or son by a former marriage. Nothing else is known about Frank except that his occupation is listed as working on a Gasoline Boat. The one thing that can be said with certainty is that this is the only "Fannie A. James" who shows up anywhere in the United States on the 1910 census.

Federal Census, Washington District, Richmond County, Virginia—May 6, 1910.

Back in Palm Beach County, big changes were in the works for Fannie. In December 1910, she sold both of her old homesites to PBFC, including the six remaining acres of her original waterfront homestead and 150 acres of the second homestead site. Although the *Lakeworth Abstract of Title* shows her receiving only $10, which has given rise to rumors of coercion, county records show that, in fact, she received $1,124 in the form of two $562 notes, payable in 1911 and 1912, respectively.

As a stipulation to the deal, Fannie insisted on preserving a ten-foot-by-ten-foot reserve, "where Samuel James is now buried" to protect his gravesite after incorporation. The original town plat clearly marks the location of the reserve on L Street, between 3rd and 4th Avenues South.

After consummation of the deal with PBFC and the sale of her homes, where she had lived for 24 years, Fannie had to move.

Where did she go?

Chapter 30: When Fannie Was Not Welcome Here —Segregation Settles in

As part of the legal procedure for incorporating the town and establishing a municipal government, the Lake Worth Charter was adopted June 4, 1913. It borrowed much of its language from the charters of other Florida cities. An original handwritten copy of the Charter can be found in the Lake Worth City Clerk's public records.

Among its many provisions, Article III, Section 38 presented a special challenge to Fannie James and other African Americans. It provided for racially segregated neighborhoods, white districts where blacks could not reside, and "negro districts" where whites could not reside. The wording of the segregation provision was identical to that found in the Saint Petersburg, Florida, charter. Similar language was used by neighboring towns; Boynton when it was incorporated in 1920 and Lantana when it was incorporated in 1921.

"To establish and set apart in said Town separate residential limits for districts for white and negro residents to distinguish, establish and set apart the territorial limits or districts of said Town within which white persons may reside and separate territorial limits or districts of said Town within which negroes may reside: to prohibit any white person from taking up or establishing a place of residence with the territorial limits or districts of said Town so set apart and established for the residence of negroes and to prohibit any negro from taking up or establishing a place of residence with the territorial limits or districts of said Town so set apart and established for the residence of white persons: to define the terms, 'resident,' 'residents' and 'place of residence.'"

Despite a pretense at "separate but equal" neighborhoods, no provision was made for black neighborhoods. After 1913, there would have been no place within the city limits of Lake Worth where Fannie could have lived.

White supremacist practices were typical in that era throughout Florida, but Lake Worth went further than most communities. In promotional brochures from the late teens to the early '20s, Bryant & Greenwood advertised, "Lake Worth is the only city in Florida without negroes," and "No property is sold to colored people." (McCabe, "Pioneer's Will Reveals More Surprises.")

Chapter 31: During Jim Crow, Where Did Fannie Go?

In 1910, when Fannie sold her land to the developer, she must have known that the racial climate would not permit her to stay in her home near the grave of her beloved Samuel, or for that matter, live anywhere in the new city. It is hard to know what motivated her to sell. She certainly was not in want of funds, as she took notes instead of cash. Perhaps she felt her age and the responsibility of looking after her many land holdings had become burdensome.

The price Fannie received for her property was about average, perhaps a little below average considering the six waterfront acres included in the deal. If she had held out, she might have received a better price, as others did a year or two later. On the other hand, her holdings were so central to the new town that if a deal had not been struck, PBFC may have had to continue to search for a more affordable site.

Regardless of the precise reason, Fannie decided to downsize. After securing a deal to reserve her beloved Samuel's burial plot, she sold her 150-acre farm and moved.

Where did Fannie go? Although she may have done some initial traveling, she maintained her base in Palm Beach County. Recorded transaction documents show her either selling property or acting as power of attorney for her sister Lucy (who lived in Baltimore, Maryland) in April 1910, December 1911, September 1912, January 1913, and June 1914.

One of Lucy's holdings was 100 acres of the old Gudmundsen homestead. It is unknown whether Fannie moved into a preexisting house or had a new one built, but later she was living there, just south of the new city limits on the County Road that would later be called Dixie Highway. Significantly, the location, outside Lake Worth, meant that she would not run afoul of the Jim Crow laws.

County records are incomplete and have not preserved the whole sequence of transactions. Lucy sold the land to Fannie in September 1912, yet somehow Lucy regained possession. In the end, Fannie owned only the 1.25-acre farmette, Lucy having sold the remaining 98.75 of the Gudmundsen 100 acres to Harold Bryant (of developer Bryant & Greenwood) for $6,250. This price amounted to about four times what Fannie had received for her 150-acre homestead just a couple of years earlier. It is possible that confusion or disagreement over these transactions led to the troubles between Lucy and Fannie that were soon to emerge.

In any event, Fannie ended up living on the 1.25-acre plot with a horse barn and a chicken coop. Located at the junction of what were then known as Osborne Road and County Road (now 12th Avenue South and Dixie Highway), she could make ready use of her horse and buggy.

Another possible benefit of Fannie's move would be proximity to the emerging Osborne community, which was just across the tracks. Even though the "Osborne Colored Addition" was not officially platted until 1917, blacks were likely already settling in the no-man's-land between Lantana and Lake Worth, as they were not welcome to reside in either town.

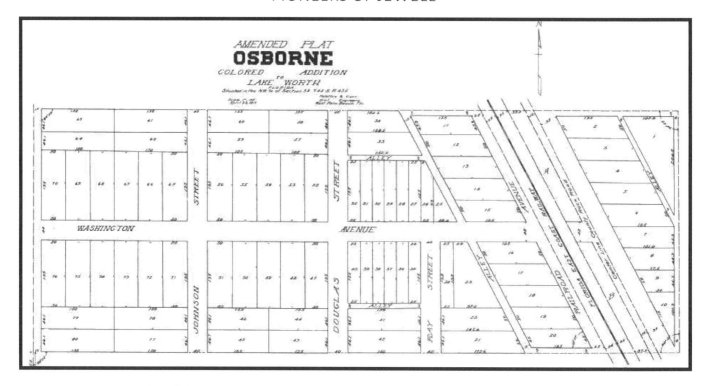

1917 Plat of the Osborne Colored Addition as filed with the Palm Beach County Clerk.

The new Osborne neighborhood got its official name from its proximity to Osborne Road and Lake Worth. Colloquially, however, it was commonly known as the "Quarters" as many of its first residents were farmsworkers who lived in barracks-style long houses built by growers and packing companies. ("70 Lake Worth Negroes Protest at City Hall," *Palm Beach Post*, July 15, 1966; oral history, Grady Lowe.)

County real estate transaction records confirm that Osborne residential lots were being sold to investors before the plat was filed. Purchasers included Mandy Marshall Gooden, Jesse Jerry, E. W. Bunker, Emma Reynolds, Annie Allen and Mallie Holt. Of those, six residential lots were sold in 1914 alone. Likely these properties were rented to agricultural workers.

Specifically, the *Lake Worth Herald* (March 18, 1915) refers to a "negro" by the name of James Allen who resided "a short distance south of Lake Worth." The location chosen for the Colored Addition may have been deemed appropriate if a nucleus of blacks already lived there. (For further information on the Osborne neighborhood, see Chapter 45: Zooming in on Lake Worth's Segregation Era.)

From Fannie's farmette, downtown Lake Worth was just a mile away. Although people "of color" were not allowed to live within the town, they were permitted to shop, bank, or work there. Lake Worth was growing rapidly. Within the space of a few years, Fannie had ready access to downtown shopping, a bank, and a new Lake Worth train station.

Lake Avenue in downtown Lake Worth, February 1914. Storm sewer was being installed and the streets graveled. The Bank of Lake Worth, where Fannie James is known to have held an account, is the columned building on the far right. Courtesy of Lake Worth Historical Museum.

The Lake Worth Railroad Depot was built in 1912 and included waiting-rooms, a telegraph, and a freight office. Under magnification, "colored" and "white" signs can be seen over the waiting-room doors. Courtesy of Lake Worth Historical Museum.

Enlarged view of waiting-room signs.

Racial segregation of public accommodations had become the norm by 1912.

> Excepting Missouri all the southern states had laws separating the races in railroad cars. The dates of the enactment of these laws were as follows... Florida, 1887. (*Tuskegee Institute Yearbook, 1931–1932*, 57.)

If Fannie chose to ride the train, which would have been the most convenient way for an older woman to get to West Palm Beach, she would have had to suffer the indignities of second-class accommodations.

Chapter 32: Fannie's Death and Funeral

Sadly, there are signs that Fannie may have begun to slip mentally in the last few years of her life. Starting in 1913, errors appear in her real estate contracts that had to be corrected and refiled. Previously she had signed her name proudly on dozens of legal documents, but in the last year of her life, she witnessed contracts with "her mark" instead, apparently no longer able to sign her name.

Although her health was good enough that she could drive her horse and buggy alone to West Palm Beach, a round-trip of 20 miles, the account of her death in a tragic traffic accident in March 1915 may indicate that she was in something of a confused mental state.

The *Daily Tropical Sun* reported that on May 6, Fannie James was heading north on the County Road toward West Palm Beach. Just before reaching the city limits she encountered a friend, A. B. Decker, driving a wagon for the Dade Lumber Company the opposite way. They both stopped. Fannie pulled her buggy to the side of the road and crossed over to speak with Decker.

Meanwhile, W. L. Flowers was in his motorcar headed south to Miami with D. B. Diellaway in the passenger seat.

According to Flowers' account of events, he slowed to about 15 mph as he approached Fannie and Mr. Decker and honked his horn. He thought he had plenty of room to pass between the parked vehicles and was sure Mrs. James saw him coming. Just at the wrong moment, Fannie darted across the road, perhaps with the intent to calm her horse as the car noisily passed. Whether she was confused or did not allow herself enough time to safely make the crossing will never be known.

Flowers's vehicle knocked Fannie off her feet and crushed her under its front wheels.

She was rushed to the Emergency Hospital at West Palm Beach in the automobile of Lake Worth neighbor J. M. Bedell. Fannie underwent emergency surgery, "but her advanced age was against her and a few hours after being injured she expired."

The cause of death on her Death Certificate provides more details on her injuries. "Accidental – struck by automobile, fractured left arm, left leg, ribs on right side and internal injuries."

Medical bills submitted to her estate show the efforts that were made to save her life:

Emergency Hospital—Operating Room—$25

Dr. W. L. Nutter—Surgeon—$110

Dr. R. O. Cooley—Assistant Surgeon—$25

Mrs. John London—Trained Nurse—$20

Dr. Frank E. Gavlas—Unspecified Medical Services—$75

It is interesting to note that West Palm Beach had a phone system at the time. Invoices give the phone number of the hospital as "3-0" and Dr. Cooley as "19."

Thomas Hazelwood, a white neighbor, paid the $225 for her funeral and burial, a fact confirmed by the County Clerk's probate records as well as records from Ferguson Undertaking. The *Lake Worth Herald* printed a front-page story about her passing. (See full article in Appendix A.) Despite the racist climate of that time and place, Fannie continued to be loved and respected in both the white and black communities.

Several noteworthy facts are cited on the Death Certificate including the names of Fannie's parents, their birthplaces, and Fannie's date of birth. Her race is listed as "mixed." Her sister "Lucy Jones" is listed as "Informant," e. g., the source of information on the form. (These details will be discussed a bit later in the context of Fannie's genealogy.

Chapter 33: Samuel & Fannie's Burial Site

The exact whereabouts of Samuel and Fannie's final resting place has been a topic of intense debate.

Samuel's death certificate states only that he was "buried on his farm 6 ½ miles south of W. Palm Beach."

Fannie's death certificate records that she was buried in Lake Worth.

Ferguson Undertaking (now Quattlebaum-Holleman-Burse) is shown as the undertaker. Quattlebaum records are still on file. They confirm that Fannie's funeral was held at the funeral home and that she was buried in Lake Worth.

The *Lake Worth Herald* obituary provides more detail explaining that Fannie was to be buried next to her husband and cited to a plan to later move their bodies to the Lake Worth cemetery. However, no such cemetery existed before Pine Crest Municipal Cemetery was established in 1923.

Perhaps spurred by Fannie's burial in a residential neighborhood, the City Commission began to think about establishing a municipal cemetery about the same time. It commissioned a study, but no action was taken for many years. A later report explains:

> … Lake Worth was incorporated in June 1913.… However, there was no cemetery.
>
> In 1915, the Lake Worth governing body appointed a committee to scout around and find suitable location for a cemetery. The committee members reported that there was a 9.2 acre parcel adjoining the southwest corner of the town, immediately west of A Street between 9th Avenue South and 12th Avenue South. The city commission was urged to buy the land before the price went up, which they did, paying $10 per acre for a total of $920.
>
> What happened during the next eight years is unknown because the first recorded burial in the new cemetery wasn't until July of 1923. (*Municipal Cemeteries of Lake Worth, vii.*)

There is no record of the Jameses' bodies having been moved to Pine Crest or elsewhere.

In 1999, the *Palm Beach Post* published a series of six articles, written by Scott McCabe, investigating Samuel James's final resting place, wherein he identified the location of the burial site.

> Land records at the Palm Beach County courthouse prove what 70-year-old rumors couldn't: Lake Worth's first settler was buried in what is now the front yard of the house at 315 South L St. But the case isn't closed. The documents only raise more questions.
>
> When Samuel died… Fannie sold their land, except for the 10-foot-by-10-foot plot where she buried her husband, according to a deed filed Dec. 7 of that year.
>
> The first registered map of Lake Worth, drawn in 1912, shows the tiny square where James rested, smack in the middle of what is now the front yard of… (McCabe, "First Settler's Grave Site Confirmed.")

Public records confirm McCabe's investigation. When the Palm Beach Farms Company acquired the land that was to be platted into the Town of Lake Worth, it performed a legal title search, track-ing ownership from the U.S. Government, through homestead grants and property sales and showing transfer of title up to and including the company's purchase.

For the benefit of prospective buyers of lots, it published the results of the title searches in a single volume called *Abstract of Title for the Town of Lucerne in Palm Beach County Florida, now known as Lakeworth.* (Lucerne was the name given to the town before being rejected by the U.S. Post Office Department due to similarity with another site in Florida.)

The abstract gives a full legal description of two parcels that Fannie sold to PBFC and exempts Samuel's burial plot just as McCabe reported.

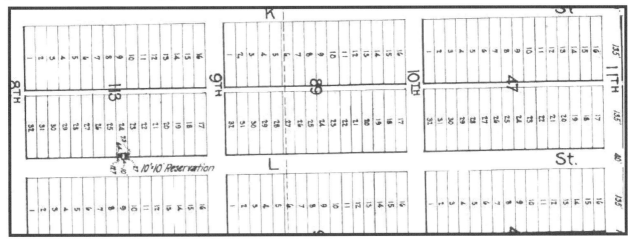

Note the last line in the sale description of land:
"excepting a parcel 10 feet by 10 feet upon which Samuel James is now buried."

The original plat map recorded with the Palm Beach County Clerk provides the location of Samuel's grave site with amazing precision.

"10' x 10' Reservation" from Book 2, Pages 29–40 of official county records. Note that east-west street names have since changed. The property in question is Block 113, Lot 24, or 325 S. L Street.

To this day, neighborhood rumors persist that the house is haunted (from private conversation with neighbors who wish to remain anonymous).

Magnification of the burial plot reveals that, rather than lying completely in the front yard, the grave site straddles the property line with a portion of the Reservation under the sidewalk in the L Street right-of-way.

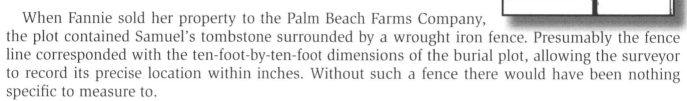

Note that the length of the upper boundary of the reserve is given as two figures, measured from each side of the property line, adding up to 10 feet. Thus 7.3 feet is the portion on the residential lot and 2.7 feet extends into the L Street right-of-way.

For the lower boundary, only one figure is shown, indicating that the distance from the southwest corner of the plot to the property line is 6.4 feet, leaving 3.6 feet extending into the right-of-way.

The reserve is shown 12.7 feet north of the line dividing Lots 23 and 24.

When Fannie sold her property to the Palm Beach Farms Company, the plot contained Samuel's tombstone surrounded by a wrought iron fence. Presumably the fence line corresponded with the ten-foot-by-ten-foot dimensions of the burial plot, allowing the surveyor to record its precise location within inches. Without such a fence there would have been nothing specific to measure to.

Given the fact that the burial and fence predated the survey, is it not surprising to find that the reserve boundaries do not square up with true north but skew a bit to the west.

Jean Child Addison, a lifelong resident who grew up in Lake Worth in the 1920s, used to talk about the scary wooded lot where the grave site stood and its clandestine removal. Men came "in the dead of night… with shovels and lanterns" and removed the grave, Addison said. She did not say whether they dug up the bodies or merely removed the marker and the fence, but she did say that when a house was put up on the lot a few years later, they built a curved sidewalk that went around what had been the burial site. (McCabe, "The Mystery of the Lost Grave.")

This private residence stands on the lot containing the Jameses' burial plot. Approximately a third of the plot lies under the frontage sidewalk with the rest under the front lawn. A curved entry sidewalk circumvents the area where the grave marker and fence would have been.

In June 2013, the burial plot was scanned with ground penetrating radar and probed to a depth of seven feet. The results indicated a soil disturbance consistent with burial plots, but the presence of coffins or bodies could not be confirmed. (*Lake Worth Herald*, June 20, 2013)

Chapter 34: Discovery of Fannie's Lockbox Makes Headlines

Fannie James was a popular figure in her own lifetime. Public interest was high. Both the West Palm Beach and Lake Worth press ran numerous articles covering her death. (Complete articles can be read in Appendix A.)

On the front page of the *Daily Tropical Sun*, two weeks after Fannie's passing, headlines reported the surprise discovery of her safe-deposit box at the Pioneer Bank in West Palm Beach. Bank cashier, Barney Maxfield was the only one who knew about the existence of the lockbox. Following instructions left by Fannie prior to her death, the box was opened in the presence of two unnamed witnesses, who refused to discuss what they found with reporters.

There has been much speculation as to whether Mrs. James left a will and as to the amount of the fortune which she left. The disposition of her estate is also looked forward to with great interest by the citizens of the county. It is reported that the deceased woman was the owner of a large amount of valuable property at the time of her death.

Those who were acquainted with her say that she was never known to divulge her intentions as to what the provisions of her will would be and it is generally believed that she wrote the will herself.

Daily Tropical Sun, **March 20, 1915.**

FANNIE'S WILL AND PROBATE

As it turned out, the safe-deposit box did contain Fannie's Last Will and Testament, dated June 16, 1913, two years before her death. The will and her county probate case provide fascinating details on Fannie's life and family which was scattered around the country. Three sisters, two nieces, two nephews, and a great-nephew are named. . By its terms, Fannie's estate assets were to be divided among her relatives as follows:

- One-third to her sister, Nancy W. P. Webster.

- One-sixth to her niece, Emma Charlton of Boston, Massachusetts, and one-sixth to her niece Ada W. S. T. Mitchell of Creedmore, "daughters of my deceased sister Eliza."

- One-third to her nephew, Alonzo T. Anderson.

Two nephews were names as the will's executors, Alonzo T. Andersonand W.T.B. Jones. Helpful for tracing Fannie's family background is the fact that the home addresses of both are given in pro-

Shortly before her death, Mrs. James left instructions with Barney Maxfield that in the event of her death the lock-box which she used in the Pioneer Bank was to be opened by Mr. Maxfield in the presence of two men, whose names Mr. Maxfield refused to divulge. One of the men arrived in the city several days ago but the bank officials refused to open the box until the arrival of the other man.

Both of the men called at the bank yesterday and the box was opened. "What was in the box," was asked Mr. Maxfield, to which he replied that he could not give out this information as it was strictly a private affair. He was then asked if a will had been found in the box by the men, but he also refused to answer this question.

After securing the contents from the box the two men left for the James residence at Lake Worth.

bate documents. Anderson was from Washington Court House, Ohio, and Jones from Knoxville, Tennessee.

Fannie's will was admitted to probate in Palm Beach County on May 7, 1915. W.T.B. Jones submitted a letter to the court in which he declined to serve as executor for reasons of ill health. His son, Fannie's great-nephew, A.T.B. Jones, also of Knoxville, Tennessee, was assigned as executor in his place.

Daily Tropical Sun, **March 20, 1915.**

Chapter 35: Through the Probate Door —A Look Inside Fannie's Life

The Daily *Tropical Sun* reported that two unnamed men from out of town were present at the bank when Fannie's lock-box was opened. It is reasonable to assume that the men were Fannie's executors, Alonzo Anderson and A.T.B. Jones. After securing the box's unspecified contents, the two "left for the Jameses' residence at Lake Worth," presumably Fannie's farmette.

The will provided that the two executors be reimbursed for their expenses, including railroad fares from Ohio and Tennessee and room and board while in Palm Beach County settling the estate, as well as receive compensation for services amounting to 6% of the estate value.

Fannie's longtime attorney, William I. Metcalf of West Palm Beach, was appointed local agent for the estate.

The probate records on microfiche at the Palm Beach County Clerk's office contain 198-pages of material describing the legal process of paying off Fannie's debts, liquidating her assets, and distributing cash in several payments over a number of years to the heirs.

Included is an accounting of Fannie's debts, revealing details of her purchases and lifestyle. Bank accounts, investments, real estate holdings, and personal possessions are listed in the inventory of her assets. These documents provide specific details on the surprising wealth that Fannie accumulated during her lifetime, and her connections with bankers and lawyers, all of which paint a vivid picture of Mrs. James's prominence in the community.

Fannie James's assets included:

- Savings deposit in Bank of Palm Beach of $2000
- Savings deposit in Pioneer Bank of $100
- Three mortgage loans valued at $6,600 plus $570 in outstanding interest
- 41 acres of land in West Palm Beach, "value unknown"
- 1¼-acre homesite in Lake Worth, "value unknown"
- Household goods including two old sewing machines, carpets, furniture, "old horse & buggy," "one rusty stove," "old Victrola (nonusable)," "new wheelbarrow"

The executors ran an ad in the *Lake Worth Herald* to arrange for the sale of Fannie's household goods:

.THE HOUSEHOLD GOODS, ALSO horse, buggy and chickens of the late Fannie A. James will be sold at private sale to anyone wanting same. Call at residence on rock road, one miles south of Lake Worth before 9 o'clock a. m. or after 6 p. m. any day up to May, 18, 1915. Alonzo T. Anderson and A. T. B. Jones, executors Fannie A. James. 52

Lake Worth Herald, May 13, 1915—
Classified ad for Fannie's Estate Sale.

The horse and buggy went to S. B. Garlington for $50. J. Truax Café bought one of Fannie's carpets for $3. Of note is the description of the location of the sale; "on rock road… south of Lake Worth". Apparently there was only one rock road in the vicinity. No address is given indicating that there were not many homes in the area. Simply saying that the residence was one mile south of downtown Lake Worth would have been enough information for interested parties to find it.

The total estate was estimated to be worth $12,000 in addition to the two real estate properties of "unknown value."

Debts settled by the executors included:

$3 per week paid to Jay Irwin for feeding her horse and chickens

$4.25 paid to an unnamed girl who was left "in charge of house" at time of Fannie A. James's

death A bill for horse and chicken feed was paid, $18.43

Outstanding milk bill, $1.05 for seven quarts

Property taxes, $35

Outstanding legal bills, $55

An interesting insight into Fannie's business affairs comes from an invoice from her attorney, W. I. Metcalf. Prior to her death, she had an outstanding balance for legal fees, itemized as "retainer in Mengel case" and "retainer in Carrol case." Nothing further is known about either of these legal matters, but apparently Fannie was no stranger to Metcalf's law office.

The estate also paid expenses for Fannie's doctor and hospital bills for the attempt to save her life after the car accident.

IN THE COUNTY JUDGES COURT IN AND FOR THE COUNTY OF

PALM BEACH, FLORIDA.

IN RE:

ESTATE OF FANNIE JAMES, DECEASED.

The undersigned executors of the Estate of Fannie
James, deceased respectfully show your Honor, that the Estate
of said deceased consists of some money in bank, of two mortgages, one of $2500.00 and one of $3800.00, forty acres of
land and a home, and some personal property, in all of the
value of about $12000.00; that said $2500.00 mortgage given to the
Pioneer Bank by the Palm Beach Fair Association and assigned
to said Fannie James, long past due, that the executors have
an opportunity of realizing on the same, its full value, by
sale and assignment, and they believe it will be for the best
interests for the Estate that it be so realized upon by said
assignment and sale.

Wherefore, your petitioners pray for an order of the
Court authorizing said disposition of said mortgage as above
set forth and for such other order as may seem to the Court
just and proper therein.

Alonzo T. Anderson

A. T. B. Jones.
Executors Estate Fannie James

STATE OF FLORIDA,) SS.
COUNTY OF PALM BEACH.)

Alonzo T. Anderson and A. T. B. Jones, being
first duly sworn, as executors of the Estate of Fannie James,
say the foregoing facts in the petition are true.

Alonzo T. Anderson

A. T. B. Jones.

Sworn to and subscribed to before
me this 15th day of May 1915.

William J. Metcalf
Notary Public

APPLICATION FOR LETTERS TESTAMENTARY

R. O. Davies Publishing Co.

In Court of the County Judge, State of Florida.

Estate of

Fannie A James

Deceased

Palm Beach County

TO THE HONORABLE *D. F. Pettishall* JUDGE OF SAID COURT:

The petition of *W. I. Metcalf* respectfully showeth that he is a resident of *Palm Beach* County, State of *Florida* that on the 6th day of *March* A. D. 1915 *Fannie A James* of *Lake Worth* in said *Palm Beach* County, departed this life at *Lake Worth Florida*, leaving a last will and testament, duly signed and attested, as your petitioner believes, which he now presents to your Honor for probate; that said testator in said will nominated your petitioner *Alonzo T Anderson and W. J. B Jones* *without Bond* executor thereof; that said deceased left property and effects as follows: *4.1 acre of Land in Palm Beach County Actual Value unknown, 1¼ acre Lake Worth Value unknown Savings Deposit in Bank of Palm Beach $2000, Saving Dep Pioneer Bank $100 and about $600 of Mortgage Notes*

That said deceased left surviving *one sister Lucy Jones, also Darmie, widow, the wives Nancy H P Koster, Knoxville Tenn, Alonzo T Anderson, Washington Court House, Ohio, Ada W S T Metchell Grand niece N C Emma Carlton Boston Mass said Lucy Jones not named in the will the only heirs at law; that your petitioner resides at West Palm Beach Flo and said Alonzo T Anderson, and A. J. B Jones son of W. J. B Jone who is unable to act, are willing to accept and undertake the trust confided to them in said will.*

Wherefore your petitioner prays that the said will may be admitted to probate, and Letters Testamentary thereon may be issued to *Alonzo T Anderson and A. J. B Jones in place & stead of W. J. B Jone* after proper hearing and proof, and that all other orders necessary may be made.

W. I. Metcalf

State of Florida
County of Palm Beach

W. I. Metcalf being duly sworn, says that the foregoing petition by *him* supported is true.

Sworn to and subscribed before me this 7th day of May A. D. 1915.

D. F. Pettishall

County Judge.

State of Florida
Palm Beach County

Be it remembered that on this 7th day of May A. D. 19 15 I have duly recorded the foregoing Application for Letters Testamentary in the Public Records of said County.

D. F. Pettishall

County Judge.

Washington, C. H., Ohio,

June 1, 1917.

Estate of Fannie A. James, deceased, in account with Alonzo

T. Anderson, executor of the estate.

The Executor charges himself with monies received

on behalf of said Estate, as follows:

1915		$2020.00
May 8	Bank of P. Beach Sav. acct.	100.00
" 8	Acct Pioneer Bank	13.76
" 11	Lake Worth Bank Acct.	.65
"	Refund from Tropical Sun	4.40
" 13	Sold D. H. Chambers H. H. goods	1.00
"	Amanda Joiner H. H. goods	5.50
May 17	Joe Brooker H. H. goods	50.00
" 20	S. B. Garlinghouse Horse & Buggy	28.50
" 17	" " " " " H. H. goods	.75
" "	Lantern 50¢ Jelly Glasses 25¢	3.00
" 18	J. Truax cafe L. W. carpet	.50
	C. J. Suffett lantern 25¢ bucket 25¢	2500.00
	P. B. Fair Association note	72.21
	Interest on same	3.75
May 20	Amanda Marshall H. H. goods	3.00
June 14	Sold W. S. Anderson watch	24.48
Sept 28	Interest on Kidd note	
1916		474.48
Feb. 24	Interest on J. I. McDonald note	
		$5305.98
	TOTAL RECEIPTS	
	To amount on hand	$ 905.20

DISBURSEMENTS.

Bal. bro't forward, $ Bal. bro't forward, $

Executor claims allowance for disbursements and expenses as follows:

	1916			
1	May	15	Acknowledgment first account	
2	June	5	" satisfaction Ella Kidd note	25
3	July	11	Second acknowledgment Ella Kidd note, would not accept 1st	25
4	Aug.	8	Paid by check deposit box at Bank	25
5	"	9	Telegram charges Tedder & Moorehead	1 00
6	"	10	Exchange Bank of Palm Beach	72
7	"	14	O. C. Miller preparing Kidd satisfaction	85
				5 00
9	Oct.	30	Taxes James' real estate	
	1917			3 5 29
10	Jan.	3	E. L. Bush acknowledgment McDonald sat. would not accept 1st	
11	May	3	Acknowledgment assignment McDonald note to Bank Palm Beach	25
12	"	11	H. L. Bussey services	25
13	June	1	Palms Publishing Co. notices	5 00
14	"	14	Western Union Tel. Co.	7 00
15	"	26	Acknowledgment first account returned for correction	2 70
16	"	27	Wash. Savings Bank exchange Bank of Palm Beach	25
17	July	24	W. I. Metcalf services	5 49
18			acknowledging this account	3 5 50
19			Stationery and postage	25
20			Registered letters, six	2 46
Sept.	17		Paid W. I. Metcalf attorneys fees	60
22			Amount claimed by Executor for further allowance in closing of Estate	
23			Court costs for recording annual account	27 5 00
24			Court costs on final accounting	1 06
			Balance in hands for distribution to legatees	6 00

Sept. 17   *Thomas Hazelwood services, Mrs. James funeral*   16 60

26 " "   *Amount allowed Executor first account*   455 45

Total Disbursements   9 1063

Balance in hands for distribution to legatees   454010

To the estate of Mrs F. A. James.

"Itemized expense account

March 8th Ticket from
Knoxville to Lake Worth

March 10 Fish .15
1915
  " Bread .20
  " Butter .10
  11 meat .10
  13 Bread .20
  " meal .10
  " Bread .20
  " Bacon .10
  " Sausage .10
  16 Fish .10
  " meal .10
  " Buckwheat .10
  18 meat .20
  " Bread .10
  19 cheese .13
  " Bread .5
May 17 Fish .10
     2.13

and return $41.40

Type written document   .35

May 7th telephone   .10

Lunch in route   .75

" " Return   .75
     $43.35

For caring horse chickens
Chopping wood and cooking
two months $25.00

Railroad ticket from Knoxville and return 43.35
(and other items mentioned above)

Food provision   2.13

Total $70.48 Reimb

My prorata 6 pro of 4800.27   144.00 Com.
       $214.48 total

Received payment.   A. F. B. Jones

The $144.00 horse chorn & hold to deducted from $288.00 check, cover

Lake Worth Fla

1915
Mch 25.
To 1 bale of Hay } $3.31
        50 lbs oats
April 2nd 1 bale of hay and 50 lbs oats   3.23
    " 12th oats 50 lbs   1.30
    " 13th Hay for horse 1 bale   2.03
    " 21st Oats 50 lbs   1.30
    " 23rd One bale of Hay   2.16
    " 30th 50 lbs oats   1.30
May 3rd 1 bale of Hay   = —   1.75
    " "   Shoeing Horse   .75
    " 8th   50 lbs oats   1.30
April 29. Witness fee To Harry Noble   2.70
            Total $21.13

The above feed was purchased by
me from Wm Crown of Lake Worth
before and during the will contest and
was reimbursed by check by Executors
Jessica estate.
                Alonzo T. Anderson

Chapter 36: Zooming in on Fannie's Mortgages

A sign of Fannie's business skill can be seen in the way she handled her financial affairs. From the proceeds of real estate sales, she acquired substantial sums of cash. Yet only a relatively small portion was left in bank deposits. The majority of her funds were loaned out at interest in the form of mortgages that were duly recorded with the County Clerk.

The Palm Beach Fair Association was an organization of West Palm Beach business leaders who started and operated the annual Palm Beach County Fair. It borrowed $2,500 from Fannie on July 7, 1914, for a term of nine months at 8% interest. The mere fact that a group of prominent men knew Fannie and borrowed from her is another indication of how well connected she was in the West Palm Beach community.

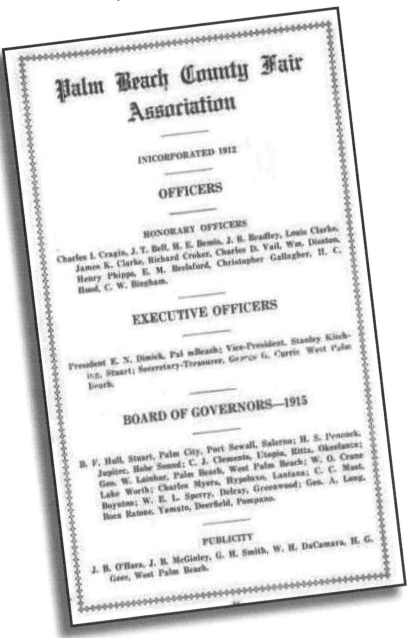

Advertisement in *1915 Directory of West Palm Beach & County*.

In May 18, 1915, the estate sold the mortgage note to the Pioneer Bank for its full face value of $2,500 plus $72.21 in interest.

Fannie was also active in lending to purchasers of Lake Worth residential lots. The *Lake Worth Herald* of December 18, 1913, indicates that G. Rae Eubank repaid his loan to her for two such lots. A mortgage to Mrs. Ella Kidd for a lot located at E Street and 2nd Avenue North (Block 10, Lot 5) was still in her possession when she died. The estate sold the mortgage to the Bank of Lake Worth for its full value of $300 plus $24 in interest on May 10, 1916.

Another personal loan was made to Joseph I. McDonald and his wife. The couple borrowed $3,800 from Fannie in the form of a mortgage note issued on August 24, 1914, for a two-year term at 8% interest. The estate sold that note to the Bank of Palm Beach at full value plus $474 in interest on June 18, 1916.

The breadth of Fannie's business contacts can also be seen in the fact that Fannie and her executors worked with three different banks in three different cities, Pioneer Bank in West Palm Beach, Bank of Lake Worth, and Bank of Palm Beach. It is quite remarkable that Fannie's reputation was such that neither race nor gender was a barrier to her business dealings.

Pioneer Bank, West Palm Beach, *circa* 1915. Courtesy of State Archives of Florida.

These facts give substance to the praise Fannie received in her obituary that ran in the leading West Palm Beach newspaper of the day.

Daily Tropical Sun, March 8, 1915.

Mrs. James was well beloved by all who knew her and enjoyed a wide acquaintanceship among the residents of the county.

Chapter 37: Fannie's Sister Contests Her Will

The executors' responsibility was to include an unexpected and unpleasant task. Fannie's sister, Lucy Jones, was hurt when she learned that she was left out of the will. She hired well-known attorney, Gordon R. Broome and moved quickly to file suit contesting the will. Broome submitted the necessary documents to the court, advocating his client's position.

Lucy Jones prayed that said Will not be admitted to Probate because of undue influence being brought to bear on Fannie A. James at the time of the making of her Will and also that she was *non compus mentus* at the time of the making of said will and for other reasons.

> Lucy Jones is a sister by the whole blood, of the said Fannie A. James, deceased and is one of the heirs and legatees and devisees under said Last Will and Testament, or is an heir at law… intends to file a petition to contest… the will… on the ground that said Last Will and Testament is unartificially drawn, is vague, uncertain and misleading in its terms and is not… executed according to the laws of the State of Florida. (Palm Beach County Probate Court Records, filed April 2, 1915.)

A hearing was held on May 3, 1915. The estate paid the cost for a stenographer. Records of the trial are not included in the 198-page probate file and have presumably been lost.

The only surviving evidence from the hearing is a sworn statement submitted by the defense that E. S. Ferguson, David Summers, and H. L. Bussey witnessed Fannie's signature of her will and that it had been properly recorded in the county judge's office in Will Book #3, page 103.

The court handed down a quick verdict stating that the will was valid. Lucy Jones's petition that she be included among the heirs was denied.

In the County Judges Court in and for the
County of Palm Beach and State of
Florida.

****
In re Contest of Will of
Fannie A. James Will.
****

JUDGMENT.

The contest petition filed in re will of Fannie A. James by Lucy Jones by her attorney, Gordon R. Broome, Esq., coming on to be heard and the evidence offered by the Contestant and the Contestees being fully taken in writing and the Court being fully advised in the premises, the judgment of the Court in the said matter is that the allegations in the said petition were not sustained by the evidence and it is, therefore, the judgment of the Court that the will of Fannie A. James filed in the office of the County Judge in and for the County of Palm Beach and State of Florida expresses the desire of the testatrix in the disposition of her property and that said will was made and executed by said testatrix while in her right mind and that no undue influence was was used on her by any one to induce her to so dispose of her property.

Done and ordered this 3rd day of May, A. D. 1915 at West Palm Beach, Florida.

D. F. Parrishall

County Judge of Palm Beach County, Florida.

State of Florida, } SS.
County of Palm Beach

Be It Remembered, That on this the 5 day of May A.D. 19 15
I have duly recorded the foregoing Judgment

in the Public Records of said County.

In Witness Whereof, I have hereunto set my hand and official seal.

D. F. Parrishall County Judge.

By _____ Clerk.

Chapter 38: Zooming in on Fannie's Real Estate Holdings

During their lifetimes, Samuel and Fannie had acquired, bought, subdivided, and sold over 600 acres of real estate. When Fannie passed, she still owned 42.25 acres in two parcels. A 41 acre-acre parcel left over from the Stephan estate in what is now the College Park neighborhood, west of Federal Highway, and a 1 ¼-acre parcel at 12th Avenue South and Dixie.

The responsibility to sell these two parcels and distribute the proceeds to her heirs fell to her executors. While most of the estate's business was concluded by 1917, it took much longer to sell the real estate. The 41-acres were sold in 1919 to Edwin C. Davis for $5,000.

The second parcel was the 1.25-acre farmette, Fannie's home at the time of her death. It provided just enough land for her to keep her horse and chickens. Interestingly, not only was Fannie's homesite outside the original town boundary, but special treatment was given to the tract when the surrounding properties were annexed into the town in 1917. Note the blank area on the Addition 1 map in the midst of platted blocks and lots. In this way promoters could continue to claim that no negroes were allowed to live within Lake Worth.

Fannie's farmette, where she lived 1910–1915, represented by blank area in the Lake Worth plat of Addition #1, above. Note FEC tracks angling NW – SE. "County Road" is Dixie Highway. The stub of 12th Avenue South runs in from the east.

This last piece of the Jameses' property remained in the hands of Fannie's family until 1925. County records disclose that her heirs, Alonzo Anderson (Ohio), Emma Gray (Massachusetts), Ada Mitchell (North Carolina), and Nancy Webster (then having moved to Tennessee), were each sent separate handwritten documents to sign and have notarized in their home states approving the sale to banker Earl Reed. Public records do not disclose the sale price.

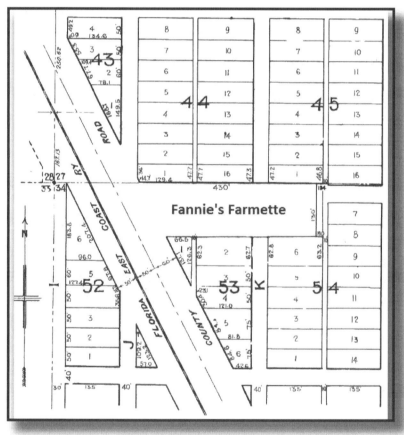

A portion of the plat of Addition 1-Town of Lake Worth, 1917, showing that Fannie's property was excluded from annexation.

The late date of this final estate transaction, ten years after Fannie's death, highlights the complexity of Fannie's business dealings and the amount of work required by her executors, Alonzo and A. T. B. Jones, in settling her affairs and disposing of her assets.

Chapter 39: Jameses' Business Acumen

Their business connections and financial skills reveal that the Jameses were sophisticated people. Nothing is known of their education. The fact that Fannie could read and write indicates that she probably had at least a few years of schooling. Samuel may have had none. Nevertheless, through their friendships with successful people, their natural ability and life experience, they gained the skills they needed to be financially successful.

The Jameses' proximity to William G. Stewart in Tallahassee is instructive. Stewart served as an elected official in multiple capacities, including Tallahassee treasurer and Florida state legislator. He was postmaster of Tallahassee when the Jameses lived next door. Fannie's interest in becoming a postmaster could well have developed through her link with Stewart.

When Samuel James first came to the lake region, he met Edwin Bradley, who showed him vacant land available for homesteading. Bradley also was the person James turned to when Stites and his friends inquired about for potential homestead properties. For many years, the Bradley's were the Jameses' nearest neighbors.

The Pierces also aided the Jameses in learning the homestead process and went so far as to take Fannie's nephew on the *Bessie B.* voyage to the Gainesville Land Office.

Hannibal Pierce, as postmaster, and George Potter, as county surveyor, both played important roles in helping the Jameses through both the post office application process, Potter providing the required maps.

John C. Hoagland was justice of the peace and one of the first people that Samuel met when he first visited Palm Beach in December 1884. In 1887 Hoagland took up a homestead along the lakefront adjacent to and just north of the Jameses. As his nickname indicates, the Squire was an influential man throughout the county and a good friend to have.

Owen S. Porter is another example. He opened one of the first real estate companies in the lake area. Samuel befriended Owen, who made a homestead claim on the property north of Hoagland. Together Samuel and Owen built Porter's house.

Several valuable points can be gleaned from the fact of their relationship. First, Porter was financially well off and would not need to hire a second-rate carpenter. As such Porter's choice of Samuel James was a testament to his skill. Second, during construction, the two spent a fair amount of time together and most likely hit it off on a personal level. Together they built a house, an outside kitchen, a shed, and a 300-foot-long wharf. Third, Porter ran a highly successful real estate business. It would not be surprising if Samuel learned valuable lessons about marketing, mortgages, and the legalities of real estate transactions from Porter.

Subsequently, Samuel subdivided his property, sold most of it to his Palm Beach contacts, and made some good money. He even sold 20 acres to Porter.

Eventually, Fannie and Fannie's sister Lucy took over Samuel's end of the real estate business, acquiring, subdividing, and selling parcels in the old Gudmundsen and Stephan properties. Issuing mortgages became standard practice for them, yielding easier sales and larger profits. When Fannie passed away, it came as no surprise that her assets were chiefly in mortgages and land.

In contrast, Fannie received only meager compensation for her work as Jewell postmaster. Mail was delivered initially three times and later six times per week. Her pay averaged $62 per year, or just over $1 a week, at a time when the Jameses were making hundreds, and in some cases thousands, of dollars on a single real estate transaction. Nevertheless, the postmaster job afforded her opportunities to establish contacts with the community, running for a time, her small general store and perhaps helping promote property sales.

The biennial Official Register of the United States shows how low Fannie's postmaster earnings were. (Figures are available only for the years shown.)

1891—$44.71

1893—62.96

1895—44.91

1897—61.84

1899—79.41

1901—80.62

Meanwhile, the Jameses' farming operations were both successful and profitable. Samuel went into the pineapple and vegetable-growing business with Josiah Sherman, and their partnership prospered. He became well-known for his large watermelons, as Fannie was known for her chickens. Fannie later ran a pineapple operation on the old Stephan estate, hiring workers and overseeing planting, fertilizing, and harvesting. She became a large producer during the era when pineapple was king. (*Tropical Sun*, June 9, 1906)

SAMUEL JAMES

and wife have charge of the post-office at Jewell, and have a good profitable investment in the contiguous lands. A large number of pine-apples and vegetables have been planted by Mr. James and his partner, Mr. Josiah Sherman, who owns a valuable property at Oak Lawn. A long, substancial wharf has been erected by the two men, and farming has been entered into with fair prospects for success. Rich, low lands furnish fertile soil for the cultivation

Tropical Sun, August 18, 1891—James/Sherman partnership.

On top of their farming and real estate ventures, there is the curious remark in the 1896 Dade County Directory that describes the Jewell Post Office as "the only public stopping place between Lantana and West Palm Beach." Unfortunately, no further details are provided. Mention of a public stopping place could simply have meant that boaters could find a secure place to tie up at the Jewell wharf during storms.

However, a more common usage of the term in pioneer days was in reference to a place where travelers could stop overnight for room and board.

PINEAPPLE CULTURE IN DADE COUNTY

At West Palm Beach among those who have large fields are G. C. Matthams, W. C. Clough, Ben Potter, Dr. Potter, W. C. C. Branning, George G. Currie, J. R. Anthony, Sr., D. A. Allen, A. B. Marvin, Mrs. Fannie James, W. H. Means, John Clark and others.

Tropical Sun, June 9, 1906—Fannie listed among major pineapple producers of West Palm Beach.

By 1855, during the heat of the Gold Rush, there were five hotels or stopping places located along the twelve miles of the winding rough dirt road between Shasta and the Tower House…. A public "stopping place" wasn't much to brag about though. Usually all it consisted of was a barroom in the front of the building, a dining room with long tables and benches (no tablecloths), and one or more bunkrooms for the overnight guests. (http://blogs.redding.com/dsmith/archives/2009/10/the-public-stop.html)

Perhaps, like others in the lake area, the Jameses had an extra bedroom or two that they let out on occasion. Samuel and Fannie owned two houses, one on the lake and one nearer the FEC tracks, so it would not be surprising if they had used an extra room or two to accommodate overnight guests.

Interestingly, there is another historical reference to the Jameses' interest in the hospitality industry. Edwin Bradley's comment about a potential hotel at Jewell (in the August 12, 1891, issue of the *Tropical Sun*) shows there was talk of a larger, though similar, enterprise.

Another example of the Jameses' business skills is seen in Fannie's sale of option contracts on the sale of real estate, a type of transaction that would be considered a sophisticated transaction even today. Records show that in August 1910, just as the Palm Beach Farms Company was busy acquiring land for the townsite of Lake Worth, Fannie James sold an option on her 156 acres to Elmer Anderson. The sale garnered Fannie only $78, but if Anderson had exercised his option, the purchase price would have been $15 per acre or some $2,300 in total. Anderson was no doubt speculating that he could "flip" the property for a handsome profit. Ultimately, Anderson did not exercise his option and Fannie sold directly to PBFC for about $7 per acre. Significantly, Fannie continued to be successful in her real estate dealing even after Samuel's passing.

Looking at the broad picture, the Jameses' business skills were finely honed, their ability to work with lawyers and government bureaucracies was well developed, and their enterprising nature was equal to their neighbors. All this is remarkable for folks of their background and lack of advanced education. Undoubtedly, the Jameses' social skills and their knack for traversing class and racial divides, as well as their general likeability, were virtues that contributed greatly to their financial success.

Chapter 40: Bird's-Eye View of the Jewell Homestead Era

Land speculation was rife in South Florida during the Homestead Era, as in later times. Those with means bought land to hold for a number of years and then resold it at considerable profit. Others, less well off, used the provisions of the Homestead Act to acquire title to large tracts of public land, fulfilling the bare requirements of the law and then leaving the area. Some, like the Stiteses and Gudmundsens, were virtual snowbirds. Others, like Orville Fulton and Harvey Geer came south to seek their fortune on the tropical frontier without a real commitment to building the lake community. Simply put, many homesteaders took the money and ran.

How Long Did Homestead Era Pioneers Stay?

	Arrival Date	Moved	Died	Length of Residence
James Murrin	1878	b. 1885		less than 7 years
Robert Stringfellow				never lived on property
Samuel James	1885		1909	24 years
Fannie James	1885		1915	30 years
Harry Stites	1885	1887		2 years
Harry Stites Return	1893	1894		1 year
Orville Fulton	1885	c. 1885		less than 1 year
William Hartzell	1885	c. 1885		less than 1 year
Benjamin Himes	1885	c. 1885		less than 1 year
William Stephan	1885		1897	12 years
John Hoagland	1887		1894	7 years
Owen S. Porter	1889	1893		4 years
Olai Gudmundsen	1889	b. 1897		8 years
Ella Dimick-Potter				never lived on property
Thurza Earnest	1892	1908		16 years
Harvey Geer	1892	b. 1900		less than 8 years
Ernest Crenshaw	1903	b. 1910		less than 7 years

Key: b. indicates "before"; c. indicate "circa" (around)

The above chart illustrates the mobility of the pioneer population. Of the original 16 who attempted or completed a homestead claim, only two individuals, besides the Jameses, remained there for the rest of their lives. Most either returned home or moved on to larger, better-established communities. Many who owned acreage in Jewell were investors rather than residents.

When the Jameses arrived, they sailed into a trackless wilderness surrounded by swamp and accessible only by boat. When they built their first house, the nearest neighbor was two miles away. Creature comforts were rare and hard to obtain. The only stores were in-home affairs that carried salt, sugar, mosquito bars, and a few simple staples. Fewer than 350 people lived in the entire county, that then stretched from the St. Lucie River to Miami. Nevertheless, a growing community took root. Eventually, people came to stay. During the 30 years, 1885 to 1915, that Fannie James lived at the lake, conditions changed dramatically, facilitating settlement.

```
Population Growth Dade and Palm Beach Counties
(Palm Beach split off from Dade County in 1909)

                 Dade              PB County
1860              83
1870              85
1880             257
1885             333
1890             861
1895           3,322
1900           4,955
1905          12,089
1910          11,933              5,577
1915          24,536              9,669
```

Data source: U.S. and Florida censuses.

Before Fannie passed, she lived on the edge of the Town of Lake Worth, which had a growing population of more than a thousand. Even in its first few years, the downtown business district provided access to luxuries she could only dream of since leaving Cocoa. Her home had an icebox, a soft bed, carpets, and a Victrola. If she needed a lawyer or to pick up supplies, she could drive her horse and buggy down an improved County Road, or jump on the train and be in downtown West Palm Beach in minutes.

The rapid progress that Fannie witnessed was truly remarkable. From the scanty Jewell Thirteen in 1889, the population mushroomed to 800 in 1912 and 1,300 by 1915. Fannie was subjected to the injustices of racism at the end of her life but, nevertheless, handled herself with dignity and maintained friendships across racial lines. Her designations as "first lady" and "first citizen" of Lake Worth are well-deserved.

Fannie and Samuel were unique in their perseverance in the wake of both natural and societal obstacles. They braved the loneliness, the betrayal of neighbors, the heat, the flooding, the mosquitoes, and the crop failures and stuck it out when so many others threw in the towel. The Jameses were, in every sense, a tribute to the American pioneer spirit.

Daily Tropical Sun, March 8, 1915
—Fannie's obituary.

> Mrs. James and her husband were pioneer settlers on the east coast of Florida. They at one time owned the greater portion of the land upon which is now located the city of Lake Worth. Mr. and Mrs. James came to this section from the Indian river region, about 25 years ago. They took a homestead on the present site of Lake Worth and were instrumental in building up this section of the county. Mrs. James was well beloved by all who knew her and enjoyed a wide acquaintanceship among the residents of the county.

Part 4

Jewell in Historical Context

===

BEFORE & AFTER

"If you don't know history, then you don't know anything.

You are a leaf that doesn't know it is part of a tree."

— Michael Crichton

NEGROES ARE BARRED

Lake Worth, Sept. 15—As result of complaints that negroes live in a division recently annexed to Lake Worth, action will be taken to enforce the ordinance that allows no person of that race within the corporate limits of the city.

Palm Beach Post, September 16, 1926.

Chapter 41: How the Lake Became the Intracoastal Waterway

In the earliest recollection of the American settlers, Lake Worth was a freshwater lake separated from the Atlantic Ocean by a long ridge of sand dunes. No substantial rivers or creeks flowed into the Lake. Rather, it was fed by a steady oozing of overflow from the Everglades. Its shores were lined with saw grass and other swamp vegetation. Its waters teemed with alligators and freshwater fish.

However, centuries earlier, during the period of the first European explorers, the lake had been a saltwater lagoon. For example, the 1588 Le Moyne map shows Lake Worth labeled "Aestuaria," i.e., saltwater estuaries with wide openings to the sea at both its north and south end.

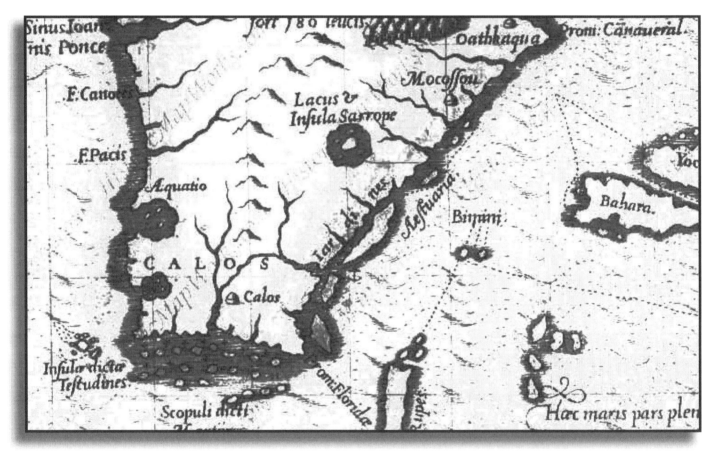

Part of map drawn by the French artist Jacques Le Moyne de Morgues *circa* 1565 and published by Theodore de Bry in 1591. This magnificent work was the first French map of the Florida peninsula. Interestingly, the area to the west of the lagoon, including the future City of Lake Worth is called "Iardines," meaning "gardens."

Spanish records likewise indicate that during the 1600s and 1700s Lake Worth was open to the sea. Several old maps depict "Rio Jaega" (sometimes spelled "Jega", "Gega" or "Xega") emptying into the Atlantic at the point along the coast that later became Palm Beach County. This fact requires some explanation since Lake Worth blocked the flow of freshwater from the Everglades to the ocean along its 22-mile length. No flowing river could have existed along that stretch of coast. Evidently, what Spanish explorers found were transitory outlets from the lake to the ocean across the narrow barrier island. Drainage from the Everglades raised the level of the lake water and from time to time force temporary outflows to the sea that resembled running rivers.

Rio Jaega is, therefore the earliest known name for the body of water now called Lake Worth. (Wheeler and Pepe, "The Jobe and Jaega of the Palm Beach County Area," 224, 225, 237.) ("Hypoluxo" was a later 1800s Seminole term. The name used by the Jaega themselves has been lost to time.) Early map makers depicted the South Florida Atlantic Coast as a series of inlets and islands, with the inlets designated as "rios" or "rivers." The name "Indian River," which is still used for the saltwater lagoon in Brevard County that runs north of the Saint Lucie inlet, is a remnant of the old Spanish nomenclature.

Gibson's 1763 map, which used older Spanish place names. South of the Saint Lucie River are found Rio Jobe (Jupiter inlet), Rio Jega (Lake Worth inlet), Rio Seco (Spanish River), and Boca de Ratones.

During the period that the British occupied Florida, some places were given English names. Rio Jobe became "Shark's Head River" while the inlet was renamed "Grenville" (1794 Romans map) or "Jupiter Inlet." (A form of the name "Jobe" survives in "Hobe Sound.") Rio Seco was, logically enough, translated to "Dry Inlet."

Notably, maps from the mid-1800s continue to alternately depict the lake with and without an outlet to the sea.

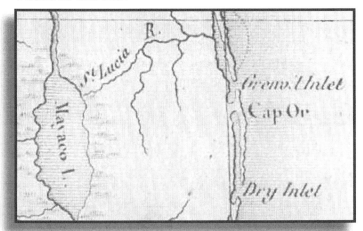

1825 Lucas map showing Grenville Inlet and Lake Worth with a natural "dry" inlet at its southern end, near the site of the current Boynton inlet.

1850 Radefeld map showing Lake Worth as a "Fresh Water Lake" without inlets.

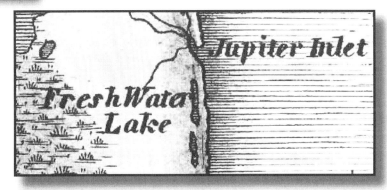

According to early pioneer accounts, the Seminoles called the lake Om-Pi-Let-Kee in Miccosukee or O-Po-Lus-Kee in Creek, meaning "water all around, no get out," referring to the landlocked nature of the lake during the mid-1800s. The Pierces derived Hypoluxo from the Seminole name. Other authorities believe that the Seminole word refers to the island, rather than the lake. (PLSF 54, 254)

During the Seminole Wars, various army men and engineers visited the lake. Capt. A. A. Humphreys described his 1841 observations:

> Lake Worth is a pretty sheet of water, about twenty miles long and three quarters of a mile in width: bounded on the west by pine barren, on the east by sand hills of the beach, which are sometimes twelve or fifteen feet in height, and covered with cabbage trees, wild figs, mangroves, saw palmetto, etc... Below, along the eastern border of the lake are long strips of cultivable land... formerly tilled by the Indians who had large villages in the neighborhood. (Capron, "First in Palm Beach," 60–61.)

Shortly after the Second Seminole War, the lake was christened "Lake Worth" to honor war hero Col. William Jenkins Worth, the Indian fighter who went on to fight the Mexicans in Texas and for whom Fort Worth is also named.

In sum, it is clear that the waterway went back and forth between lagoon and lake on numerous occasions. The narrow ridge of sand dunes was easily breached by storms, creating temporary inlets that would later silt up. The geological as well as cartographic evidence points to the fact that the water has alternated between being brackish and fresh. Over its history, freshwater inflow from the west and saltwater intrusion from the east have fought a seesaw battle and radically changed the lake's flora and fauna time after time.

> Archaeological excavations along the Lake Worth Lagoon uncovered an abundance of oysters, indicating that it had been salt water during a much earlier time. But when the first settlers arrived in the mid-1800s, Lake Worth Lagoon was an enclosed freshwater lake.... Natural inlets opened and closed occasionally due to storms, high water levels in the lake, and extreme high tides and waves. (http://www.pbchistoryonline.org/page/lake-worth-lagoon-and-intracoastal-waterway)

At the time of the arrival of the first permanent settlers in 1873, the lake was brackish and showed signs of recent change. Charles Pierce described his observations both at the northern and the southern ends of the lake :

> The inlet was small and shallow and admitted only a small quantity of ocean water each day. As there were no fresh water streams entering into the lake, only a seepage from the west shore through the swamps, the mixture of fresh and salt water was kept at an even grade.

> Alligators (fresh water dwellers) were... plentiful... conclusive proof that the water had been salty for only a short time. (PLSF, 48, 210)

HISTORY OF THE INLETS

The rapidity with which temporary inlets could open and close is demonstrated by the experience of merchant Michael Sears and his son George on their voyage from Miami to Titusville in a small schooner in the fall of 1866. There were no inlets between Boca Raton and Jupiter when they sailed north. On their return trip to Miami, after a period of heavy rain, they saw a large stream of water gushing from the lake into the Atlantic. They were able to sail against the current, enter the lake, and explore the "inside waters" of Lake Worth for the first time.

The opening came to be called "Lang's Cut" due to the belief of some that August Lang had dug the inlet. Others contend that the "heavy rain" would have been enough to open a natural inlet and that temporary inlets formed fairly frequently on their own. There may be some truth in both opinions.

> Lang said at this time Lake Worth was fresh water and while he was there, there came a great deal of rain and filled the lake up high. He said he was walking over the beach and he come to a place where the water was almost breaking over so he picked up a peace [sic] of board and dug a small dich [sic] across, got the water started and almost had to run to keep from being washed away. In a few minutes it was a large inlet there. He said in a few days there came thousands and thousands of dead fish where the salt water had killed the fresh water fish. (Joseph Priest, as quoted in *Tropical Frontier*, 321)

> The fish all died and floating ashore died by the cartloads, making such a stench that Lang had to clear out to find cleaner air. (Dr. J. M. Hawks, as quoted in *Tropical Frontier*, 321)

Lang's Cut stayed open for the next seven years without human aid. But it was unstable, tending to silt up frequently and drift south. The currents were treacherous. During high tide, water from the sea would rush into the lake and then reverse at low tide. Navigation through that inlet was never reliable.

The first verified attempt at constructing a permanent, navigable inlet was made in 1877. Settlers around the lake selected a location about a mile north of Lang's Cut where a rock formation called the Black Rocks provided some protection. The barrier island was only about 300 feet wide at the new location, but the dune ridge was 20 feet high and covered with heavy growth. Twenty volunteers performed the excavation over a period of several weeks with hand tools, shovels, and wheelbarrows.

James Henshall vividly described his 1878 experience of entering the lake through the treacherous currents of the newly dug inlet:

> The inlet… (is) quite narrow, and has an angle in its channel at the worst possible place… through an opening in the beach bluff, running due east and west, some fifty yards wide and of about the same length. From its north side is a long ledge of black rocks running out into the sea, and trending toward the south-east about one hundred and fifty yards, on which the breakers dash and roar with tremendous fury…. The tides rush in and out through this narrow passage with great force and swiftness.

> We sailed down below the ledge…. At about seventy-five yards from the end of the ledge the channel turns suddenly to the west, through the inlet proper into the lake; and in making this turn Dye (the pilot) put down the helm… too soon, causing her to run on a submerged reef…. Dye and Sandlin immediately sprang overboard and towed her off into the channel and so into the lake…. The water was not over four feet deep, even in the channel.

I made the turn to the west (heading through the inlet) but we came under a group of palmettos on the south shore of the inlet, which shut off the wind. The sail shaking, the Blue Wing lost her headway, and soon began making sternway [heading backwards] toward the reef of rocks outside (the inlet), both wind and tide carrying her in that direction, where she would soon have been knocked to pieces by the breakers.... In imitation of Dye and Sandlin, (Frank and Ben) jumped overboard and towed her into the lake and around into a sandy bight just above the inlet. After the turn of the tide, I pointed out a school of sharks in the inlet. (Henshall, 84–85)

While construction of the 1877 inlet was an important step toward improving navigation, it failed to permanently solve the problem. Over time, the inlet migrated south as the current wore away the southern bank and deposited sand on the northern bank. Within a matter of years, the inlet had moved a mile south, and in 1886 it completely silted up during a storm. Another attempt at a permanent inlet was subsequently made just south of the Black Rocks.

It took a number of years and several attempts before the Palm Beach inlet was once and for all established. In 1894 Henry Flagler had the inlet enlarged by the crew that was working on his Florida East Coast Railway. In 1915 the Florida Legislature commissioned the construction of another new inlet on the site of the original Lang's Cut, which eventually became the Port of Palm Beach.

Construction of the South Lake Worth (Boynton) Inlet began in 1925 and was completed in two years. This second opening to the Atlantic created circulation driven by the ocean tides and diminished the level of pollution from the growing lake population.

HISTORY OF THE CANALS

While successive attempts were being made to improve the "outside route," efforts were also underway on the "inside route." In 1885, the Florida East Coast Canal and Transportation Company completed a navigable, 15-mile waterway between the Jupiter inlet and the lake. They widened Lake Worth Creek, dredged the swamp, and replaced old alligator crawls with a real canal. The U.S. government provided an incentive of 1,265 acres of land for every mile of canal constructed.

Access to the lake from the south had to wait 10 years. It was not until 1895 that the canal connecting Lake Worth to the Boca Raton, Hillsborough, and New River (Fort Lauderdale) inlets was completed. The immediate result was increased settlement in that formerly vacant zone, including the founding of Linton (Delray Beach) that same year. (*1896 Directory*, 32)

Tropical Sun, May 23, 1895—Opening of south canal.

> The canal was opened to New River on Saturday night and Sunday the lake was full of floating debris washed out by the removing of the dam

Eventually, the canals at the north and south ends of the lake became part of a larger transportation system that provided conduits for the movement of people and goods up and down the Atlantic Coast. Today the lake is often called the Intracoastal, due to being part of a man-made waterway that runs from ports in Texas on the Gulf of Mexico to Maryland and Chesapeake Bay.

DRAINAGE CANALS

North-south canals were primarily for transportation, but the east-west canals had a different purpose. They were designed to lower the water level in the Everglades, transform swamp into tillable land, and open up western areas to agriculture.

The architect of the first drainage plan was industrialist and real estate developer Hamilton Disston. In 1881, he purchased four million acres of Florida land, mostly in the Kissimmee area of Central Florida, reportedly the largest land purchase every by a single individual in world history. Original plans called for a sea level canal between Lake Okeechobee and Lake Worth, but its effect would have been to completely drain all the freshwater lakes in southeastern Florida.

Although his efforts encouraged investment and settlement in Florida, the plan proved to be too expensive and environmentally impractical. Disston was ultimately unsuccessful in draining the Kissimmee River floodplain or lowering the surface water around Lake Okeechobee and in the Everglades. He was forced to sell much of his investments at a fraction of their original costs.

Edwin Bradley contemplated the effect of the project on the Lake Worth community, its fishery, and irrigation.

Tropical Sun, September 9, 1891
—Impact of a sea level canal.

> Anathemas cover our canal company like a pall, but here comes Hamilton Disston who proposes to dig a large canal from the south end of Okeechobee straight to the ocean and Mr. Merkle will have to go hence for his black bass and my irrigation scheme has got the jim-jams, for the seventeen feet of fall between Lake Osborn and Lake Worth will be reduced to *nil* and my hopes to *desperandum*.

Muck land had enormous economic potential, but remained valueless while underwater. Talk of draining the Glades persisted after the Disston effort, but no real progress was made for decades.

> Since the year 1906, when plans to reclaim the land were undertaken by the state through trustees of the Internal Improvements Fund, the project has progressed so far that all doubt of the ultimate success has been removed, and we know that it is only a matter of time when most of this vast area will be made fit for cultivation. (Florida Governor N. B. Broward, *Florida Fruit Lands Review*, November 1909 as quoted in *UF Digital Colllection*, 91)

Dredge "Okeechobee" removing 4.5 cubic yards of much per second—*UF Digital Collection*, 91

By 1915, a series of canals was complete that siphoned water from the swamps and carried it east to the Intracoastal.

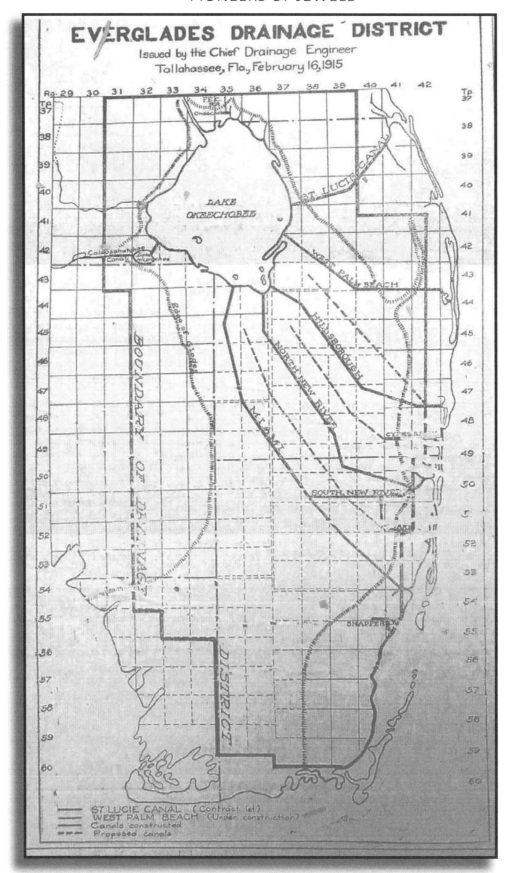

West Palm Beach Canal, also known as the C-51 canal, shown running through the middle of Lake Clark. The C-51 canal forms the current city limit between West Palm Beach and Lake Worth. The drop in water level from the canal to the Intracoastal can be seen at the dam in Spillway Park. —*UF Digital Collection*

Chapter 42: Seminole Community

The vast majority of Seminoles were driven from South Florida in forced deportations after the Seminole Wars. Those few hundred who remained were clustered around Miami or Big Cypress Swamp in the southwestern part of the state or secretively living in the Everglades.

Nevertheless there is evidence of smaller populations, perhaps a few dozen individuals, in the Palm Beach County area during the beginning of the Homestead Era. Customarily, they would move from campsite to campsite in search of game. One such campsite is said to have been located at the head of Lake Worth Creek, apparently abandoned most of the year. (PLSF, 45)

Charles Pierce describes an encounter with a group of Indians who may have been camping at the Lake Worth Creek site. When a steamer wrecked on the breakers off the Jupiter Inlet in 1872, seven canoes full of Indians arrived and began hauling off the salvage. Boxes and barrels by the hundreds were floating in the water, containing goods such as perfume, butter, cloth, whiskey, and even a sewing machine. Indians and lighthouse keepers helped themselves to the spoils.

> When the Indians arrived at Jupiter they were dressed in regular Seminole style with fancy colored shirts that reached to their knees. Some of them also wore brown tanned buckskin leggings and large turbans made from red and black checked shawls… The Indians remained for about an hour, but then, all of a sudden, they started for their canoes, the squaws and piccaninnies trailing along behind. They went up Lake Worth Creek for a short distance and made camp, prepared to stay until there was nothing left to pick up from the wreck.

> The Indians were frequent visitors at the light at all times. They would bring fresh venison, honey, or buckskin to swap for such stores of food as the people of the light could spare. They had one set price and never varied it, ten cents a pound for venison and one dollar for a buckskin. (PLSF, 37, 35, 43)

Seminoles at Jupiter Lighthouse, 1887— Courtesy of *Lake Worth Herald*.

Seminoles also frequented the south end of the lake. Pierce described an encounter on Hypoluxo Island, by which the island got its name.

> After we moved into our new house a party of two Indian men and three squaws... made camp a short distance east of the house. The men went deer hunting in the pine woods on the west shore, leaving the squaws to keep camp. Mother asked one of them what the Indian name of the lake was. She answered "Hypoluxo," and when asked what the name meant she said "Water all around, no get out." She meant, evidently, that it was a landlocked lake, without inlet or outlet.... We all agreed that it was a good name... and so it has remained. (PLSF, 54)

When the Henshall party walked the beach between Hypoluxo and Miami in 1878, they stopped "over at Lauderdale for a visit to the Indian village near the headwaters of the New River." (PLSF, 109)

Dr. Richard Potter had earned the Seminoles' trust when he had lived on Biscayne Bay, and they continued to seek out his care on Lake Worth after the Potters moved to the lake in 1881, as his niece, Marjorie Potter Stewart, recalled:

> I heard him tell about one old Indian that came in with his leg nearly gone with snake-bite, and he cleaned that out and the old Indian got well, and they thought he was sort of a miracle man. (From a 1962 interview, http://www.pbchistoryonline.org/page/medical-care.)

When George Potter moved from the east to the west side of the lake in 1893, he built a house on a bluff at the foot of Hibiscus Street. "Seminole Indians occasionally camped under the pine trees on his lakefront." (http://www.pbchistoryonline.org/page/george-wells-potter)

The August 30, 1888 issue of the *Florida Star*, published a brief report about a typical visit of the Seminoles to Palm Beach to sell "game."

Apparently, the Indians did not want to reveal where their home was, but it seems unlikely that they would haul fresh meat any great distance. The "home" was most likely in the northern Everglades, between Lake Worth and Lake Okeechobee. Oral histories report one such "hidden village" about 9 miles west of the southern tip of the lake.

> Indians have been here lately, supplying our residents with game, but left on the 19th, for home.

> The Seminole Indians farmed and hunted out west near their hidden villages... near the current Faith Farms Ministries on U.S. 441.(*Foundations of Faith*, 39)

Canoes were the main mode of transportation for the Seminoles and they were well acquainted with water routes through the Everglades. Instead of dealing with the surf and currents of the Atlantic, they preferred the "inside route" and would travel in small fleets of canoes between Miami, New River, Lake Worth and Lake Okeechobee. At times, they would serve as guides to adventuresome whites. The *Tropical Sun* of November 24, 1892, reports one such arduous canoe trip by a Mr. James Ingraham and party from Biscayne Bay to New River "under the guidance of old Indian Charlie – the white man's friend, and came through the inside route by canoe."

There are also reports of Seminoles visiting M. B. Lyman's Store and Indian Trading Post in Lantana.

Indians came periodically to trade furs and hides for white man's goods. The whole family would come in from the Everglades and camp nearby while the braves did the trading and the pioneer and Indian children played together. One pioneer remembers playing with Indian children as late as 1906. (*Early Lantana,* **29**.)

As was typical throughout the United States during that period, settlers would often romanticize the natives, imagine them living a carefree existence and paint a rosy picture of their war-ravaged condition.

The 1905 Florida Census reports 20 "Indians" in Fort Lauderdale. By 1915, Indiantown was on the map in northwestern Palm Beach County with a reported population of 74 "Indians."

Tropical Sun, June 3, 1892
—Seminole lifestyle.

The large islands in the glades, some of which are a mile square, are occupied by the Indians, who have corn, rice, coffee, cocoanuts, bananas, sweet potatoes, tobacco and sugar-cane growing in large quantities. They can be seen in large fleets of canoes going to Miami to trade. They are always equipped with the best that can be had in market, and Mr. Brickle caters specially to their tastes, always dealing fairly with them.

In these glades the alligators abound, so do the otter and other valuable fur animals. The deer are hunted largely in the pine woods.

The Indians of this country are well off financially, as they are at no expense, and all they sell brings good prices. One Indian showed me a leather bag with $4,000 in it that he kept in his hut. There is no danger of theft, as a crime of this kind with them is punished with death, and at present no white man dare attempt to steal from them, so they are safe. They seem glad to have good white men near them, and will give them all the venison and birds they want. The white man has only to be kind to them and, as the old saying is, "keep to his own side of the fence." "Little Tiger" is the chief among them now, but his power is very limited and is only recognized when the corn dance is being celebrated. Each household governs itself.

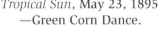

The great annual festival is called the Green Corn dance, which takes place during the "little moon in June," usually the second week. Indians come from all about, from the unknown islands of the Everglades, and even a few from the Big Cypress. They get together and eat green corn, dance and drink wyome (whisky). The dancing lasts four or five days, but it is intermittent, and most of it is done on the first day. The women tie seven dry land turtle shells, containing stones or beans, to each leg and stamp about, keeping time with the dancers.

Tropical Sun, May 23, 1895
—Green Corn Dance.

Seminole women and children in traditional garb. Courtesy of *Lake Worth Herald.*

Over time, white settlers invited the natives to town and organized annual festivals where the two cultures could coexist for a few days a year. West Palm Beach held its first annual Seminole Sun Dance festival in 1916.

Local resident Thomas Tipton "T. T." Reese Jr. described the doings:

> They'd import a whole Indian village—Sammie Tommie and Billy Bowlegs and one of the Indian tribes would come—[it'd] be a couple a hundred Indians. Everything would stop almost to a standstill for a week. And everybody'd dress up in Indian costume and they'd have street dances in the middle of Clematis Avenue.
> (http://www.pbchistoryonline.org/page/fun-and-games-becomes-culture)

WHAT ABOUT JEWELL?

Surrounding communities—Jupiter, Palm Beach, Lantana, Figulus, and Hypoluxo—all report periodic visits by the natives. Of particular significance is the Pierce report that the Indians would go deer hunting on the west shore across the lake from Hypoluxo Island (PLSF, 54). It would be most strange if Jewell settlers did not have similar occasional contacts.

WERE THE JAMESES BLACK SEMINOLES?

One question that can now be answered with certainty concerns the suggestion that the Jameses' may have been Black Seminoles, runaway slaves who came to Florida before the Civil War and lived with the Indians.

Undoubtedly, there was a scattered population of Black Seminoles living a nomadic hunter-gatherer lifestyle in South Florida alongside the Indians both before and after the arrival of white settlers from the north. The 1890 U.S. Census report refers to Seminoles living in the swamp areas of Dade County "among whom are counted some persons of more or less negro blood." Oral traditions tell a similar tale. (*Foundations of Faith*, 38; "Pioneer's Will Reveals More Surprises", Scott McCabe, *Palm Beach Post*, June 10, 1999)

From 1890 US Census, Volume 10—Report on Indians Taxed and Not Taxed in the United States, page 231. http://www.census.gov/prod/www/abs/decennial/1890.html

> ## FLORIDA.
>
> The civilized (self-supporting) Indians of Florida, counted in the general census, number 171, 97 males and 74 females, and are distributed as follows: Brevard county, 23; Dade county, 134; other counties with 3 or less in each, 14.
>
> There is a small remnant of the Seminoles, mainly in the swamp regions of Dade county, among whom are counted some persons of more or less negro blood. The Indians live by hunting, fishing, and the cultivation of semitropical vegetables.
>
> The difficulties of penetrating the swamps where they live keep up a great mystery as to these Indians and lead some persons to estimate their number as vastly greater than can be authenticated by any substantial authority.
>
> 231

However, the Jameses did not lead the life of the Indians, nor were they part of the Black Seminole community. Fannie's family sought freedom in Ohio, rather than in Florida. During their early years in Florida, the Jameses' lived in urban centers in Tallahassee and Cocoa, not in Seminole villages. They were introduced to the lake area through contacts with the settler community in which they were well integrated. Throughout her life, Fannie maintained ties with her relatives in the north. At the time of her death, she had relatives in six states: Georgia, Maryland, Massachusetts, North Carolina, Ohio and Tennessee. Homesteading, farming, selling real estate, running the post office and the general tenor of their lives indicate that they were settlers, rather than Seminoles. As intriguing as it might be to link the Jameses with the Black Seminoles, the suggestion runs counter to the available evidence.

Chapter 43: Fannie's Genealogy

Everyone is curious to know more about Fannie's background. The good news is that the names of many of Fannie's relatives are known through her will, her death certificate, and the U.S. Census. The bad news is that there are holes in the available information and a complete family tree cannot be constructed. Thus, it is sometimes impossible to tell exactly how Fannie's sisters, half-sisters, nieces and nephews were related to her and to each other.

Records from the U.S. Census are particularly patchy. Fannie, although born in 1843, is not found until 1880. There is one listing for Fannie's mother in 1850, nothing for her father, and disconnected records for other relatives, 1850 to 1910.

The identities of Fannie's heirs, named in her will, provide the best point of departure for investigating her family background. Significantly, most of her heirs were members of the Anderson clan. Specifically named are her nephew, Alonzo Anderson, her sister, Eliza Anderson, two of Eliza's married daughters.

THE ANDERSON CLAN

The 1860 census shows the Andersons living in Granville County, North Carolina. All were "mulatto" and "free inhabitants." (Slaves were listed on a different census form that did not include their names and listed only their owner, with the number of slaves he owned, their ages and genders.)

Three Anderson households left Granville County, during the early years of the Civil War, sometime between 1860 and 1863. Escaping Confederate territory, they relocated to Fayette County, Ohio. The 1870 census shows that the three families, including Fannie' sister, Eliza, and nephew, Alonzo, took up residence in three adjacent dwellings. Eliza was 46 at the time and Alonzo was seven.

An examination of the ages of the children and their respective places of birth reveals the time of their move from North Carolina to Ohio. Those children born in 1860 or before were born in North Carolina, while those born in 1863 or thereafter were born in Ohio. Accordingly, their move to Ohio must have taken place between those two years.

It would be interesting to know more about their journey, such as what prompted their move, their mode of transportation, and the impact the ongoing war may have had on their trip. Hopefully, future research will shed light on these questions.

WHY FAYETTE COUNTY, OHIO?

One possible motive for leaving North Carolina may have been to escape the war zone at a time when tensions were high and anyone of African American blood was suspected of being a Union sympathizer. In contrast, Fayette County, Ohio, had been a hub of resistance to slavery long before the Civil War. Specifically the towns of Bloomingburg and Washington Court House were known for their sympathies toward runaways and ex-slaves.

Native son and historian, Frank Allen, described the place of Fayette County in the abolition movement and its role in providing refuge from the storms of slavery and racial oppression:

It should ever be remembered that Bloomingburg as a station on the "underground railroad" (a system by which slaves were secreted and at the time unlawfully spirited to the North)... Here the runaway slaves were fed and clothed and sent on their way toward the north star and freedom in Canada... These exertions were prompted by an intelligent conviction that human slavery was not right. The Presbyterians were ardent supporters of the anti-slavery cause and in 1834... drafted a constitution for the organization of the anti-slavery society—among the first, if not the first in all America.

Slave hunters had but little use for Bloomingburg after this society's organization. Here the cabin, the garret, stable, hay rack and barns, as well as the kitchen and parlors were open to the weary wanderers in search of freedom. Hundreds of them, in need of food, clothing and money, found the true Samaritan here with open hands. (*History of Fayette County Ohio*, 334–335.)

The Anti-Slavery Society of Paint Valley (Bloomingburg) formed in April 1833 and quickly spread to neighboring Union Township (Washington Court House). The Reverend William Dickey, a native of South Carolina and minister of the Presbyterian parishes in Bloomingburg and Washington Court House, preached against slavery for over 40 years. He and his wife, Ellen Ghormly, were operators on the Underground Railroad who led slaves from one safe haven to the next.

The Quakers of Washington Court House were also ardent abolitionists and provided a vital link on the pathway to freedom. Fayette County "was one of the destinations for slaves manumitted [freed] by the North Carolina manumission societies" organized by Quakers.

The colored folks appreciated these things and after the Civil War had forever set them free, many came here and located permanently. (*Underground Railroad*, 347.)

The existence of a route on the underground railroad running between North Carolina and Fayette County, Ohio, raises the possibility that the Andersons made use of its friendly way-stations on their trip from Confederate to Union territory.

Fayette County, although by no means free of race discrimination, was light-years ahead of other areas of the country.

Public schools for "negro" children were in operation before 1855. And unlike the voter suppression in the former Confederate states, people of color in Fayette County retained the right to vote in the same proportion as whites. In 1910, 28% of white county residents were registered to vote, as compared to 31% of blacks. (*History of Fayette County Ohio*, 335, 208, 269).

Illustrative of the racial climate of Fayette County is the story of the prejudicial attitude of one Henry Kirk, "a Democrat of the Southern school," and the community's response.

He (Kirk) firmly resolved never to sit on a jury with a negro, and kept that resolution throughout his whole life. At one time he was chosen as a jurist, but when he saw that there were already two negroes accepted for jury service he refused to serve. The judge told him that he could not excuse him on such grounds and that he must abide by the law or be imprisoned. (*History of Fayette County Ohio*, 537.)

The Andersons' selection of Fayette County, Ohio, as their new home not only allowed them to live with greater dignity, but also opened up opportunities for their children. Fannie's ability to read and write may well have been one of the beneficial outcomes of that decision.

		Name	Age	Gender	Color	Occupation	Real Estate	Personal Estate	Birth
764	744	Anderson Bolen	49	m	m	Laborer			N. Carolina
		— Eliza	46	f	m	Keeping house			N. Carolina
		— James	3	m	m	Farm Laborer			N. Carolina
		— Maggie	21	f	m	House serv.			N. Carolina
		— Eliza	14	f	m	At school			N. Carolina
		— Whileman	5	m	B				Ohio
765	745	Anderson Betzy	35	f	m	Keeping House	800	100	N. Carolina
		— Alphine	12	f	m	At school			N. Carolina
		— William	10	m	m	" "			N. Carolina
		— Alonzo	7	m	m				Ohio
		— Emma	3	f	m				Ohio
		Spears Nelson	26	m	m	Laborer			Ohio
766	746	Anderson King D	36	m	m	Butcher	2500	1200	N. Carolina
		— Emily	28	f	m	Keeps House			N. Carolina
		— Dora	12	f	m	At school			N. Carolina

Section of 1870 Census for Union Township, Fayette County, Ohio. Columns represent, from left to right, Dwelling number, Family number, Name, Age at Last Birthday, Gender—Male (M), Female (If), Color—White (W), Black (B), Mulatto (M), Chinese (C), Indian (I), Occupation, Value of Real Estate (home), Value of Personal Estate (net worth), State or Country of Birth.

ELIZA ANDERSON

Fannie's sister, born *circa* 1824, would have been 18 years her senior. She was married to Bolen Anderson in Granville County, North Carolina. The couple moved to Washington Court House, Ohio, during the Civil War with their children and two other Anderson households, headed by Betzy Anderson, apparently widowed, and King David Anderson. The race of all three families is shown as mulatto.

Eliza died sometime before Fannie's death in 1915. Fannie's will provided for Eliza's daughter, Emma, and granddaughter, Ada.

ALONZO T. ANDERSON

Fannie's nephew was born in Ohio in June 1863. He was shown on the 1870 census as seven years old and living in the Washington Court House household of Betzy Anderson. Eliza Anderson, Fannie's sister, lived next door. The exact nature of their relationship is unclear. Alonzo's race was listed as mulatto (1870) or black (1910).

Alonzo is likely the nephew reported by Charles Pierce as visiting Aunt Fannie in Florida in 1886. He accompanied Pierce and other neighbors on the *Bessie B.* when a group from the lake traveled to the Gainesville Land Office to file homestead claims.

In 1891 he was back in Ohio and married to Hattie A. The couple had two children, Willie S (born 1892) and Margaret E. (born 1894).

Alonzo was appointed as one of two executors of Fannie's will. He was the one who took the lead in settling her affairs and made numerous train trips to Lake Worth from Ohio between 1915 and 1925 when the last of Fannie's property was finally sold. He inherited one-third of Fannie's estate as well as receiving compensation for his services as executor.

EMMA CHARLTON GRAY

Born around 1867, Emma Gray was a niece of Fannie through her "deceased sister Eliza." At the time of Fannie's death, Emma was living in Roxbury, Massachusetts, married to Robert S. Gray. She was named in Fannie's will as heir of one-sixth of her estate.

On the 1870 census, Emma Anderson was shown as three years old and living in the household of Betzy Anderson along with Alonzo, who presumably was her older brother.

There were several other children in Betzy's household. One puzzle is the usage of the name "Whiteman" for a child, age five. Whiteman's race was given as black while the rest in the Anderson households were mulatto. One cannot help but wonder if Whiteman was of a darker complexion and the name an ironic-tongued nickname. Or perhaps someone was pulling the leg of the census enumerator. The name "Whiteman Anderson" does not appear in any other census.

ADA W. S. T. MITCHELL

Ada Anderson was born around 1877. She was listed on the 1880 census as age three, the grand-daughter of Bolin and Eliza Anderson, and living in Washington Court House.

In 1915, Ada was living in Durham, North Carolina, when she received her inheritance of one-sixth of Fannie's estate. No other biographical information is known about her.

KING DAVID AND JAMES ANDERSON

King David, born around 1834, was married to Emily Anderson. He was shown on the 1850 and 1860 censuses as "free" and "mulatto." He moved from North Carolina to Ohio with the rest of the Anderson clan during the Civil War. He enlisted in Company G of the U.S. Colored Infantry, Regiment 42, in September 1864.

James Anderson, born around 1839, was the oldest son of Fannie's sister, Eliza. In August 1864, he enlisted in Regiment 45, Company D, of the U.S. Colored Infantry.

Military records for both men confirm the information found on the U.S. Census. Both were born in Granville County, North Carolina, and enlisted in the U.S. Army in Ohio. Both were fairly short and light-skinned with blue and gray eyes, respectively.

NANCY W. P. WEBSTER

Nancy Webster was Fannie's sister, born around 1847, making her five years younger than Fannie. Nancy married Robert Webster around 1870. The couple lived in Jackson County, Florida, (per 1880 census) and then in Monroe County, Georgia (1900 and 1910). She received one-third of Fannie's estate. By 1915, she had moved again as legal papers and checks from the estate were sent to her at a Knoxville, Tennessee address.

A | 42 | **U.S.C.T.**

King David Anderson

..........., Co. ...., 42 Reg't U. S. Col'd Inf.

Appears on

Company Descriptive Book

of the organization named above.

DESCRIPTION.

Age 29 years; height 5 feet 7 inches.

Complexion *Lt.*

Eyes *Blue* ; hair *Dk.*

Where born *Granville Co. N.C.*

Occupation *Carpenter*

ENLISTMENT.

When *Sep. 29* , 1864.

Where *Columbus, O.*

By whom *Cap. Nesbitt* ; term *one* y'rs.

Remarks: *M O by reason of Expiration of term of service Nov. 13/65*

C. E. McLaughlin

(383g)   Copyist.

A | 45 | **U.S.C.T.**

James Anderson

..........., Co. D ...., 45 Reg't U. S. Col'd Inf.

Appears on

Company Descriptive Book

of the organization named above.

DESCRIPTION.

Age 25 years; height 5 feet 8 inches.

Complexion *Yellow*

Eyes *Grey* ; hair *Sandy*

Where born *Granville Co. N.C.*

Occupation *Farmer*

ENLISTMENT.

When *Aug. 29,* 1864.
× mustered *Aug 30 1864*

Where *Washington Ohio*
× " *Hillsboro Ohio*

By whom *Lt. W. B. Logan* ; term *1* y'rs.
× " *Capt Marley*

Remarks: *Credited to 51st Sub Dist Marion Tp. Fayette Co. 6th Dist of Ohio. Assigned to Company Oct. 17 1864 In Hospital during the Spring campaign of 1865 Sick almost continually from date of joining Co. though a good soldier as far as health would permit Mustered out at Fortress Monroe Va. June 2 1865 in obedience to G.O. 77. AGO. April 28 1865*

N. H. Minick

(383g)   Copyist.

LUCY MANGURN

Fannie's mother was born *circa* 1803. She was listed on the 1850 census as age 47 and living in Granville County, North Carolina, near the Andersons. Her race was shown as white, and she was listed as the mother of three mulatto children, Polly (age 25), Betsy (age 19), and Emily (age 14). No Eliza or Fannie is shown.

At that time, Lucy Mangurn was sharing a household with another single white mom with two mulatto children. Under North Carolina law, mixed-race children inherited the "free" status of the mother, even when the father was a slave. (Taylor, *"The Free Negro in North Carolina,"* 5.)

In 1850, Fannie would have been seven or eight years old. Perhaps her absence from the household can be explained by the fact that her mother was single and poor. The census shows various Mangurn children living with other families in the area, including one four-year-old boy named "Anderson Mangurn" in the "poor house." (Could Anderson Mangurn be a conflation of his father's and mother's names?) Under such circumstances, it would seem plausible that Fannie went to live with her older sister Eliza.

LUCY A. JONES

Lucy was Fannie's "sister of full blood" who lived next door to Fannie and Samuel in Tallahassee in 1880. She was dark-skinned enough to be reported on the census as "black." Although she was a widow, no information about her deceased husband is available. Jones was apparently her father's name. Lucy later moved to Baltimore, Maryland, from where she sent Samuel a pair of new shoes. She also collaborated with Fannie on real estate deals in Lake Worth.

W. T. B. JONES

William T. B. Jones was Fannie's nephew, born October 1848 in North Carolina. U.S. Census records show him living in Knoxville, Tennessee, continuously from 1880 to 1920. He worked as a barber. Fannie's will appointed him co-executor with Alonzo Anderson, but he deferred to his son, A. T. B. Jones, for reasons of health.

A. T. B. JONES

Algernon Theodore B. Jones was Fannie's great-nephew, son of W. T. B. and Ella Jones, born May 1872 in Tennessee. He was a jeweler in a repair shop (1930 census). His education was limited to the sixth grade (1940 census). Along with Alonzo Anderson, he served as executor for Fannie's will, making several trips by train from Tennessee to Lake Worth between 1915 and 1917. He appears on U.S. Census reports as living in the household of his father with variants of his name being Theodore B., Theadore, Algernon T., and A. T. B. He was apparently single all his life.

HENRY JONES

According to her death certificate, Fannie's father was Henry Jones, born in North Carolina. Based on the fact that Fannie was of mixed race and assuming, based on the 1850 census, that her mother "Lucy Mangurn" was white, it would follow that her father, Henry Jones, would be a man of African ancestry. A search of the U.S. Census, however, fails to identify anyone matching the required description.

Attempts to trace Fannie's reported slave background encounter the same set of problems previously discussed relating to Samuel. If Fannie's father was a slave, a search for him would entail looking for a slave owner with the name "Jones" living in Granville County, North Carolina, around 1840 with slaves in the right age and gender brackets. One possibility is the household of Henry W. Jones, who had a large contingent of slaves. The 1840 census gives the following demographics:

Free White Persons—Under 20: 8

Free White Persons—20 thru 49: 3

Slaves—Males—10 thru 23: 4

Slaves—Males—24 thru 35: 2

Slaves—Males—36 thru 54: 1

Slaves—Females—Under 10: 4

Slaves—Females—10 thru 23: 1

Slaves—Females—24 thru 35: 1

Total All Persons—Free White, Free Colored, Slaves: 24

An overview of Samuel's and Fannie's known relatives a picture of the family's mixed racial background. The following chart summarizes the census data.

Fannie & Samuel James Relatives - Evidence of Slave and Race Status - By Census Year													
			1830	1840	1850	1860	1870	1880	1885	1900	1910	1920
	Relation	Date of Birth										
Samuel James		1827-8	slave??					mulatto	mulatto			
Joseph James	Father	???	slave??									
Mrs. James	Mother	???	white??									
Fannie James		1842-3						mulatto	mulatto			
Henry Jones	Father	???		slave??								
Lucy Mangrun	Mother	1803			white							
Polly Mangum	Sister?	1825			free mulatto							
Betsy	Sister?	1831			free mulatto							
Emily	Sister?	1836			free mulatto							
Eliza Anderson	Sister	1824		free colored			mulatto	mulatto				
Bolding Anderson	Brother-in-law	1813		free colored			mulatto	mulatto				
Emma Charlton Gray	Niece	1867					mulatto	mulatto			black	mulatto
Ada Mitchell	Grandniece	1863						mulatto				
Nancy Webster	Sister	1849						black		black	mulatto	
Lucy Jones	Sister	1860						black			mulato	
Betzy Anderson	Sister ?	1836					mulatto	mulatto				
Alonzo Anderson	Nephew	1867					mulatto	mulatto		white?	black	black
W. T. B. Jones	Nephew	1848						mulatto		black	colored	mulatto
A. T. B. Anderson	FJ Grandnephew	1872						mulatto		black	colored	mulatto
Notes:													
??? = unknown; ?? = indirect evidence; ? = circumstantial or conflicting evidence													
1890 Census Records have been destroyed due to fire. 1885 Records represent Florida State Census only.													

Without question, Fannie was of mixed race, as were all of her siblings, their spouses, and their descendants. Although the bulk of the evidence points to Samuel also being of mixed race, the case is not as clear. What is clear is that in an age when the racial divide was widening, the Jameses had the skills to straddle the gap and exist as members of both the black and white communities.

WHERE DID FANNIE'S MIDDLE INITIAL COME FROM?

Fannie often used the middle initial "A." Yet what the "A." stood for is a mystery. Fannie's sister likewise used "A.," signing her name "Lucy A. Jones" while never providing a full middle name. In view of their close relationship with the Anderson clan, is it possible that both women adopted "A." for Anderson? Although census data is lacking, there is a likelihood that at some point the two had lived some portion of their childhood with their older sister, Eliza, perhaps after their mother died. Eliza was married to Bolding Anderson and, demonstrating the strength of their family ties, Fannie named Eliza's daughter, Emma, and granddaughter, Ada as her heirs.

FANNIE'S INDIAN HERITAGE

Lillie Pierce Voss is our sole source for the information on Fannie's indian heritage. In her recently published memoir, she said:

> Mr. and Mrs. Fanny James who were light colored ex-slaves, and well thought of by everyone. Mrs. James was part Indian. ("Pioneer Mail Service," 21)

As Charles Pierce's younger sister, Lillie grew up on Hypoluxo Island, across the lake from the Jameses. Evidently she was quite taken with Fannie. Samuel's name had been forgotten, so she refered to the couple as "Mr. and Mrs. Fanny James." From her detailed description of the Jameses' house and dock, it seems likely that Lillie had visited Fannie from time to time and received her information about Fannie's slave and indian background directly.

In the Carolinas, where Fannie was born, people of mixed African and Native American blood were known as "mustees." Members of the Yamasee, Tuscarora, Cherokee and Creek tribes were among those captured and enslaved. Before the American Revolution, "black and red Carolinians continued to share slave quarters and intimate lives; many wills continued to refer to "all my Slaves, whether Negroes, Indians, Mustees, or Mulattoes." (The American Religious Experience website.)

> It is not commonly known that in all southern colonies Indian slaves were bought and sold and kept in servitude and worked in the fields side by side with negroes up to the time of the revolution... Furthermore, as the coast tribes dwindled they were compelled to associate and intermarry with the negroes until they finally lost their identity and were classified with that race, so that a considerable proportion of the blood of the southern negroes is unquestionably Indian. (Mooney, *Myths of the Cherokees*, 233.)

While the full details of her lineage are unknown, Fannie James apparently had European, African and Native American ancestors; her mother being white, her father black with traces of indian blood. As her death certificate states, she was truly a person of mixed race.

Chapter 44: African American Community During the Homestead Era

As far as is known, the first African American in the lake area was a cook and housekeeper named Aunt Betsy. When Margretta Pierce fell ill during their first year out on Hypoluxo Island, (1876), her husband, Hannibal, sent for her.

> After the first of June father sent Frank Small to Fort Pierce to get Aunt Betsy, an old Negro woman who had befriended us during our first days in Florida. Father wanted her to keep house and do the cooking for the family as mother was not well. Ten days later, Frank came sailing in with Aunt Betsy and her four-year old daughter, Liz. (PLSF, 73)

Although Aunt Betsy did not take up residence on the lake, her story provides insight into the isolation of life during those early homestead years. Imagine sailing for 10 days to pick up someone for work.

Of the 150 people or so who lived on the lake in 1885, about 15 were of African descent. (1885 Florida Census) Included were single men, married couples, and families with children. They came primarily from Georgia or the Bahamas. Occupations of the men were given as either "servant" or "laborer," employed, for the most part, as domestic help or field workers.

One sign of the growing affluence in West Palm Beach can be seen in households that had live-in servants. A number of African Americans, working as domestics, can be found on the 1900 census, just six years after the city's founding. One notable example is the George Potter household where a 32 year old black woman named Christina Floyd worked as a live-in cook.

As agricultural production grew from family farms to larger enterprises, employment opportunities drew more and more newcomers to the lake. Many of the new jobs were filled by blacks from Georgia or the Bahamas. Not all early efforts met with success. The nascent industry went through growth pains as the secrets of cultivation in muck soil were learned by trial and error.

> J. Gingrass, then living... on the Indian River bought all the muck land on the west shore south of Hypoluxo, (now Boynton Beach).... He sent his son-in-law, Tony Canova with a team of mules and a bunch of Negroes to raise a crop of tomatoes on this very black, rich-looking soil.... But the crop was an almost complete failure.... Some years later it was learned that all this land needed was to be sweetened with hardwood ashes. When ashes were used, about a ton to the acre, wonderful crops of tomatoes were produced. (PLSF, 201

Blacks, including many Bahamians, worked in agriculture. Courtesy of *Lake Worth Herald.*

The Jameses were the only ones to file a homestead claim, but there were other African Americans who were independent farmers. L. A. King and Samuel Cade were farmers in the Boynton area for years before the arrival of white settlers. (*Foundations of Faith,* 39). Dillard King, Ebbie Roberts, and Nathaniel Major are shown on the 1910 census as farming their own land.

Jake Gildersleeve grew vegetables in the Riviera Beach area, just west of the Oak Lawn Hotel. His wife, Millie was well known as a midwife, assisting Dr. Richard Potter, who would call for her in a naphtha launch at the hotel dock with a toot on his whistle. Together they attended both settlers and Seminole Indians.

It seems virtually certain that Millie and Fannie knew each other in light of their mutual ties to Dr. Potter, but there is no record to confirm their possible friendship.

As the hotel industry developed on Palm Beach, a community of black workers arose to serve as cooks, laundry service personnel and general labor. Cocoanut Grove Hotel started as an eight-room addition to "Cap" Dimick's house in 1880 and grew to 50 rooms. It was located just south of where the Flagler Museum now stands. Room and board was $6 per person per day.

Cocoanut Grove Hotel, first hotel in Palm Beach, as seen from the lake in 1891. A young black girl stands at the end of the dock and a young black man on the lawn. Courtesy of Florida Archives.

When Flagler started work on Royal Poinciana Hotel in 1893, separate housing arrangements were made for black and white workers. A community called the Styx quickly grew up north of the resort area. Some of the homes were substantial but many were rough shacks. The population was large enough to support two churches: Tabernacle Missionary Baptist and Payne Chapel African Methodist Episcopal. After Flagler built the hotel in 1894, the call for African American workers rapidly expanded.

Automobiles were banned from the grounds of the Royal Poinciana Hotel. Bicycle driven rickshaws, popularly called 'Palm Beach Chariots' and later 'Afromobiles' were used for leisurely afternoon drives. Courtesy of Lake Worth Historical Museum.

The Styx neighborhood experienced growth pains, poor planning, and prejudice. There were complaints about haphazard construction and lack of proper sanitation. Most of the residents paid rent, but there were also squatters. (http://www.pbchistoryonline.org/page/teaching-and-preaching)

Rumor has it that the settlement was intentionally burned down one day while its inhabitants were away at the circus, but former Styx residents question such reports.

Payne Chapel AME, 1894.
Courtesy of Historical Society of Palm Beach County.

The legend of the Styx has been passed down by oral tradition and is accepted as gospel by many. But the evidence all but dismisses it. The shantytown sprang up on Palm Beach's County Road, north of the Royal Poinciana Hotel, in the 1890s for more than 2,000 black workers at nearby hotels. The story is that Henry Flagler was eager to oust the residents so he could develop the land. He had it condemned on health grounds, then hired a circus to set up across the Intracoastal Waterway in West Palm Beach, gave black residents free passes, and while they enjoyed the show, burned their homes down.

Inez Peppers Lovett, who was born in 1895, said in 1994, a year before her death, that she recalled packing up and leaving the Styx (in 1906) but remembers no fire. (http://www.historicpalmbeach.com/eliot-kleinberg/2010/04/the-legend-of-the-styx-outgrew-reality/)

The Styx around 1906.
Courtesy of Historical Society of Palm Beach County.

In any case, the Styx was gradually dismantled and replaced by black communities on the other side of the lake in West Palm Beach, where black churches, businesses, and homes quickly sprung up. The first and only African American school of record in 1895 operated out of the Tabernacle Baptist Church on Clematis Street. It is likely that the newspaper notice below, stating that "J. E. Jones, colored" had passed the teacher's exam, was in reference to one of its teachers.

C. P. Jackson and L. L. Kidner, white; and J. E. Jones, colored, took the recent examination for teachers. The grading was 77 7.10, 77 1/2, 75 5.11 respectively.

Tropical Sun, May 23, 1895

From its inception, West Palm Beach was a boomtown, and although relegated to second-class status, the African American community enjoyed a measure of prosperity. Pleasant City was created there in 1905 as a middle-class "negro" neighborhood of doctors, businessmen, and professionals. By 1915, there were over 150 "colored" property owners (families and individuals) listed in the City Directory.

Sample extract from 1915 Directory of West Palm Beach and County, 49ff).

COLORED SECTION
WEST PALM BEACH—PROPERTY OWNERS ONLY

A
Akery, P., 831 Clematis Ave.
Ambrose, Allen, 818 Second Ave.
Andrews, D., 533 First Ave.
anderson, E. A., 915 Fourth Ave.
Anderson, Sadie H., 527 Clematis Ave.
Artson, W. H., 910 First Ave.

B
Bird, B., 809 Althea St.
Bird, Chas., 802 Fifth Ave.
Blaine, A. H., 708 Second Ave.
Blaine, Carrie, 415 Division St.
Bland, Richard, 611 Second Ave.
Bolding, G., 706 Tamarind St.
Boyd, Lottie, 817 Banyan St.
Brennan, Joseph, 720 Douglas St.

F
Finley, 912 Althea St.
Francis, E., 820 Banyan St.
Franklin, J., 828 Fern St.
Franklin, Phyllis, 928 Third Ave.
Frederick, Nat., 802 Althea St.

G
Cee, B. F., 825 Datura St.
Gibbons, Mary, 922 Althea St.
Gilbert, John, 528 First Ave.
Giradeau, Hattie, 902 First Ave.
Goins, Sam, 614 First Ave.
Green, Carrie, 905 Althea St.
Green, Forest, 915 Third Ave.
Green, S. C., 315 S. Tamarind St.
Griffin, Chrissie, 639 Third Ave.

Meanwhile there were also emerging black communities further south in Linton (Delray), Boynton and Lantana. As early as 1894, there were 14 African American and Bahamian families living in Linton, with enough children to petition Dade County for their own school. The request was granted and Dade County "Colored School" #4" opened the following year.
(http://www.delraybeachhistory.org/timeline.aspx;
http://www.palmbeach.k12.fl.us/SDSpadyES/SpadyHistory.htm)

At the southern end of the lake, where the City of Boynton Beach now stands, there was a population of African Americans and Bahamians farming the land in the early 1890s out of sight of the larger lake community. They are sometimes referred to as "squatters" as is it unclear whether or not they had legal title to their farmlands.

When Major Nathan S. Boynton settled here in 1894, he was befriended by the local Seminole Indians and African American settlers.... African American families like the Kings, McCades and others taught Major Boynton and other white settlers how to farm. The muck soil along the shore of Lake Hypoluxo now called Lake Worth was very fertile and produced excellent crops of all types. (*Foundations of Faith,* 39)

Everyone avoided the white community out of fear and mistrust. (*Foundations of Faith,* 36)

M. B. Lyman took up residence in January 1888 at Lantana Point, two miles south of Jewell. A small but thriving town soon developed with a cluster of black households on its west end. The Lymans are said to have employed an African American woman named "Aunt Susan" to do their laundry. She, like Millie Gildersleeve, was "a midwife and a nurse." (*Early Lantana,* 75)

The 1900 census lists the following blacks living in the Lantana area:

Joseph Houston, family head, age 40, born in Georgia, married one year, worked as a "day laborer."

Anna Houston, wife, age 34, born in Virginia, married one year, had given birth to four children, only one of whom survived.

Alex Dawxy, family head, age 34, born in Virginia, married 11 years, worked as a "day laborer."

Judie Dawxy, wife, age 35, born in South Carolina, married 11 years, had given birth to four children, three of whom survived.

Levina Dawxy, daughter, age 18, single.

Abiah Dawxy, daughter, age 7, single.

Sarah Combs, servant in household of Olwell Wood, age 31, born in Florida, single.

July Jenkins, boarder in Wood household, age 25, born in Georgia, single.

Frank Nelson, boarder in Wood household, age 24, born in Florida, single.

John Jones, boarder in Wood household, age 20, born in Florida, single.

The growth of both agriculture and the hotel industry resulted in an increasing demand for inexpensive labor. By 1905, the population of Dade County had grown to over 12,000 including 4,000 "negroes". The state census of that year shows the population by race and city. Figures for Lantana were included in the totals for Boynton, showing 338 residents, 151—or 45%—of them "negro."

Thee1915 figures likewise include the Lantana area in the Boynton count. Total population had grown to 806 residents, 247, or 30%, of them black.

During the Jameses first years on the lake, the black population would have been small and distant from Jewell. But given their pattern of associating with the black community while living in Tallahassee and Cocoa, it would have been natural for them to have sought out their ethnic community as the demographics changed and the opportunity for contact afforded itself. Despite that lack of recorded

TABLE NO. 7—(*Continued*)—POPULATION OF FLORIDA BY MINOR CIVIL DIVISIONS: 1905 AND 1900.

MINOR CIVIL DIVISIONS.	1905			1900
	White	Negro	Total	Total
1 Dade County	7,880	4,181	1 12,089	4,955
Precinct 1, Stuart	215	22	237	......
Precinct 2, Jupiter	198	50	248	......
Precinct 3, West Palm Beach, including West Palm Beach town.	1,076	731	3 1,808	......
West Palm Beach town	883	397	1,280	......
Precinct 4, Boynton	187	151	338	......
Precinct 5, Delray	309	190	499	......
Precinct 6, Pompano	76	2	78	......
Precinct 7, Ft. Lauderdale (20 Indians)	161	38	4 219	......
Precinct 8, Ojus	212	70	282	......
Precinct 9, Lemon City	622	252	874	......
Precinct 10, Miami, including Miami city	3,893	2,329	5 6,228	......
Miami city	2,983	1,744	6 4,733	......
Miami suburbs	108	183	291	......
Precinct 11, Cocoanut Grove......	398	221	7 620	......
Precinct 12, Cutler..............	145	29	174	......
Precinct 13, Naranja	212	1	213	......
Precinct 14, Deerfield	31	47	78	......
Precinct 15, David	144	49	193	......

1 Owing to entire redistricting of the county, comparison cannot be made with precincts existing in 1900.

2 This total includes 28 persons of other races.

3 This total includes 1 person of other races.

4 This total includes 20 Indians.

5 This total includes 6 persons of other races.

6 This total includes 6 persons of other races.

7 This total includes 1 person of other races.

Third Census of the State of Florida: Taken in the year 1905, 26–27.

documentation, it would seem likely that the Jameses would have found black friends and attended a black church either in Lantana, West Palm Beach or both.

On the 1915 chart, Lake Worth was listed separately as it was by then an incorporated town. The effectiveness of efforts to make Lake Worth a white-only community is evident from the data. Among the 1915 residents, not a single "Negro" is shown.

TABLE No. 9—POPULATION OF FLORIDA BY MINOR CIVIL DIVISIONS: CLASSIFIED BY RACE: 1915

MINOR CIVIL DIVISIONS	1915			1910 (U.S.) Total
	Total	White	Negro	
Palm Beach County	*9,669	6,499	3,062	5,577
Precinct 1, Stuart, including Stuart town	1,053	843	210	457
Stuart town	599	484	115	......
Precinct 2, Jupiter	459	306	153	398
Precinct 3, including Palm Beach town and part of West Palm Beach city (1)	465	446	18	......
Palm Beach town	113	101	12	......
West Palm Beach city, part of (1)	320	314	5	......
Pecinct 4, Boynton	806	559	247	671
Precinct 5, Delray (2), including Delray town	1,262	756	476	904
Delray town	839	421	418	......
Precinct 8, Utopia	137	137	......	......
Precinct 9, Indian town (3)	110	34	2	......
Precinct 10, West Palm Beach, including part of West Palm Beach city (1)	654	649	4	......
Precinct 11, including part of West Palm Beach city (1)	1,375	1,169	205	......
Precinct 12, including part of West Palm Beach city	1,988	412	1,576	......
Total West Palm Beach city (4)	4,090	2,307	1,780	1,743
Precinct 3, part of (1)	320	314	5	......
Precinct 10, part of (1)	654	649	4	......
Precinct 11, part of (1)	1,275	1,081	193	......
Precinct 12, part of	1,838	262	1,576	......
Precinct 13, Ritta (1)	201	200	......	......
Precinct 14, Lake Worth, including Lake Worth town	705	705	......	......
Lake Worth town	612	612	......	......
Precinct 15, Gomez	242	102	140	......
Precinct 16, Salerno	212	181	31	......

* Total includes 34 persons of other races and 74 Indians.
(1) Total includes 1 person of another race.
(2) Total includes 30 persons of other races.
(3) Total includes 74 Indians.
(4) Total includes 3 persons of other races.

Fourth Census of the State of Florida: Taken in the year 1915, 44.

Chapter 45: Zooming in on Lake Worth's Segregation Era

Nationally, segregation fervor reached its height in the 1920s. Klu Klux Klan and White Citizens Councils sprang up in community after community. By 1925, Klan ranks had swollen to three million throughout the country. A large Klan rally was held in Washington, DC, on August 8, 1925, when 50,000 men and women marched in support of the Klan's racist agenda. The purpose of the marches and cross burnings was to keep the black community in fear and through intimidation force subservience, hold down demands for equal rights, and ensure compliance with segregation laws.

Klan rally in Gainesville, Florida, 1922. Courtesy of National Archives.

KKK tentacles reached down into South Florida. George Greenberg recalled seeing a Ku Klux Klan parade in downtown Lake Worth in the 1920s:

> All these men… and their cars were covered with white sheets and it was sort of a scary thing for a young kid to see that. I know my dad said he knew who they were. He recognized them all. Of course, in those days it was a small town, so everybody knew everybody else. (http://www.pbchistoryonline.org/page/african-american)

Although many remained in hiding behind the KKK's traditional white hoods and sheets, others were bolder and operated openly. The Lake Worth Klan boasted in nationally syndicated Klan publications of its plans to build a two story headquarters in the city (*Hooded Americanism*, 211). Lake Worth's auxiliary WKKK (Women's Klu Klux Klan) likewise operated in the open and ran a free day nursery school, claiming that Catholic teachers had ruined public education. (*Fiery Cross*, October 10, 1924). Naming itself the George B. Baker Klan, after Palm Beach County's popular first sheriff, it claimed to be a bulwark against the forces of lawlessness.

During the first decades of its existence, Lake Worth also saw white supremacist attitudes displayed in a variety of ways, though not necessarily tied directly to Klan activity. For example, a petition with 66 signatures was presented to the City Commission requesting that "white labor be given preference on city work." (Minutes of the Commission of the City of Lake Worth, October 2, 1917.) Although the motion to formalize racist hiring practices was tabled at that meeting, such attitudes eventually had an impact on hiring practices. When the city entered into an arrangement with George W. Hulme for the upkeep and maintenance of the municipal golf course, the contract prohibited the employment of black workers:

> **The party of the second part agrees to employ at his own expense a sufficient number of laborers… to keep said grounds in proper condition and repair at all times during the term of this contract, but that he will not employ any person who is not of the Caucasian race. (Minutes of the Commission of the City of Lake Worth, October 15, 1931.)**

The situation for African Americans in Lantana was equally intimidating. From the 1890s, a mixed black population of Bahamians and Georgians had settled in and around Lantana, providing a labor pool for pineapple and vegetable growers. Through segregation statutes and KKK intimidation, they were forced out. (*Jewel of the Gold Coast*, 248) By 1917, perhaps earlier, blacks started relocating to the unincorporated area between Lake Worth and Lantana. Black churches, which had been founded in Lantana, followed.

This area had originally been part of the Gudmundsen homestead. Fannie James acted as power of attorney when her sister Lucy bought the property in in February 1903. Later Lucy, working with Fannie as her intermediary, followed the long established business plan of subdividing and selling off various parcels. Included among those sales was a 15 acre lot, purchased by Will D. Griffin in 1907. The parcel changed hands several times during the next few years.

Ott M. Carmichael and Vincent Oaksmith acquired the 15-acre property in 1913. They were businessmen from West Palm who engaged in real estate speculation on the side. They had the parcel surveyed and platted the Osborne Colored Addition. The plan created eighty lots and was conceived as an addition to the Town of Lake Worth, just south of the city limits. At that time, however, the Town was in no mood to annex the area and thus change the whites-only status of the town.

When Lantana was incorporated in 1921, its charter also implemented a racial segregation policy, similar to and in some ways harsher than Lake Worth's. Blacks, as well as "foreigners," were prohibited, although clearly Swedes and Germans were not considered "foreigners" under the segregation policy.

> **When these black families left Lantana, many of them moved to the Osborne section of Lake Worth, which lies between Lantana (Road) and 12th Avenue South in Lake Worth, immediately west of the Florida East Coast Railway. They had been asked to leave when the town was incorporated, but they refused to do so. Later the Klu Klux Klan forced the move. Lantana has a provision in its charter that says no blacks nor foreigners are allowed, which is unenforceable under federal law but remains on the books at least until 1972. (*Early Lantana*, 75)**

The area between the northern city limits of Lantana and the southern limits of Lake Worth became a no-man's-land where many displaced blacks moved. In 1922, Grant AME Chapel followed its parishioners and moved from Broadway Street in Lantana to Ray Street in the Osborne Colored Addition. At that time, the AME church served both Bahamian and African American populations. (Later, in 1927, a Saint John's Episcopal Church split off to better meet the Anglican orientation of the Bahamians.)

In 1925, a revised city charter annexed all previously unincorporated land that lay between Lake Worth and Lantana. Thus, the Osborne Colored Addition finally became part of the City. However, even after annexation, the City Commission did not immediately implement the charter provision for a "district in which negroes may reside." Subsequently, complaints began to be heard that blacks were living in the city illegally.

These complaints are best understood in the context of the city's successful white-only policy. The Florida State Census of 1925 surveyed the "population of cities, towns and villages" throughout Florida, counting "White" and "Negro" separately. Lake Worth had 4,617 white residents and zero negro residents. Of all the municipalities in the state with populations over 1,000 Lake Worth was unique in having no African-American population whatsoever. Lantana likewise had no negroes, but its population was less than 200. (*Fifth Census of the State of Florida: Taken in the year 1925.* Commissioner of Agriculture, 71–77.)

Then on November 22, 1926, 13 years after the city's incorporation, an ordinance was approved that created a "negro district" within the city where it was legal for persons of "that race" to reside. In addition to the area defined by the 1917 Osborne Colored Addition plat, the negro district included the Latona Court area and a narrow strip south to the Lantana city line.

> **NEGROES ARE BARRED**
>
> Lake Worth, Sept. 15—As result of complaints that negroes live in a division recently annexed to Lake Worth, action will be taken to enforce the ordinance that allows no person of that race within the corporate limits of the city.

Palm Beach Post, September 16, 1926.

THE 1926 ORDINANCE READ, IN PART:

An ordinance establishing, designating and setting apart in the City of Lake Worth District in said city within which only Negroes may reside.

Be it ordained by the City Commission of the City of Lake Worth, Florida;

That the following described district within the City of Lake Worth is hereby established, designated and set apart as the territorial limits and district in said city within which only Negroes may reside....

[Legal description of the boundaries of the "negro district," which included the Osborne Colored Addition as platted in 1917 and added the area south to the Lantana city limits.]

Be it further ordained, that white persons are hereby prohibited from establishing a place of residence within the territorial limits above described in the said city so set apart and established for the residence of negroes.

Any person violating the provisions of this Ordinance shall be punished on conviction by a fine not exceeding five hundred ($500) dollars or imprisoned in the city jail for a period not to exceed thirty (30) days or both such fine and imprisonment, and each ten (10) days of prohibited condition shall constitute a separate offense. (passed November 22, 1926. See also *Tuskegee Institute Yearbook, 1931–1932,* 67.)

As a result of the 1926 segregation ordinance, "negroes" could, for the first time, live within the city limits of Lake Worth as long as they stayed within the designated ghetto boundries. Penalties for violating the ordinance were severe, especially when considering that 30-days of jail time or a $500 fine could be imposed for each 10-days of residence in the wrong neighborhood. In 1926 dollars, $500 would be equivalent to more than $6,000 today.

By 1930, the workers' barracks of the Quarters had been remodeled to accommodate families. The Federal Census of that year shows 22 married couples, 18 of whom had children.

During that period, the neighborhood still retained its predominately Bahamian character. Of the 92 residents in the Quarters, 60 were of Bahamian heritage with the remainder being African Americans from Georgia, North Carolina and other southern states.

The changing demographics resulted in diversification in the types of jobs held by the black population. While in the earlier period agricultural work was dominant, the census lists a broad range of occupations include 15 laborers doing "odd jobs," laundresses, cooks, housekeepers, painters, carpenters, and beauticians, as well as one grocer and one chauffer. Only two were full time fruit pickers. A number of black women were housekeepers at the newly built Gulfstream Hotel.

HOMEOWNERS IN THE QUARTERS - 1930

Name	Marital Status	Home Value	Age	Place of Birth	Occupation
Berry Joseph Berry	Husband	$400	48	Florida	Laborer
Anna Berry	Wife		45	Florida	Homemaker
Frank Deal	Husband	$800	33	Long Island, Bahamas	Laborer
Sada Deal	Wife		24	Long Island, Bahamas	Homemaker
Thomas Geslow	Husband	$1,500	35	Georgia	Laborer
Bertha Geslow	Wife		40	Georgia	Domestic Worker
Donald Gibson	Husband	$1,500	36	Nassau, Bahamas	Landscape Gardener
Henrietta Gibson	Wife		29	Nassau, Bahamas	Homemaker
Harold Glinton	Husband	$500	35	Long Island, Bahamas	Farm Worker
Celest	Wife		33	Long Island, Bahamas	Takes in Laundry
Claude Knowles	Husband	$800	35	Long Island, Bahamas	Fruit Picker
Elizabeth Knowles	Wife		29	Long Island, Bahamas	Takes in Laundry
Edmund Knowles	Widower	$1,000	47	Long Island, Bahamas	Laborer
Richard Knowles	Husband	$800	33	Long Island, Bahamas	Laborer
Allice Knowles	Wife		21	Long Island, Bahamas	Homemaker
Emma Marshall	Divorced	$800	23	Florida	Takes in Laundry
Wilfred McPhee	Husband	$1,500	31	Long Island, Bahamas	Retail Grocer
Leona McPhee	Wife		27	North Carolina	Homemaker
Ida Pratt	Widow	$1,000	59	Nassau, Bahamas	Laundress
Leon Pratt	Husband	$200	21	Long Island, Bahamas	Domestic Worker
Carry Pratt	Wife		23	Georgia	Cook in Café
A. Hap. Watkins	Husband	$1,000	43	Florida	Landscape Gardener
Maztis Watkins	Wife		40	Florida	Homemaker

Twelve other families rented homes or rooms paying between $3 and $20 per month.

After annexation, few, if any, city services were provided to the negro district. Streets were unlit and unpaved. There were no public schools until after World War II when the Osborne School was built. (Unofficial schools were set up in churches in the Osborne area and were run by the community.) The annexation, however, did allow city police to gain jurisdiction over the negro neighborhood enabling enforcement of segregation statutes.

According to Lake Worth City Clerk's records, in 1938 residents of the Quarters petitioned the city to pave its unpaved streets and install sanitary sewer. Through the 40s and 50s city services gradually improved, adding garbage collection, street lighting, city water and a public school.

Parkview Heights, now Latona Court, was to be a new upscale subdivision, in the expanded "Negro Section," south of the Osborne Addition.

In 1949, the City Commission voted to expand the "Negro Section" further. The new boundaries ran up to 12th Avenue South. Eighty acres to the west were also added including a "colored" cemetery (now I. A. Banks Memorial Park) and a sports field (now Howard Park). The bulk of the 80 acres, however, became a sanitation dump and was never used for residential purposes.

The Palm Beach Post - Jul 29, 1946

PARKVIEW HEIGHTS
New Colored Subdivision in Osborne Addition, Lake Worth
These choice building lots, on wide paved street, opposite new schoolhouse site in Osborne Addition to Lake Worth, now being offered for sale at prices from $125 to $450. Terms if desired. Better grab one quickly—they wont last long at this price. Sold exclusively by
M. C. BAKER, Realtor
909 Lake Ave., Lake Worth. Ph. 104

Despite its genteel description as a neighborhood with "choice building lots" and "wide paved streets," the Quarters was a literal ghetto, hemmed in from every side and designed to keep blacks and whites apart. A wall blocking all access to Lantana on the south end, combined county dump and barbed-wire-topped wall on the west, and the FEC tracks running NE–SW enclosed the triangle-shaped neighborhood. Residents were allowed to leave during the day but were required to be within its confines at night. (See description of life in the Osborne neighborhood in the 1950s by Reverend Wade Hardeman as found in *Jewel of the Gold Coast*, 256.)

Section 9. That property described as follows shall be designated as "H" District, Negro Section.

"H" DISTRICT

(1) In Addition No. 1 to Lake Worth, the following: All of Blocks 70, 71, 79, 80, 81; also Lots 1, 2, 3 and 4, Block 72.

(2) All of Osborne Colored Addition lying West of the F. E. C. Railroad.

(3) All of Latona Court.

(4) All of Hancock Court.

(5) All of Lantana Osborne Addition

(6) That land lying between Broadway and Lantana Osborne Addition and South of Latona Court.

(7) The South half of the Northeast quarter of Section 33, Township 44 South, Range 43 East.

Article XXV of 1949 Revision of Lake Worth Charter.

During the height of the Jim Crow era, not only were black residents confined to dwelling in the Osborne district, but they were also subject to a variety of segregation measures throughout the city. There were separate white-only and black-only water fountains downtown at Lake Avenue and J Street. Gas stations had four restrooms: men's and women's white and men's and women's colored. Only the Lake Theatre movie house downtown permitted blacks, and it had a separate "colored-only" balcony.

African American children attended colored schools, first at Saint John's Episcopal Church and after 1946, at the three-room Osborne Colored School. High school students went to Carver High School in Delray Beach. Lake Worth High, Lake Worth Middle, Barton, and other elementary schools were white-only. Blacks were not welcomed at the public beach. As late as 1962, a black high school student was arrested for attending a beach party with her white friends. ("Kanu Broke Palm Beach School Segregation Barriers," *Muse,* Dreyfus School of the Arts, October 11, 2011.)

Jordan Family from the Quarters in the 1940s.
Courtesy of Herman Jordan.

Chapter 46: Lake Worth Loosens Up

Things began to change during the 1960s. Though there were troublesome incidents, public schools were, for the most part, peacefully integrated. The process was a gradual one, starting with two black students at Lake Worth High in 1961 and ending when the Osborne Colored School finally closed in 1969. After the implementation of federal integration mandates, many white parents chose, for a time, to send their children to all-white private schools rather than to allow racial mixing. New, all-white private schools sprang up overnight, especially for younger grades. Little by little, however, attitudes mellowed. After a few years, "integration-avoidance" private schools closed as both parents and students adjusted to public education in the age of equality.

Federal fair housing laws outlawed segregated neighborhoods. As a result, the black population, while still concentrated in the old Osborne neighborhood, began to scatter throughout the city.

"Mural of Unity", on Wingfield Street, transformed a ghetto wall into a tribute to diversity in 1994.

Barbed wire stringers are a reminder of the wall's former purpose.

Lake Worth today takes pride in its reputation as a haven of diversity. The Quarters retains strong Bahamian and African American cultural ties with six active black churches and a black cemetery, but it has also become an integral part of Lake Worth as home to a municipal recreation center, ball fields, and the municipal gym.

In 1994, the city took steps to amend its segregationist past. An act of the Florida Legislature was required, but the name of the former negro district legally was changed from the "Osborne Colored Addition" to simply the "Osborne Addition," removing a stigma from the city's racist past.

A steady stream of changes, both symbolic and substantial, has transformed the face of the city. Haitians, African Americans, and Caribbeans now live side by side with Latinos and whites in every neighborhood. The old segregation wall still stands as a relic of the past but is graced with a "Mural of Unity" depicting scenes of race amity.

A block-long "Pathway to Freedom" and an MLK Fountain occupy a prominent place in the downtown Cultural Plaza, proudly celebrating the end of the ugliness of segregation and the current status of the former site of Jewell as a haven for diversity.

Pioneer Osborne community fights racial stigma legally affixed in 1917

By ANGELA HORNSBY
Palm Beach Post Staff Writer

LAKE WORTH — Osborne. Born from unpaved roads, palmettos and Australian pines. Recognizable by a strong line of black families who settled and remained: the Jacksons, the Knowleses, the Grimeses. Sustained by church and neighborly get-togethers.

Osborne. This five-block, 10-acre community, west of the railroad tracks on the city's south side, has another distinctive mark. It's the only neighborhood in Palm Beach County ever legally designated as "colored." That was in 1917 in the county's plat book.

The name still exists.

For many residents, the "Osborne Colored Addition" has and continues to

be a steady reminder of their place in society. The description has appeared on mortgages, property tax assessments, deeds, job licenses and other legal documents. About 80 homeowners currently are affected.

The name has outlived some pioneer families. In city hall, it has gone unchanged through 26 mayors and more than 100 commissioners, none of whom were black.

Now community leaders say it's time to erase that symbol of racial

Please see **OSBORNE/4B**

THE PALM BEACH POST   SUNDAY, SEPTEMBER 11, 1994

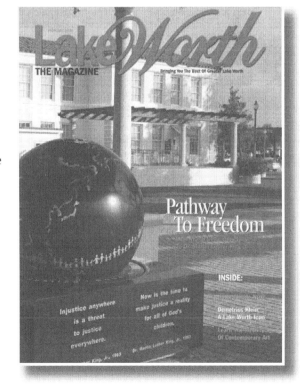

Martin Luther King Jr. Memorial Fountain in downtown Lake Worth, *Lake Worth* magazine cover, February 2005.

Interview with former Lake Worth Commissioner Retha Lowe

February 5, 2013

WHEN DID YOU GET INTERESTED IN LAKE WORTH HISTORY?

Really, it was little by little. I was born in Tallahassee. My family came to Delray when I was young. I went to Poinciana Elementary in Boynton from first grade to the eighth grade. I never really knew anything about Lake Worth.

Now in 9th grade all the high school kids had to be bused to Carver [High School] in Delray, even though we had a couple of high schools in Boynton. Boynton had a high school right on Ocean Avenue. And there was Seacrest [High School]. They were all-white schools. But we had to go to the black school at Carver. Even the black kids from Deerfield and Boca were bused up to Carver.

That's when I started to meet people from Lake Worth. I heard about the Osborne colored neighborhood and how all the black people lived together [in one community]. I knew all the families from the Osborne community because of the kids that went to school with me in Delray. I knew the Glintons. I knew the Knowles, the Smiths, the Jordans. I knew the Greens and Johnny Green, who was the first black boy to integrate Lake Worth High School. Theresa Jakes, too, she was the first [black] girl to attend Lake Worth High.

WOULD YOU SAY YOU GOT A GOOD EDUCATION IN THE ALL-BLACK SCHOOLS?

I think so. The schools didn't have a lot of money and they didn't pay the teachers all that much, but the teachers were very good in the black schools. They treated you just like you were their own kid. They treated you like your own mother and father and I feel we got more discipline, more love. There was a family feeling and we lost it when we integrated.

WHY DID YOU MOVE TO LAKE WORTH?

My husband, Grady Lowe, was from Lake Worth. We moved to this house on 12th Avenue South in 1975. At that time, people would say, "You moved to the Quarters" but I didn't know what they were talking about. I lived in Lake Worth, but people were still used to segregation and they would tell me, "No, you didn't move to Lake Worth. You moved to the Quarters."

So I asked Grady, "What was the Quarters?" And I started doing some digging to find out why it was called the "Quarters?" Why was it called "Osborne Colored?" I found out that around

Lake Osborne and Lake Worth, was where all the white people lived. But the black people lived in the Quarters.

Back then the farms owned the houses where their field workers lived. So they called it the Quarters. The people worked in pineapple fields and tomato fields. The houses were all cut up into efficiencies. A whole family would stay in one room with four or five kids. You could not stay there unless you and your kids worked. If you had three teenage kids and one of them said, "Mama, I'm not going out there in that hot field to work" that kid could not stay there. Oh, yeah.

Later on I ran for the City Commission. Mayor Rodney Romano got together with me and other people in the community to talk about the "Osborne Colored Addition". He said to me, "We're going to take that "Colored" off of there and change the name to "Osborne Addition." And that's when we started to work with the County Clerk to remove the word "Colored" and we got it done. Yet even to this day, there are some older people, not too many left now, who still call it the Quarters. After segregation ended, it took some time for them to realize that black people could live anywhere in Lake Worth.

WHAT WERE THE NAMES OF THE COMPANIES THAT PEOPLE WORKED FOR?

I really don't know the names of the owners, but there were farms all around and there was one construction company in Lantana that had houses for their workers. That's just the way it was done back then.

The Knowles, they owned a pineapple field in Hypoluxo. In Hypoluxo all that area was in pineapple farms. The employer owned the houses… some of those same houses in the Quarters lasted until I was on the City Commission. They were old and run down, so we had to take them down.

Retha Lowe was the first African-American elected to the Lake Worth City Commission. She served from 1995 to 2001 and again from 2003 to 2009. Among her many accomplishments, Commissioner Lowe helped to heal old wounds and to revitalize the Osborne community through improved city services, new housing, a municipal gymnasium, as well as the transformation of a segregation era wall into a Mural of Unity.

Chapter 47: Summing It All Up.
What It Means.

Many current Lake Worth residents are transplants from other parts of the United States and the world, with a natural curiosity about their new hometown. It is hoped that studies such as this one help newcomers to put down roots by seeing current affairs in a broader context.

The City of Lake Worth, formerly known as Jewell, has a rich and intriguing history. Recent research, aided by the internet, has uncovered a generation of previously unknown homesteaders who entered a tropical wilderness and began the process of building the City as it is known today. This new information supplements the well-documented history of the City since its incorporation.

Briefly, Lake Worth's history can be divided into five time periods.

- The Indigenous Period of the Jaega and early Spanish Explorers, prehistoric to 1700s.

- The Seminole Period, when both natives and blacks took refuge in the Everglades, 1700s to 1870s.

- The Homestead Era, when the pioneers of Jewell formed a thinly populated rural community, 1870s to 1912.

- The Early Urban Era, when the town was incorporated and defined itself as a racially divided community, 1912 to 1960s.

- The Diversity Era, the current period when the city has made strides to redefine itself by embracing its multicultural population.

Struggles with issues of race and culture have been a major theme in Lake Worth's history, as has been true of the United States as a whole. Having first citizens, such as Fannie and Samuel James, African Americans who were well respected on both sides of the color line, set an example in harmony with the American Dream. Despite the disheartening errors of the past, the history of the Jewell pioneers reveals the city is now truer to its roots. If Fannie James were to walk into town today, she would once again be welcomed wherever she might choose to go.

Appendices

==

FROM THE JAEGA TO THE JAMESES

"There's an old saying about those who forget history. I don't remember it, but it's good."

— Stephen Colbert

The Barefoot Mailman, as depicted in this 1940 West Palm Beach post office mural by Stevan Dohanos, rows through an alligator infested swamp. Although most famous for walking along the the Atlantic beach, the Barefoot Mailman used rowboats for several legs of the three day trek between Hypoluxo and Biscayne Bay including the southern end of Lake Worth and the Hillsboro inlet.

Appendix A: Select Newspaper Ads and Clippings

Local newspapers of the day provided firsthand information on the doings on the lake, written by and for the community. While often lacking in broad perspective, archives of historic papers provide serial glimpses into the daily lives of early pioneers.

The first paper to provide coverage for lake residents was The *Florida Star,* published weekly in Titusville. Early editions included only towns that were close to Titusville, such as Cocoa and Eau Galle, but starting in 1884 it began covering places farther south including Palm Beach and Hypoluxo. The paper covered topics ranging from world events to gossip on dinner guests. Local affairs were covered in specific columns dedicated to the various communities in its coverage area. A typical column would start with rapid fire one or two line remarks on the weather, mosquito conditions, then move on to crop production, hunting and fishing exploits and boating incidents.

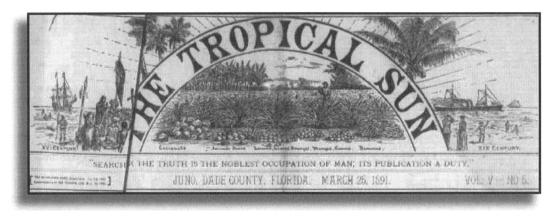

Lake residents got their own paper, when Guy Metcalf moved the *Indian River News* from Melbourne to Juno and changed its name to the *Tropical Sun* in March 1891. Its intricate masthead depicted sixteenth-century Spanish explorers on the left, tropical fruits such as mangoes, pineapples, oranges, and bananas in the center under the arch, and nineteenth-century progress on the right. The first issue published in Juno bore the confusing designation Vol. V— as a continuation of its Brevard County forerunner.

The *Tropical Sun,* like the *Florida Star* before it, ran weekly columns on each of the various lake communities. Edwin Bradley's clever chronicle, called "Lotus Cove," covered the everyday doings of the settlers "twixt Hypo and Jewell." (Bradley signed his articles as "Ruthven.") The *Tropical Sun* moved its offices to West Palm Beach in 1895.

Another paper, *The Gazette,* was briefly published in West Palm Beach from March 1894 to 1896(?). All copies have been lost. A weekly summary of contents survives in the *1896 Directory, Guide and History of Dade County, Florida, including Broward and Palm Beach Counties.*

The Daily *Tropical Sun* was a daily addition of the weekly *Tropical Sun* that was briefly published for several months in 1914–1915. (On microfiche at UF-Gainesville, Library West, third floor.)

The *Palm Beach County* started as a weekly in 1908. The name was changed to *the Palm Beach Post* when daily publication began in 1916.

The *Lake Worth Herald* is a weekly that began publication in May 1912.

Below are selected excerpts and short articles that reveal happenings and attitudes in the Homestead Era lake community.

> Neither railroad, canal, nor telegraph line has got here yet, though they are all talked about. Wonder which will get here first? The odds, if any, seem to be in favor of our being "struck by lightning" first.

Florida Star, Lake Worth column, January 5, 1888
—Telegraph or lightning?

> **Hypoluxo.**
> "There's music in the air,"
> The musquito is to hum.
> He—or she rather—judging from the name, is of Spanish origin. The plain English of it should be the "must-eat-oh," for they are indefatigable in search of a meal, and they puncture the millionaire with the same calm indifference and bill that they do the humble scribe. They are democratic in their tastes and manners, and, *per se*, inflict the "solid South" and New Jersey. The sulphurous fumes of profanity drive them not, but a pinch of pyrethrum in the smoke-pot and they are like the learned country constable's return on his writ, "*non est in veritus, in scampo up a stumpo.*" You can take your choice—patience, profanity or pyrethrum.

Florida Star, July 3, 1889—Mosquito repellant.

> The Miami mail carriers report very few turtle signs on the beach. Hundreds of them were killed last year by the conchs. Two or three schooners from the Bahamas prowled along the coast and killed turtle merely for their eggs, throwing their carcasses overboard; but a revenue cutter took one of them in, and as a result they have not showed up this year.

Florida Star, August 21, 1889
—Barefoot Mailman and scarcity of sea turtle nests.

> Indians have been here for the past eek or so, but have not been very sucssful in their hunting.

Florida Star, August 21, 1889—Seminoles hunting in the lake area without success.

> The Bradley boys returned from their successful hunt. Results—three deer, one turkey and three terrapin. The boys do not cut a big swath at the rifle range but are on deck when game is wanted.

Tropical Sun, Lotus Cove Column, August 26, 1891
—Hunting.

> Mr. A. W. Garnett takes this week's trip with the Miami mail. If length of limb were conducive of speed Mr. G. ought to come near annihilating space. He has been there before—and made a first-class record for promptness and efficiency.

Tropical Sun, Lotus Cove Column, August 26, 1891
—Barefoot Mail Run.

> My sweet potatoes grin when it rains all day on the mail carrier.

Tropical Sun, Lotus Cove Column, September 9, 1891
—Smiling yams.

> It cost me three dollars to have a barrel crate of egg-plants sold in N. Y. City. *Ego non sum tam fool* enough to go and raise some more.—RUTHVEN.

Tropical Sun, Lotus Cove Column, September 30, 1891
—Latin eggplant.

I wonder why Dade Co., is not entitled to a finger in the Worlds Fair pie. United effort would make a display superior to any single county in the United States. Who will make the first move? Call a meeting, somebody; set the date of same far enough ahead so that *all* will have time to ponder, plead and prepare to pucker, and see if it is possible to be unanimous, for once.

I think it will rain soon. R.

Tropical Sun, Lotus Cove Column, October 14, 1891
—1893 Columbian Exhibition in Chicago.

While old man B. was working in his garden he was rather surprised to see five turkeys walk quietly out of the egg plants. He as quietly walked into the house, and soon Lewis B. was russian after turkey and got four out of the five and we and some of the neighbors had a premature Thanksgiving.

Tropical Sun, Lotus Cove Column, October 28, 1891
—Turkeys in the eggplants.

If it took ten men, four rollers and two bottles of whiskey to move Laubach's kithen 400 yards—how many Irish potatoes can you buy for five cents a pound?

Tropical Sun, Lotus Cove Column, November 5, 1891
—Whiskey helps move kitchen.

And now the frisky cut worm and the pesky leaf-roller get in their fine work, and the tomato grower gets on his knees, uses bad language and picks them off.

Tropical Sun, Lotus Cove Column, November 11, 1891
— Frisky cut worms.

The total eclipse of the moon arrived and departed on time Sunday evening; as Tommy Listy would say, "Moon sick too much."

Tropical Sun, Lotus Cove Column, November 11, 1891
—Seminole sick moon.

The Christmas picnic of the Hy-Lo-Zi-natives was a success in every sense of the word. The weather, location, arrangements and eatables were all first-class. The table on the brow of the beach bluff, under the shade of the giant sea-grapes commanded a view of old ocean, as well as the lake. Thirty-five noses were counted, each o'ertopping a more or less ornamental and useful mouth. It was not 90 in the shade, only 35, just cool and comfortable. There were no over-dressed ladies and the dude was not in it. The gents, if they chose, let the sea-grape limbs wear their coats and when a surfeit threatened they could jump down the bluff a couple of times and then come back and eat some more chicken pie and roast venison, tender as a 50c. shirt and juicy as a lover's first kiss (I can't help being poetical, it is heredity. My father often wood the mewses, and took the boot-jack to knock tarnal cats off the roof. The divine affright-us is neither contagious, nor infectious but epidemic, in the spring when the be silly floats on the zephyrs, and attacks weak minds. I am taking a tonic now myself.) We had no feast of reason, for Lyman was just out of reason and our souls did not flow perceptibly, but the root beer and the wit did—freely. Benson furnished the beer. We were all as merry as a married belle and we unanimously voted each other effusive thanks and congrats.

RUTHVEN.

Tropical Sun, December 31, 1891
—Christmas picnic.

We Lotus Covers were startled out of our usual beatific serenity by the arrival of Mr. V. P. Keller, the engineer in charge of the surveying party in the employ of the Disston Drainage Company, and three of his crew. They are fresh from the wilds of the Everglades and Lake Okeechobee and have the honor of being the first white men to reach Lake Worth by those over-land and water roots. To be sure it took six weeks hard work to make the trip from lake to lake, but the Almighty Dollar will make a man travel a worse route than that. Mr. Keller and party will, after taking the levels between Lake Worth and Lake Osborne, proceed to the old haul over in the "Rosie B." and ascertain the fall between the marsh and Lake Worth, and then return to Kissimmee and report. A full report of the incidents of his trip would no doubt make interesting reading.

The levels so far as ascertained have proved satisfactory.

Tropical Sun, September 2, 1891
—Surveying begins for drainage canals.

Mr. James E. Ingraham and party arrived at Lantana on Wednesday, after a long and tedious trip from Biscayne Bay. They left Guava Key, in the Everglades, under the guidance of old Indian Charlie—the white man's friend, and came through the inside route, by canoe to the Orange Grove Station, Capt. S. N. Andrews, where they were met by Lew Bradley and George Lyman. They left on the following day, by wagon and mule power for Palm Beach—taking in the fresh water lakes en route. If Mr. Flagler had used a search-light of a million candle power—he could not have found a more able or affable gentleman to represent his business interests in Florida.

Tropical Sun, November 24, 1892—Indian guide.

The gale was a little too stiff for the little mail steamer Hypo, and she laid at her moorings through it all, and was hard aground one day.

Tropical Sun, October 4, 1894—Mail steamboat.

The market-gardeners in this vicinity are beginning operations in earnest. The area of operations will be increased ten-fold and the value of our thousands of acres of muck land will be proven beyond doubt. Our increased facilities for transportation will be an incalculable boon to our truckers, and they are not slow in taking due advantage of it. Five acres is enough; that will keep three men on the jump during the season of picking and packing.

Tropical Sun, October 4, 1894—Crop boom.

It was the first call for incorporation of the Town of West Palm Beach.

It was small, then. On Jan. 1, 1894, reports the Gazette, only one house stood in West Palm Beach, the home of Capt. O. S. Potter, from whom the town site was bought. The Town of Palm Beach was prospering, and on the west side of the lake lived "the servants and household employes, together with railroad workers" employed by Henry Flagler and the Palm Beachers.

The incorporation petition was signed by Harry Stites, president of the Village Improvement Association; Joseph Elliott, chairman, H. J. Burkhardt, J. K. Marvin, C. O. Blythe, Eli Sims and A. L. Knowlton. The first reporter to record the town's happenings was C. M. Gardner, publisher of the Gazette.

The Gazette, 1894, as quoted in the *Palm Beach Post*, October 9, 1949—Harry Stites.

189

HYPOLUXO HAPPENINGS.

Uncle Fred Meyers, on the Island, has began shipping tomatoes.

Capt. W. H. Moore will soon be sending tomatoes to the Northern markets.

We are glad to hear that Mrs. W. H. Moore is out again after several days illness.

Mr. A W. Garnett still continues to ship tomatoes and cabbages from Trenton Farm.

Tropical Sun, February 3, 1898—Tomatoes, tomatoes.

Fishing was never better in Lake Os borne as W. P. Carroll and Mr. Thomas was over to the Lake Thursday and caught 150 pounds in a few hours. mostly black bass.

Tropical Sun, March 3, 1898
—Bass fishing on Lake Osborne.

STRUCK BY AUTO; INJURIES FATAL

Mrs. Fannie James Badly Mangled In Auto Accident At Lake Worth.

Was Pioneer Settler In This County And Owned Most of Site of Lake Worth At One Time.

Mrs. Fannie James, widow of the late Samuel James, died at the Emergency hospital in this city about 8 o'clock Saturday night as the result of injuries received when she was struck by an automobile about 12:30 o'clock Saturday afternoon.

Mrs. James was hurried to this city in an automobile driven by J. M. Bedell, of Lake Worth, and taken to the Emergency hospital where every effort was made to save her but it was found her body was so badly mangled there were no hopes for recovery. She died at 8:00 o'clock Saturday night.

The automobile which struck Mrs. James was driven by W. L. Flowers, of Lake Worth, who had as his passenger, D. B. Diellaway, of Miami. They were on their way to Miami on a business trip and were leaving the southern limits of the city when the accident occurred.

According to the statement made by Mr. Flowers to the coroner's jury this morning he was driving his automobile in a southern direction about 12:30 o'clock Saturday afternoon. He said that D. B. Diellaway, of Miami, was riding with him at the time. He was driving slowly and after passing the city limits had increased the speed of the automobile he was driving.

He said that after passing the city limits he noticed a wagon standing on the west side of the road and a buggy standing directly opposite on the east side of the road. Mrs. James, he said, was standing at the side of the wagon talking with A. B. Decker, an employe of the Dade Lumber Company.

Although there was plenty of room to pass between the wagon and the buggy on the sides of the road, Mr. Flowers told the jury he slowed his automobile down to about 12 to 15 miles an hour. He said he blew the horn and saw Mrs. James look back in his direction, and was sure she saw his automobile approaching.

When he attempted to pass between the wagon and the buggy Mr. Flowers told the jury the woman suddenly turned and darted in front of his automobile and was struck before he could stop or divert the course of the automobile. After the automobile struck the woman he said he turned the automobile in the direction of the side of the road and ran off into the sand.

A. B. Decker, the employe of the Dade Lumber Company, who was the driver of the wagon standing on the west side of the road at the time Mr. Flowers approached in his automobile, and who was talking with Mrs. James at the time the accident occurred, corborated the statement made by Mr. Flowers in every particular. Mr. Diellaway, the passenger in the car with Mr. Flowers, also told the same story as related by Mr. Flowers.

Mrs. James and her husband were pioneer settlers on the east coast of Florida. They at one time owned the greater portion of the land upon which is now located the city of Lake Worth. Mr. and Mrs. James came to this section from the Indian river region, about 25 years ago. They took a homestead on the present site of Lake Worth and were instrumental in building up this section of the county. Mrs. James was well beloved by all who knew her and enjoyed a wide acquaintanceship among the residents of the county.

The funeral services will be held at 9:15 o'clock tomorrow morning from the chapel of the Ferguson Undertaking Company on Clematis avenue. The body will then be taken to Lake Worth, where short services will be held at 10 o'clock. The burial will be in the family burial ground at Lake Worth.

The Daily Tropical Sun, March 8, 1915
—Details on Fannie James's auto accident.

191

THE LAKE WORTH HERALD

Aged Mrs. James Killed By an Auto

Mrs. Fannie James, pioneer of the Lake Worth district, and once owner of all the land now embraced within the town limits, was struck and killed by an automobile, on Saturday.

The driver of the auto was W. Flower, of Miami, who was placed under arrest, but later released on his recognizance, as it was shown he was not to blame in the matter.

Mrs. James had been talking with friends standing by the side of the county road, and walked in front of the Flower auto. Mr. Flower, who was running at a speed of less than 10 miles an hour, did all in his power to stop the machine, but without avail, and the woman was crushed under the front wheels.

As soon as she was taken from under the vehicle she was carred to the hospital, where everything within the power of the surgeons was done. Her advanced age was against her, however, and a few hours after being injured she expired.

Mrs. James, who was 73 years of age, had relatives in the North. They were notified at once of the accident. The body will be interred by the side of Mr. James, in the James homestead grounds, in the southern end of the city, and later removed to the cemetery.

Lake Worth Herald, March 11, 1915.

MRS. FANNY JAMES' WILL A MYSTERY

Contents of Lock Box In the Pioneer Bank Is Also Puzzling.

Deceased Woman Left Instructions With Bank Officials Before Her Death Regarding Disposition Of Contents of Safety Box.

What was in the lock-box used by the late Mrs. Fanny James, who was killed more than a week ago, when struck by an automobile near her home at Lake Worth, is somewhat of a mystery to everyone with the exception of Barney Maxfield, cashier of the Pioneer Bank and the two men who opened the box in his presence.

There has been much speculation as to whether Mrs. James left a will and as to the amount of the fortune which she left. The disposition of her estate is also looked forward to with great interest by the citizens of the county. It is reported that the deceased woman was the owner of a large amount of valuable property at the time of her death.

Those who were acquainted with her say that she was never known to divulge her intentions as to what the provisions of her will would be and it is generally believed that she wrote the will herself.

Shortly before her death, Mrs. James left instructions with Barney Maxfield that in the event of her death the lock-box which she used in the Pioneer Bank was to be opened by Mr. Maxfield in the presence of two men, whose names Mr. Maxfield refused to divulge. One of the men arrived in the city several days ago but the bank officials refused to open the box until the arrival of the other man.

Both of the men called at the bank yesterday and the box was opened. "What was in the box," was asked Mr. Maxfield, to which he replied that he could not give out this information as it was strictly a private affair. He was then asked if a will had been found in the box by the men, but he also refused to answer this question.

After securing the contents from the box the two men left for the James residence at Lake Worth.

The *Daily Tropical Sun*, March 20, 1915—Discovery of Fannie's will.

Appendix B: History of Postal Offices on the Mail Boat Route

The U.S. Post Office Department published a daily bulletin to inform its employees of changes to the mail delivery system. It reports on openings and closings of post offices, route changes, and delivery scheduling changes. These bulletins provide raw data on the development of the postal system in the Lake Worth area.

DAILY BULLETIN

OF

ORDERS AFFECTING THE POSTAL SERVICE.

VOL. X. POST OFFICE DEPARTMENT, WASHINGTON, D. C., SATURDAY, SEPTEMBER 14, 1889. NO. 2907

The Postal Bulletin.

ISSUED FROM THE OFFICE OF
GEN'L SUP'T RAILWAY MAIL SERVICE
J. LOWRIE BELL, GEN'L SUP'T.

WASHINGTON, D. C., SEPT. 14, 1889.

NOTE.—This number of the Bulletin consists of two sheets, Nos. 2907 and 2907a.

POST OFFICES ESTABLISHED

ARKANSAS.

Allegan, Pope Co., special from Gum Log, Route 29174, 3½ ms. S. E. [23 aug 89

DAKOTA.

Kaspar, Sully Co., special from Norfolk, Route 35223 Re-established. [3 aug 89

FLORIDA.

Jewell, Dade Co., Route 16235, Figulus 4 ms. N., Hypoluxo, 3¼ ms. S. [22 aug 89

Sanibel, Lee Co., special for Punta Rassa, Route 16093, 2½ N. E. [31 july 89

IDAHO.

Center, Boise Co., special from Van Wyck, Route 42213. [23 july 89

ILLINOIS.

Alworth, Winnebago Co., Route 23105, Winnebago, 1½ ms. N., Elida, 3½ ms. S. [26 aug 89

IOWA.

Kirkwood, Appanoose Co., Route 27017, Centerville, 5½ ms. W., Udell, 5½ ms. N. E. Re-established. [22 aug 89

LOUISIANA.

Quarantine, Plaquemines Co., Route 30069, Jump, 7 ms. N., Port Eads, 15 ms. S. [26 aug 89

MICHIGAN.

Stinson, Mecosta Co., special from Big Rapids, Route 24018, 7 ms. ——. [22 aug 89

WASHINGTON TERRITORY.

Daisy, Stevens Co., Route 43172, Harvey 7 ms. N., Hunters, 22 ms. S. [6 aug 89

POST OFFICE NAME AND SITE CHANGED.

ARKANSAS.

Eller, Baxter Co., to Lone Rock, 1 m. E. on Routes 29214 and 29565. [23 aug 89

CONNECTICUT.

Zoar Bridge, New Haven Co., to Stevenson, ¼ m. S. E., on Route 5133, in Fairfield County. [4 sept 89

POST OFFICE SITE CHANGED.

KANSAS.

Leland, Graham Co., 1 m. N., on Route 33250. [12 sept 89

MISSOURI.

Useful, Osage Co., 1 m. N., on Routes 28470 and 28471 [13 sept 89

Weaubleau, Hickory Co., ¼ m. E., on Routes 28147 and 28148. [13 sept 89

TENNESSEE.

Henry's Cross Roads, Sevier Co., ¾ m. W., on Routes 19199 and 19736. [13 sept 89

VIRGINIA.

Rose Mills, Amherst Co., ½ m. W. into Nelson County, on Route 11509. [12 sept 89

POST OFFICES DISCONTINUED.

The following to take effect September 20, 1889:

CALIFORNIA.

Hites Cove, Mariposa Co., Routes 46313 and 46314. Mail to Darrah. [11 sept 89

COLORADO.

Routt, Routt Co., Route 38108. Mail to Lay. [11 sept 89

SPECIAL SERVICE CHANGES.

MISSOURI.

Linden, Clay Co. Authorize supply of Linden from Kansas City, Jackson Co., Mo., instead of from Barey. [13 sept 89

SPECIAL SERVICE DISCONTINUED.

ALABAMA.

Arbacoochee, Cleburne Co., from Oswalt. From September 15, 1889, on Route 17258. [13 sept 89

WEST VIRGINIA.

Shannon, Ohio Co., from West Liberty. From September 30, 1889, on Route 12234. [13 sept 89

STAR SERVICE ESTABLISHED.

ALABAMA.

Route 17652. Argus to Saville, 6 ms. and back six times a week, by a schedule of departures and arrivals not exceeding 2 hours running time each way. From October 1, 1889, to June 30, 1890. [13 sept 89

Route 17653. Patsburgh to Live Oak, 3 ms. and back, three times a week, by a schedule of departures and arrivals not exceeding 1 hour running time each way. From October 1, 1889 to June 30, 1890. [13 sept 89

Route 17654. Julian to Rutledge, 4 miles and back, six times a week, by a schedule of not exceeding 1½ hours running time each way. From October 1, 1889, to June 30, 1890. [13 sept 89.

FLORIDA.

Route 16285. Punta Gordo to Myers, 22 ms. and back, three times a week, by a schedule of not exceeding 7 hours running time each way. From October 1, 1889, to June 30, 1890. [13 sept 89

INDIANA.

Route 22607. Fruits to Waynetown, 4 ms. and back, twice a week. From October 1, 1889, to June 30, 1890, by a schedule not exceeding 1 hour running time each way. [13 sept 89

OHIO.

Route 21949. Stockport, by Todd's, to Chester Hill, 8½ ms. and back, six times a week. From October 1, 1889, to June 30, 1890, by a schedule not exceeding 2¼ hours running time each way. [13 sept 89

Route 21950. Malta to Pennsville, 6½ ms. and back, six times a week. From October 1, 1889, to June 30, 1890, by a schedule not exceeding 2 hours running time each way. [13 sept 89

STAR SERVICE CHANGES.

NORTH CAROLINA.

Route 13215. Moretz Mills, N. C., to Trade, Tenn. Modify order of August 21, 1889, (BULLETIN 2887) so [as to state increase in distance as .48 m. [13 sept 89

VIRGINIA.

Route 11588. Rustburgh to Mount Zion. From October 1, 1889, extend route to embrace and end at Twedy's, increasing distance 2¾ ms. [13 sept 89

Route 11606. Lexington to Collierstown. From September 13, 1889, supply Collierstown as its new site without change in distance. [13 sept 89

Route 11609. Collierstown to Alphin. From September 13, 1889, supply Collierstown at its new site without change in distance. [13 sept 89

RAILROAD SERVICE ESTABLISHED

COLORADO.

Route 38041. Lake Junction (n. o.), Colo., via Allen, to Lake City, Colo. Denver & Rio Grande R. R., 36.18 ms. and back, six round trips per week, or as much oftener as trains may run. From October 10, 1889. [13 sept 89

ILLINOIS.

Route 23106. Sparta to Coultersville. Centralia & Chester R. R., 8.29 ms. and back, six times a week, or as much oftener as trains may run. From October 1, 1889. [13 sept 89

MICHIGAN.

Route 24085. Buchanan to Berrien Springs. Saint Joseph Valley Rwy., 11.88 ms. and back, six times a week, or as much oftener as trains may run. From October 1, 1889. [13 sept 89

MISSOURI.

Route 28070. Tower Grove Station (n. o.) to Oak Hill Junction (n. o.), Mo. Saint Louis, Oak Hill & Carondelet Rwy. 7.09 ms. and back, six times a week, or as much oftener as trains may run. From October 1, 1889. [13 sept 89

RAILROAD SERVICE CHANGES.

CALIFORNIA.

Route 46025. San Anselmo (n. o.) to San Quentin. North Pacific Coast R. R., 6 ms. From October 1, 1889, extend service from San Anselmo (n. o.) to San Francisco, Cal., increasing distance 16 ms., making lap service over Route 46016. [13 sept 89

INDIANA.

Route 22023. Oakland City to Mount Vernon. Louisville, Evansville & Saint Louis Rwy., 88.63 ms. From July 1, 1889, pay the Louisville, Evansville & Saint Louis Consolidated R. R. Co. for service on this route instead of the Louisville, Evansville & Saint Louis Rwy Co., evidence of change of title having been submitted. [13 sept 89

Route 22032. Evansville to Jasper. Louisville, Evansville & Saint Louis Rwy., 54.38 ms. From April 1, 1889, pay the Louisville, Evansville & Saint Louis Consolidated R. R. Co. for service on this route, instead of the Louisville, Evansville & Saint Louis Rwy. Co., evidence of change of title having been submitted. [13 sept 89

Route 22031. Rockport to Rockport Junction (n. o.) Louisville, Evansville & Saint Louis Rwy., 16.35 ms. From April 1, 1889, pay the Louisville, Evansville & Saint Louis Consolidated R. R. Co. for service on this route, instead of the Louisville, Evansville & Saint Louis Rwy. Co., evidence of change of title having been submitted. [13 sept 89

Route 22048. Louisville to Oakland City. Louisville, Evansville & Saint Louis Rwy., 99.26 ms. From April 1, 1889, pay the Louisville, Evansville & Saint Louis Consolidated R. R. Co. for service on this route, instead of the Louisville, Evansville & Saint Louis Rwy. Co., evidence of change of title having been submitted. [13 sept 89

Route 22052. Kercheval to Cannelton. Louisville, Evansville & Saint Louis Rwy., 22.50 ms. From April 1, 1889, pay the Louisville, Evansville & Saint Louis Consolidated R. R. Co for service on this route, instead of the Louisville, Evansville & Saint Louis Rwy. Co., evidence of change of title having been submitted. [13 sept 89

MICHIGAN.

Route 24037. Kalamazoo to Hastings. Kalamazoo & Hastings Construction Co. (Limited), operating the Chicago, Kalamazoo & Saginaw Rwy., 31.08 ms. From October 16, 1889, extend service from Hastings by Coates Grove and Woodland to Arvid (n. o.), Mich., increasing distance 13.67 ms. [13 sept 89

VIRGINIA.

Route 11002. Washington to Lynchburgh. Richmond & Danville R. R., 174.04 ms. Amend the order of July 6, 1889, (BULLETIN 2848) so as to extend service to begin at Washington, D. C., from July 1, 1889, instead of July 10, 1889. [13 sept 89

RAILROAD SERVICE DISCONTINUED.

CONNECTICUT.

Route 5024. Bethel to Hawleyville, Housatonic R. R., 6.07 ms. From September 30, 1889. [13 sept 89

R. P. O. CAR SERVICE CHANGES.

INDIANA.

Route 22010. Cincinnati to East Saint Louis, Ohio & Mississippi Rwy., 338.14 ms. From July 1, 1889, and August 5, 1889, add to pay for railway post office cars for 338.14 ms. for the two daily lines of 60 feet railway post office cars between Cincinnati, Ohio, and East Saint Louis, Ill., superseding one line of 50 feet railway post office cars and one line of 45 feet railway post office cars, being in accordance with the order of March 18, 1889, (BULLETIN 2756.) [13 sept 89

OHIO.

Route 21028. Cincinnati to Parkersburgh. Cincinnati, Washington & Baltimore R. R., 195.30 ms. From July 1, 1889, and August 5, 1889, add to pay for railway post office cars for 195.30 ms. for the two daily lines of 60 feet railway post office cars between Cincinnati, Ohio, and Parkersburgh, W. Va., superseding the two daily lines of 50 feet railway post office cars, being in accordance with the order of March 18, 1889, (BULLETIN 2756.) [13 sept 89

R. P. O. CAR SERVICE CHANGES.

VIRGINIA.

Route 11002. Washington to Lynchburgh. Richmond & Danville R. R., 174.04 ms. From July 1, 1889, establish railway post office service between Washington, D. C., and Alexandria, Va., as follows: One line of 60 feet, one of 50 feet and one line of 40 feet railway post office cars. Transferred from Route 11018. [13 sept 89

WEST VIRGINIA.

Route 12002. Grafton to Parkersburgh. Baltimore & Ohio R. R., 103.80 ms. From July 1 1889, and August 5, 1889, add to pay for railway post office cars for 103.80 ms. for the two daily lines of 60 feet railway post office cars between Grafton and Parkersburgh, W. Va., superseding the two daily lines of 50 feet railway post office cars, being in accordance with the order of March 18, 1889, (BULLETIN 2756.) [13 sept 89

R. P. O. CAR SERVICE DISCONTINUED.

VIRGINIA.

Route 11018. Washington to Alexandria. Alexandria & Washington R. R., 7.22 ms. From June 30, 1889, discontinue one line of 60 feet, one line of 50 feet and one line of 40 feet railway post office cars on this route, the same having been established on Route 11002. [13 sept 89

MAIL MESSENGER SERVICE ESTABLISHED

ILLINOIS.

Route 87077. Chicago, Cook Co., from Cottage Grove Station to Hyde Park, 1,150 feet. North Division Station to Lake View Station, 190 rods. Northwest Station to Humboldt Park, 2¼ ms., often as required. Mails to be carried in regulation wagons, such as are used on Route 23200. From September 23, 1889. [13 sept 89

MAIL MESSENGER SERVICE DISCONTINUED.

ILLINOIS.

Route 87052. Chicago, Cook Co., from Lake View Station to Chicago, Milwaukee & Saint Paul Rwy. From June 30, 1889. [13 sept 98

POSTMASTERS COMMISSIONED

Commissioned September 12, 1889

FOURTH CLASS OFFICE.

Joseph Hopper	Hopper, Ark
Peter Cloos	Ironton, Ark
David Goss	Buffalo Gap, Dak
Andrew A. Fvipaa	Elliott, Dak
Chas. B. Scoll	Chattahoochee, Fla
Wm. S. Broderick	De Leon Springs, Fla
Chas. R. Whitehurst	Dargo, Fla
John Evans	Narcoossee, Fla
Wm. Sniffin	Bowyer, Ill
Wm. H. Piper	Egan City, Ill
Calvin B. Crawford	Nachusa, Ill
Chas. R. Barnett	Smithshire, Ill
Wm. H. Sturgis	Bonny Eagle, Me
Wm. H. Everett	Kenduskeag, Me
John D. Rowland	Arvon, Mich
Wm. H. Chase	Bethel, Mich
Louis H. Tovatt	Sterling, Mich
John P. Tillotson	Summit City, Mich
Wm. B. Sanford	Baker, Miss
George Boswell	Ingomar, Miss
Lucius Higgins	Rancher, Mont
Franklin Patterson	Turkey, N J
Frank E. Vosburgh	Alabama, N Y
Francis M. Acker	Lakeville, N Y
Irvin E. Brigden	Mesopotamia, Ohio
Rensaler Bagley	Rockwood, Ohio
David R. Hooker	Gibson Wells, Tenn

Post Office Name Changed.

John A. Cockrum, Lone Rock, late Eller, Ark

Samuel Stephens, Stevenson, Fairfield Co., late Zoar Bridge, New Haven Co., Conn

New Offices

Wm. L. D. Ewing, Allegan, Pope Co., Ark

Gustina R. Spencer, Kaspar, Sully Co., Dak

Fannie A. James, Jewell, Dade Co., Fla

Laetitia A. Nutt, Sanibel, Lee Co., Fla

Chesney Keeney, Center, Boise Co., Idaho

John C. Van Derhoof, Allworth, Winnebago Co., Ill

John Powell, Kirkwood, Appanoose Co., Iowa

Harry Hayward, Quarantine, Plaquemines Co., La

Herbert S. Tenny, Stinson, Mecosta Co., Mich

Samuel L. Magee, Daisy, Stevens Co., Wash

Note in the left-hand column, Jewell, Dade Co. listed under New Post Offices Established.
In the lower right corner, Fannie A. James appears under New Offices.

CHRONOLOGICAL HISTORY OF POST OFFICES ON THE LAKE

TUSTENEGEE PO

Briefly established by James B. Brown, February to October 1877. Reestablished by Albert Geer from November 1877 until March 1879. Located in what is now the center of Palm Beach.

LAKE WORTH PO

Often considered the area's first permanent post office, established May 21, 1880, at the north end of Palm Beach in the home of Valorus Spencer. Initial population served: 26. Closed March 1901 and mail handling transferred to the Mangonia Post Office. A sign on the shore path at the halfway point between Royal Poinciana Way and the Palm Beach Inlet marks the post office's original location.

FIGULUS PO

Established January 7, 1886. Located on Palm Beach Island south of the Southern Boulevard Bridge. Initial population 60 (double counting with Hypoluxo Post Office and including summer tourists). Dr. Richard B. Potter was the first postmaster. His brother George Potter was county surveyor and a prolific artist. The name is a play on words as "Figulus" is the Latin word for "potter."

The Figulus Post Office was closed on February 25, 1891. Mail at first was transferred to Jewell and later to Palm Beach.

HYPOLUXO PO

Established May 18, 1886, on the southwest shore of the lake by postmaster Andrew Garnett. Population 60 (double counting with Figulus Post Office). Garnett served for a short time, complaining that the job paid too little and interrupted his work on his farm. Charles Pierce became his assistant and moved the post office across the lake to his home on Hypoluxo Island. Garnett officially resigned in September 1887 and Charles' father, Hannibal Pierce, was appointed in his place and served for 11 years until his death in August of 1898.

The Hypoluxo Post Office was the terminus of the mail boat route on the lake and the head of the Barefoot Mailman Route to Miami.

PALM BEACH PO

The Brelsford Brothers, Edmund and John, established Palm City Post Office January 15, 1887. Located at Brelsford's lakefront store near the present site of the Flagler Museum. Name changed to Palm Beach in October.

OAK LAWN PO

Founded on January 12, 1889. Located on the west shore at the northern end of the lake. Mattie Spencer Heyser, the first postmistress, was the wife of Judge Allen Heyser. The couple ran the post office from their Oak Lawn Hotel. The name of both the hotel and post office were changed to Riviera in 1893 and Riviera Beach in 1942. The post office was closed and mail handled by Mangonia Post Office between 1902 and 1915.

JUNO PO

Established July 16, 1889. Located at the far north end of the lake. Leahretta C. "Lettie" Field was the first postmistress. Juno served as the link between the new Celestial Railroad and the mail boats that delivered the mail to the post offices farther south.

Juno was briefly the Dade County seat between 1889 and 1899, before Miami reclaimed the title. The name of the post office was changed to Munyon Island in July 1903 and then permanently closed in April 1905. The town of Juno suffered a major fire in 1907 and never recovered.

JEWELL PO

Established August 22, 1889, by Fannie A. James. Located on the west shore of the lake. Population: 13. Mail initially delivered by boat. The post office moved closer to the FEC tracks when delivery by train began in May 1896. Closed April 4, 1903. Mail subsequently handled at Lantana. Reestablished as Lake Worth Post Office on July 22, 1912.

LANTANA PO

Established August 1, 1892, with Morris B. Lyman as first postmaster. Located near the present Old Key Lime House restaurant. Population: "20 in summer, more in winter." Delivery by train began at the same date as at Jewell in May 1896.

MANGONIA PO

Opened March 14, 1894, on west side of the lake, south of Riviera. Closed July 1906.

WEST PALM BEACH PO

Established April 17, 1894, on the west side of the lake across from Palm Beach at the time of the founding of the City of West Palm Beach.

Appendix C: Timeline of the James/Fulton Land Dispute

February 1885. Samuel James settles on Lots 1–4, Section 27, Township 44S, Range 43E. Began improvements on land. (James HA1 39, 65–66.)

March 1885. James builds a "shanty which was burnt down" and then lived in a tent while working on his frame house. (James HA1, 72)

"Early or middle March" 1885. Samuel James files his first claim application with the Gainesville Land Office. (James HA1, 14)

April 23, 1885. James leaves Lake Worth to be with his sick wife in Cocoa, Florida. (James HA1, 65) He entrusts Harry Griswold with the care of his claim. While in Cocoa, he built "a church for the colored people at Cocoa and thus raise money to go on." (James HA1, 70–74)

September 5, 1885. Land Office writes letter to Samuel James denying his application. The letter explains that Lots 1 and 2 had been under the homestead claim of James Murrin, but that the claim "has recently been cancelled due to expiration of 7 years and failure to make final proof."

There is also a problem with James's claim on Lots 3 and 4. At the time his application was filed, they were not subject to homesteading due to being "swamp and overflowed land." But now, as of August 22, swampland designation has been removed. Therefore Lots 1–4 are now officially designated as vacant and open for settlement. James is encouraged to reapply. (James HA1, 20)

September 14, 1885. James reapplies but submits an erroneous land description, i.e., Range 45E instead of Range 43E. (James HA1, 14) Land office rejects the application as land lies "under the waters of the Atlantic Ocean." (James HA1, 14)

September 18, 1885. James returns to Lake Worth from Cocoa on Captain Canova's boat. (James HA1, 65) James apparently meets the four Pennsylvania friends (Harry Stites, William Hartzell, Benjamin Himes, and Orville H. Fulton) aboard ship as they all arrive in Lake Worth on this same date.

September 18–22, 1885. Stites, Himes, and Hartzell stake out claims to the north of James. (James HA1, 85)

September 23, 1885. Stites, Himes, and Fulton visit Samuel James to inquire about vacant land for Fulton. James refers them to Bradley. Fulton "settles" on Lots 3 & 4 of Section 27. "With my ax and blankets and slept on the land that night. Then the next morning I started for Gainesville." This is the southern half of James's claim. The land dispute starts. (James HA1, 79–83).

September 28, 1885. Fulton files claim in Gainesville, ignoring James's earlier filing. (James HA1, 8, 14, 15) He states that when he filed his claim at Gainesville, Mr. James's petition was already there but that the people at the Land Office "did not understand it." (James HA1, 82) Then Fulton "went North… as I could not stand the heat and the mosquitos." (James HA1, 79–83)

December 25, 1885. James hires Thomas Jones as a farmhand. The two plan to "raise vegetables" and Jones was to receive a portion of the profits. (James HA1, 75)

February 4, 1886. With the confusion over the legal land description still pending, James refilled his declaratory statement for Lots 1–4 of Section 27, Township 44S, Range 43E, correcting previous errors and paying $2 in fees. (James HA1, 23)

March 2, 1886. James leaves Thomas Jones in charge of "house, clothing, furniture, provisions" and travels to Cocoa, Florida, to bring Fannie back to Lake Worth. Finds her sick. Stays in Cocoa 33 days, two weeks longer than planned. (James HA1, 5, 75–78)

March 22 or 23, 1886. Fulton returns to contested land after an absence of almost six months. Begins improvements, builds shanty, plants three citrus trees. (James HA1, 79–83).

April 4, 1886. James returns to his claim with Fannie and discovers that his worker, Thomas Jones, had built a shanty and intended to challenge James's claim under misinformation from Stites that James had abandoned his claim. (James HA1, 76) Stites boasts that he has enough witnesses to take any land he wanted and to swear the Jameses off their claim. (James HA1, 78)

June 10, 1886. Samuel James's preemption statement declared his intention to make final proof of his claim on August 2 at Titusville is filled with the Gainesville Land Office. John C. Hoagland, Antonio J. Canova, Edwin R. Bradley, and Elisha N. Dimick are listed as potential witnesses for James. (James HA1, 42) Apparently, Fannie's nephew, Alonzo T. Anderson, made the voyage to Gainesville with Charles Pierce and other neighbors to deliver Samuel's paperwork.

July 20, 1886. From Pennsylvania, W. E. Hartzell files sworn statement in support of Fulton's claim. Hartzell asserts that he had built a shanty north of James (Lots 3 and 4 of Section 22) but James had kicked him off. Therefore James must be confused about his claim, as he cannot own all the land both to the north and south. Hartzell further asserts that James had made no improvements on Fulton claim (Lots 3 and 4 of Section 27) up until April 1, 1886, while Fulton had improvements, including house and fruit trees valued at $60. (James HA1, 45–49).

July 20, 1886. Harry Stites filed a sworn statement in support of O. H. Fulton's claim, stating that James had told Fulton that Lots 3 & 4 of Section 27 were vacant in his and Benjamin Himes' presence as they all were walking the land one evening between September 10[th]10 and September 20[th]20, 1885. Fulton then got a "blanket and an axe and made settlement at once." (James HA1 50–56).

July 28, 1886. Michael Merkel (James HA1, 7) and William Stephan (James HA1, 9) file statements on James's behalf. Both state they can confirm James's presence on his land, including Lots 3 & 4 of Section 27 in February 1885. Stephan states the he believes that Stites, Fulton, Hartzell, and Himes are "engaged in a conspiracy to defraud Mr. James" with the goal of either getting the land or a monetary settlement. (James HA1, 9)

Dade County }ss. Final Proof of Samuel James
State of Florida } Pre-emption Entry No. 1616

Personally appeared before me
William Stephan of Lake Worth in above
County and State, to me well known, and
who duly sworn deposes and says.
That he is well acquainted with Samuel
James, and knows that he was on the
land now occupied by him, (to wit; lots
No's 1, 2, 3 & 4, of section 27, in Township 44
South, a Range 40 East,) in the latter part
of February 1855, and that to his personal
knowledge said Samuel James has resided
upon and occupied, and has been improving and cultivating the same ever since.
This deponent further says that he believes
that Dr. Harry Stites, Oliver H. Fulton,
William E. Hartzell, and Benjamin Hines
are engaged in a conspiracy to defraud Mr
James out of two lots of the above mentioned
land, to wit lots No. 3, 4. For that he in
conversation with said Dr. Harry Stites, made the
remark that he would be likely to have a fuss
with Mr James, to which Dr. Stites answered,
that "they could beat him either way, either
physically with numbers, or pecuniarily, and
that they stood together as one man,
William Stephan

August 2, 1886. The hearing on contested land claims began in the Circuit Court of Brevard County by A. A. Stewart, county clerk, the judge being absent. (James HA1, 63)

Fulton and Himes testify in Fulton's behalf. Surprisingly, Fulton did not exaggerate his improvements but described them in surprisingly modest terms. His palmetto shanty was a mere 12-by-14, built with three- to four-inch-diameter pine posts and a door on hinges. The house had two tiny rooms, one for sleeping with board floor and cheesecloth siding "to keep mosquitos out and let in light and air." The second room had a dirt floor.

His household furnishings consisted of a bed and a table, both homemade, two blankets, one sheet, and 25 books. Modestly, Fulton claims to have cleared only a quarter of an acre. It is almost comical to read that Fulton planted three citrus trees and a few vegetables. Further, Fulton testified that he did not eat on his property but that "Hartzwell, Himes, and I 'bach' it together as the Hartzwell place" where they gather for meals.

James next gives testimony in defense. His house is a substantial wood frame structure, 15 x 26 feet, rather than a quickly built palmetto shanty. His improvements are also more substantial than Fulton's, having "cleared four acres of land, dug a well, planted out orange trees, pine apples, and vegetables with cocoanuts." (James HA1, 24–27, 39, 70–73).

John C. Hoagland and Edwin R. Bradley testify in support of James. Hoagland confirms that James has been on his land since January or February 1885. Further, that James had cleared land on both the extreme north end and south end of his property, contradicting Fulton's testimony to the contrary. (James HA1, 28–31, 38, 64–69)

During his testimony, Hoagland produced a hand-drawn map showing the locations of the disputants' houses. According to the sketch, the two residences were incredibly close to each other, perhaps a few hundred yards apart.

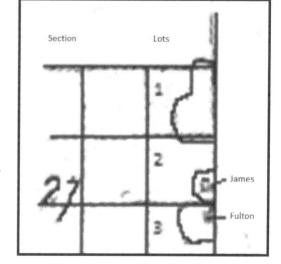

John C. Hoagland sketch (retouched) of disputed property showing the locations of Jameses' and Fulton's houses. Cleared areas outlined. Orienting this sketch map in terms of modern Lake Worth streets, the line between the James and Fulton places would be 6th Avenue South. The line on the right corresponds to the waterfront.

August 3, 1886. Fannie testifies in Samuel's behalf regarding times of Samuel's being with her in Cocoa from April to September of 1885 and 33 days in March—April of 1886. She explains that her illness was the cause for delay in Samuel's return to Lake Worth and describes an incident where Stites misinformed their hired man, Thomas Jones, and induced him to claim James's land for himself.

The record includes a word-for-word transcript of Fannie's testimony, preserving a token of her personality and sensitivities. She explains that she found the dispute with her neighbors upsetting. It had "wounded her feelings" and caused "heartache." (James HA1, 74–78) As this is the only existing record of Fannie expressing herself in her own words, a full transcript follows.

Fulton gives testimony in defense of his counterclaim, supported by Benjamin Himes suggesting that James claim was for Lots 3 & 4 of Section 22, not Section 27. (James HA1, 79–86)

August 11, 1886. Case decided in James's favor and he is granted title to claimed waterfront lots. He pays preemption fee of $232.21 for 186.57 acres at $1.25 per acre. (James HA1, 3–4)

Subsequently, Fulton had to vacate his claim. Himes and Hartzell also left the area. None of them is heard from again. Stites remained on his claim at the north end of Section 22 and eventually gets his patent. A year later, John C. Hoagland settles on the property that Hartzell had abandoned at the south end of Section 22, between Stites and James.

FANNIE'S TESTIMONY IN HER OWN WORDS

Question: State how one Thomas Jones came to be on the place, and how he came to set up a claim.

Answer: Christmas 1885, 25 December 1885, he went to work with my husband on the place to raise vegetables. He was to receive one third of what they made. He remained there with my husband until March 2, 1886, as my husband thought in good faith so did I, and said he would stay this year and make a crop.

My husband left the house, clothing, furniture, provisions and everything in the care of Thomas Jones and went up to Cocoa, and told him he would return in two weeks. He came up to get me to go to Lake Worth and to get some money that was due him to pay off some debts. He found me sick and wrote to Thomas Jones and told him he could not return at the time he had appointed, but perhaps he would be there as soon as the letter he wrote to Mr. Jones would.

He remained away from the lake 33 days, I being unable to travel as shown by the Doctor's Certificate filed herein as evidence.

When Mr. James got back he found a palmetto shanty partly built on his preemption by Thomas Jones.

We asked Mr. Jones why he did so. He stated that Mr. James had forfeited his claim by staying away over 30 days and he, Mr. James, could not get it. Jones… says that Dr. Stites told him that he could go on the land (that is Jones could claim the land since James had forfeited it.)

Jones told Mr. James and myself directly… Dr. Stites told him that if we wanted to take the land that we had better keep on the good side of them, meaning Dr. Stites, Wm. Hartzwell, Benj. Himes. And Jones said that Stites said that he, Jones, should keep on the good side of them, because he, Stites, brought men enough along to swear each other on the land. Mr. Fulton is one of Dr. Stites' party.

I know that Dr. Stites, Wm. Hartzwell, Benj. Himes have insulted us, wounded our feelings in contending for the lots that Mr. Fulton claims. They have told Mr. Jameses and myself a good many times that Mr. Fulton was their friend and if we could not be friendly to Mr. Fulton, we need not be to them.

Mrs. James cross examined by Mr. Orville Fulton, acting as his own attorney.

Question: Has Mr. James any improvements on Lots 3 & 4?

Answer: We have not had the land surveyed. Mr. Bradley showed us the north and south line. Mr. James has improvements north and south of the house, which is near the middle. And he also has land cleared on the extreme south line.

Question: About what would you suppose the improvements are worth on the extreme south end?

Answer: At the lowest calculation, $75.

Question: About how much land has he cleared and grubbed at the extreme south?

Answer: Fully an acre.

Question: Was it timber land?

Answer: It was scrub land.

Question: Did he cut down any timber or merely grub it?

Answer: He cut down small scrub bushes.

Question: Can Mr. James write a letter?

Answer: No.

Question: How do you know the Dr. Stites is assisting me?

Answer: I know it by the heartaches he has given me by his talk.

Question: Did Thomas Jones tell you that Dr. Stites told him (Jones) that he had witnesses enough and men enough along with him to swear me this land?

Answer: Yes, he told me that and another land his party could take.

Question: Did you not keep house, you and Mr. James at Cocoa between April 1885 and September 1885?

Answer: No, we were there but did not keep house.

Appendix D: James-to-Moore Land Sales Contract

From Dade County Deed Book "F," page 128, this is a typical example of contracts on file at the Palm Beach County Clerk's Office. Note the legal description of the sold property contains two parcels, ten acres of which now correspond to a strip along Lake Avenue between F Street and Federal Highway and the "Birthday Cake Castle" lot. The closing apparently took place at either the James or Hoagland home in Jewell.

APPENDIX

175

(7-178)

IN WITNESS WHEREOF, The said party of the first part have hereunto set their hand S and seal S, the day and year first above written.

Signed, Sealed and Delivered in Presence of

1. J C Hoagland
2. G M Bradley

Witnesses as to Signature of

Samuel his X mark James (SEAL.)

Fannie A. James (SEAL.)

1. _____
2. _____

Witnesses as to Signature of

(SEAL.)

(SEAL.)

STATE OF FLORIDA,
COUNTY OF Dade.

I HEREBY CERTIFY That on this Twenty fifth day of October 1894, before me a Notary Public in and for the State of Florida personally appeared Samuel James and Fannie A. James his wife, to me known to be the persons described in, and who executed the foregoing instrument, and severally acknowledged the execution thereof to be their free act and deed for the uses and purposes therein mentioned; and the said Fannie A James the wife of the said Samuel James on an examination taken and made separately and apart from her said husband, did acknowledge that she made herself a party to the said deed, for the purpose of renouncing and relinquishing her dower, or right of dower, in and to the lands, tenements and hereditaments therein described, and thereby granted and released, and that she executed said deed freely and without fear or compulsion of her said husband.

WITNESS my hand and seal at Jewell the date aforesaid.

J C Hoagland
Notary Public for Fla

STATE OF FLORIDA,
COUNTY OF Dade

BE IT REMEMBERED, That on the Eleventh day of November A.D. 1894, the foregoing instrument of writing was presented and filed for record with the subscriber, Clerk of the Circuit Court for said County, and the same being properly authenticated, I have duly recorded the same in Book "J" on page 178

By _____ D.C.

A. F Quimby. C C C.
Clerk Circuit Court.

205

Appendix E: Zooming in on Surveyors' Maps

During the Seminole Wars, the U.S. Army sent out surveyors to map the land. At first, their work was rough and approximate. But each new survey team improved upon the accuracy of the work. The 1859 survey, performed just after the end of the Third Seminole War, created maps that for the first time showed precise details of the meandering shoreline of Lake Worth and its islands.

One of the chief purposes of such surveys was to prepare for future settlement. Surveyors used a system of land description that divided the land into a grid of 160-acre homestead sites and assigned each a specific series of numbers, in terms of range, township, and sector and quarter-sector.

The range coordinates specified distance and direction from the Tallahassee meridian.

As in much of the western United States, townships were square, six miles on a side, containing a total of 36 sections of one square mile each. The original Lake Worth plat included land in Sectors 21, 22, 27, and 28 of Township 44 South, Range 43 East.

Sections could be further divided into quarters, half quarters, or quarter quarters using compass directions. A section contained 640 acres, a quarter section 160 acres, and half of a quarter section 80 acres. The famous 40-acre parcel was actually a quarter of a quarter section. For example, a particular 160-acre parcel could be cited as the northwest quarter of Section 15, Township 44 south, Range 15 east.

Rivers or lakes presented a challenge to this grid system. Natural features created irregular boundaries that could not be squared off into 40-acre parcels. To accommodate, government lots were mapped out to approximate 40 acres and given sequential numbers in each section. Thus Lot 1 of Section 27 lies on the shore of Lake Worth in what is now the north end of Bryant Park. It held 48.38 acres rather than 40 acres.

For homestead purposes, however, such lots were generally treated as 40-acre parcels. Even with the maximum claim by law set at 160 acres, the Land Office permitted claims of up to four government lots, which would often total over 160 acres. This is exactly what the Jameses did and how they ended up with the odd figure of 186.57 acres. The legal description of their first claim was for Range 43 East, Township 44 South, Sector 27, Lots 1–4.

The map on the opposite page shows subdivision of the land into townships, sections, and lots. This is the type of map that settlers used to file homestead or preemption claims.

Looking at the layout of the map, the Atlantic Ocean is on the far right. Moving left, Palm Beach Island is shown as the slim barrier island separating the ocean from Lake Worth. The original contours of Lake Clark and Lake Osborne (in the middle on the north and south, respectively) vary from their shorelines today.

Land types are also indicated. Toward the west, the swampland of the Everglades is depicted as grasslike shadings. Woodlands were shown as if small, curly treetops. Note the pine and oak woodland running east from the northern lobe of Lake Osborne. In today's urban landscape, those woods correspond to Lake Worth Road.

The sequence of horizontal lines marks sector boundaries and correspond to the approximate routes of later roadways, such as Dixie Highway, Federal Highway, Lake Worth Road, and 6th Avenue South. The line at the bottom edge of the map corresponds with Lantana Road.

Hypoluxo Island is missing. Its survey was provided on another map.

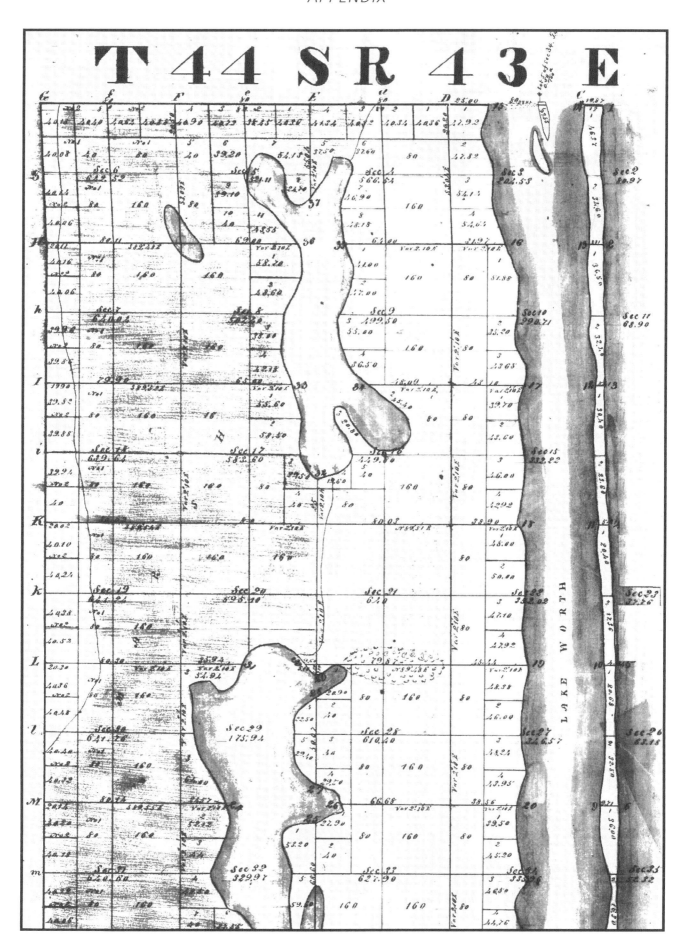

Further description of the land was provided by notes indicating the type of vegetation predominant in each sector, such as bay, pine, oak, or cypress. Would-be settlers would find this information useful when selecting a potential homestead site.

When it came to subdividing quarter sections, surveyors measured distances in "chains" according to the metes-and-bounds system. A 100-link chain, 66 feet long, was used to measure distances from lot lines or quarter section lines.

For example, when the legal description of Fannie and Samuel's original homesite is given as "the South 3.16 chains of the North 14.59 chains of Lot 2, Section 27," the precise location can be calculated as follows:

Starting with the boundary between Lots 1 and 2 of Section 27, measure 14.59 chains (or 14.59 x 66 = 962.94) feet south along the water's edge. This establishes the south boundary of the property. Then going 3.16 chains (or 3.16 x 66 = 208.56) feet north establishes the north boundary.

The line between Lots 1 and 2 corresponds today to approximately 3rd Avenue South. The north end of Jameses' original homesite approximately 750 feet south of where 3rd Avenue South meets the water's edge and the south end of their property would have been 200 feet farther southward. These measurements encompass an area in South Bryant Park between 4th and 5th Avenues South.

Appendix F: Lake Worth Timeline—Major Events From Pre-Columbian Times Until Today

INDIGENOUS ERA

11000 BCE—Beginning of Paleo-Indian Period. First human inhabitants arrive to the Florida peninsula from North America. They find a dry, desert climate inhabited by large mammals, such as mastodon, sloth, bison, camels, giant armadillos, and tortoises. Large spear points, suited to hunting such large Pleistocene game, testify to human presence during this period. (Pre*historic Peoples*, 7.)

5000 BCE—Archaic Indigenous Period. The climate becomes gradually wetter, leading eventually to the formation of the Everglades, along with Lake Okeechobee, Lake Osborne, and Lake Worth. Large mammals disappear.

1500 BCE—Transitional Indigenous Period marked by the first appearance of pottery.

500 BCE—Beginning of Glades Indigenous Period marked by appearance of sand-tempered pottery. Shell mounds and burial mounds from this period are found scattered throughout Palm Beach County. Well-established sites included Barnhill burial mounds near Boca Raton, a huge shell mound, still partially existing, near the Jupiter Lighthouse, and large settlement complex west of Boynton Beach. Canoes were used for transportation. Fishnets in evidence. Diet consisted of fish, shellfish, turtles, deer, small game, saw palmetto berries, coco plums, yucca, and sea grapes. The land was rich in resources and the population low enough that there was little, if any, need for agriculture.

1300 AD—Evidence of complex indigenous society in southeast Florida with completion of Barnhill Mounds near Boca Raton. (McGoun, *Prehistoric Peoples*, 99.)

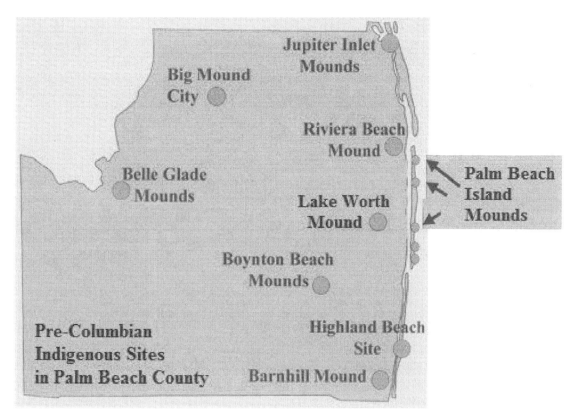

COLONIAL ERA

April 3 and *circa* July 3, 1513—Voyage of Juan Ponce de Leon along the South Florida coast as described in the account of Spanish royal scribe Antonio de Herrera. Marks the beginning of European influence and Spanish Colonial Period. De Leon reportedly came ashore at two Indian villages located south of Jupiter inlet. The first, named by De Herrera as "Abacoa," was apparently in Palm Beach County, while the second, "Chequescah" (Tequesta), was farther south, in the areas of present Broward or Dade counties. Herrera's book briefly describes how explosive encounters with the natives could be.

> Juan Ponce de Leon went ashore here, called by the Indians, who promptly tried to steal his launch, the oars, and arms and… wounded two Spaniards. (http://www.pbchistory-online.org/page/jeaga-and-jobee)

Jupiter Inlet

Cabo de Setos (Palm Beach)

Abacoa (near Lake Worth Inlet)

Rio Saltado (New River, near Las Olas, Fort Lauderdale)

Chequescha (Tequesta, now Miami)

Southeast Florida locations as identified in "Freducci Map of 1514-1515", David O. True, Collection of Florida International University, 1994.

This sketch (Freducci map) comes from the work of Antonio de Herrera (*circa* 1600) based on Ponce de Leon's original journals, now lost. This was the first map to use the name "Florida" and clearly identifies the Jupiter Inlet and the Cape of Florida. Authorities differ on the identification of the other sites shown here as well as the accuracy of the reinterpretation of de Leon's voyage ninety years after it occurred. Cabo de Setos is thought by some to be the easternmost point of the Florida coast which would be on Singer Island, north of Palm Beach.

Circa 1560—During the early Colonial Period, Spanish explorers identify the indigenous tribes along the southeast Florida coast as the Ais, north of the Jupiter inlet, the Jobe around Jupiter, the Jaega around Lake Worth, and the Tequesta farther south. The first historical reference to the Jaega comes from their encounters with the Spanish as reported by Pedro Menéndez de Avilés in 1565. Spanish maps place the "Gega," "Jaega," or "Xega" south of Jupiter inlet and north of "Boca de Ratones." The Ais and Jaega accumulated European artifacts, including iron, gold, and silver from shipwreck salvage. (Wheeler and Pepe, "The Jobe and Jaega," 224, 225, 237)

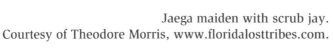

Jaega maiden with scrub jay.
Courtesy of Theodore Morris, www.floridalosttribes.com.

1564—French Protestant Huguenots found Fort Caroline, modern-day Jacksonville.

1565—The Spanish King Phillip commissions Pedro Menéndez de Avilés to drive the French from Florida. Saint Augustine founded by de Aviles to protect Spain's interests.

Circa 1600—Slave hunting by Spanish and French reaches a peak.

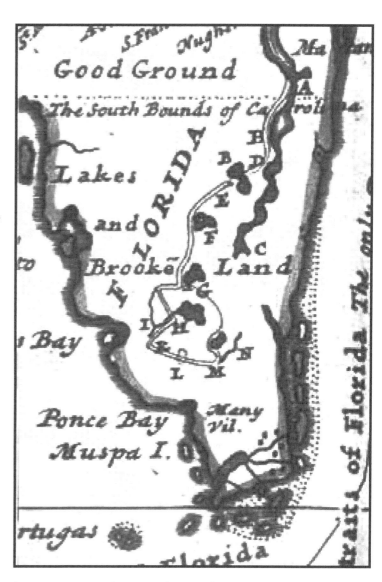

A portion of Herman Moll's 1720 map showing the route that a French slaving party took, guided by 33 Yamasee Indians. Points A. and D. mark places the party left canoes. E. marks the path they took to go slave catching. K. marks a place where they took 29 slaves and L. a place where they took six more. M. marks the place where the party met resistance from Indians with iron and fish bone harpoons, re-sulting in many deaths. From Map Division, Library of Congress.

1693—African slaves flee to Florida from plantations in the South Carolina Low Country. King Charles II of Spain grants the refugees liberty in exchange for defending Saint Augustine from the British.

1696—Jonathan Dickinson, a Quaker merchant, was shipwrecked near Jupiter while sailing between Jamaica and Philadelphia. To survive, Dickinson and shipmates walked 250 miles along the beach to Saint Augustine. As they traveled north, the party was at various times both aided and thwarted by the natives. They encountered the Jobe and Ais tribes but not the Jaega, who lived farther south along the coast. (Hobe Sound gets its name from the Jobe Indians.) Dickinson kept a detailed journal, which was published in Philadelphia in 1699 by the Society of Friends. The journal contains some of the best contemporary descriptions of the culture of South Florida natives—their houses, diets, tribal structure, customs, and religious ceremonies.

Jonathan Dickinson's Journal

or GOD'S PROTECTING PROVIDENCE

Being the Narrative of a Journey from

PORT ROYAL *in* JAMAICA *to* PHILADELPHIA

between August 23, 1696 and April 1, 1697

Edited by EVANGELINE WALKER ANDREWS *and*
CHARLES MCLEAN ANDREWS *with a New Introduction*
by LEONARD W. LABAREE   A Yale Paperbound $1.25

Circa 1730—British wars against the Indians in Georgia and Alabama cause the Creeks, Oconees, and other tribes to flee south into Florida. The Spanish welcomed them as a buffer against the British. Succeeding decades brought increasing numbers. The Seminoles formed from a mixture of "runaways," the term being a corruption of the Spanish word *"cimarrón."* The diversity of the tribe is reflected in the fact that its members spoke seven languages—Muscogee, Hitchiti, Koasati, Alabama, Natchez, Yuchi, and Shawnee. (*Official Website of Seminole Tribe of South Florida*, http://www.semtribe.com/History/BriefSummary.aspx.)

Runaway black slaves mixed with or lived side by side with the Indians, forming communities of Black Seminoles. (Porter, *The Black Seminoles,* 4.)

1738—African American refugees founded Fort Mose as the northern defense of Saint Augustine. It was the first legally sanctioned free black town in North America.

1763—Transfer of Florida to the British by Treaty of Paris; many free blacks who had come under the protection of the Spanish flee to Cuba. Remnants of the indigenous tribes, approximately eighty families, are likewise taken to Havana, Cuba. Records of the evacuation are the last historical mention of the native peoples of southern Florida. (Wheeler and Pepe, "The Jobe and Jaega," 230).

1783—Transfer of Florida back to the Spanish crown via the Treaty of Versailles in the aftermath of the American Revolution.

U.S. ERA

1817–1818—First Seminole War. The U.S. Army invades Spanish Florida in support of American slave owners seeking to recapture runaways. Andrew Jackson led U.S. forces against the Seminoles and their African American allies, and then later against Spanish forts and settlements.

1819—Signing of the Adams-Onís Treaty between the United States and Spain ends First Seminole War. According to its terms, the United States acquired Florida in exchange for renouncing all claims to Texas. Andrew Jackson was named military governor.

Circa 1820—As European American settlement increased after the U.S. acquisition, the settlers pressured the federal government to remove the Seminoles and Miccosukee from Florida. Settlers wanted access to desirable lands held by the Indians. Georgian slaveholders pressured for the "maroons" and fugitive slaves living among the Seminoles to be returned to slavery.

1830—The Indian Removal Act paved the way for the Trail of Tears, the forcible removal of the "Five Civilized Tribes"—Cherokee, Chickasaw, Choctaw, Creek, and Seminole (including the Black Seminoles)—from the southeastern United States to Oklahoma and other territories west of the Mississippi.

1832—Treaty of Payne's Landing was signed by the U.S. government and a few Seminole chiefs, wherein the chiefs agreed to voluntary deportation west of the Mississippi. Most Seminoles rejected the treaty and prepared for war.

Abraham, leader of the Black Seminoles
during the Second Seminole War.

1835–1842—Second Seminole War. The Seminoles resisted attempts to remove them from Florida and began attacking U.S. troops. The American press portrayed white settlers as massacre victims. In 1836, the U.S. Army arrived in force. Drawing on a population of about 4,000 Seminole Indians and 800 allied Black Seminoles, Chief Osceola mustered 1,000 to 1,400 warriors. They countered combined U.S. Army and militia forces that ranged from 6,000 troops at the outset to 9,000 at the peak of deployment in 1837. To survive, the Seminole allies employed guerrilla tactics with devastating effect against U.S. forces. A major battle was fought on the banks of the Loxahatchee River near Jupiter. Osceola was arrested when he was lured into a trap under a flag of truce in 1837. He died in jail less than a year later. By May 10, 1842, when a frustrated President John Tyler ordered the end of military actions against the Seminoles, over $20 million had been spent, 1,500 American soldiers had died, and still no formal peace treaty had been signed. The war had accomplished its primary goals, however—the deportation of most Seminoles to the west and an end of sanctuary to runaway slaves. The few remaining Seminoles, Indian and Black, were disorganized and scattered, most hiding in the Everglades.

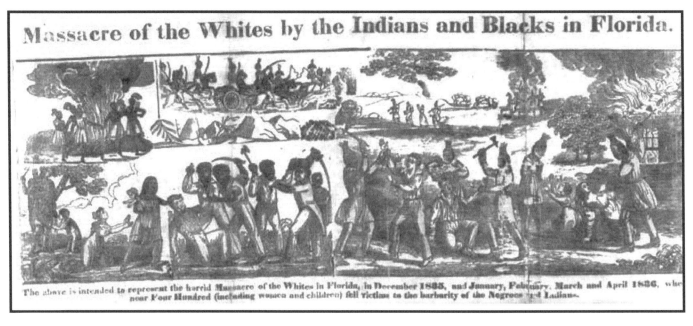

Caption reads: "The above is intended to represent the horrid Massacre of the Whites in Florida, in December 1835, and January, February, March and April 1836 when near Four Hundred (including women and children) fell victim to the barbarity of the Negroes and Indians." Courtesy of Library of Congress.

1842—The last of a series of U.S. military men entrusted with conduct of the war against the Seminoles, Col. William Jenkins Worth gives up his command on August 14.

1842—Armed Occupation Act granted 160 acres of land in the unoccupied regions of Florida to any settler willing to bear arms to defend the property for five years. The law was designed to encourage settlement after the end of the Second Seminole War and to provide for defense against the remaining Seminoles. Over 1,100 homesteading permits were issued within the nine months that the law remained in effect. Most were for Central Florida. Less than 25 permits were issued for the whole of the southeast part of the state, nine on the shores of Lake Worth. There are no records indicating who actually took up residence, but those few who attempted to settle did not stay long. By 1870, none of the Armed Occupation settlers remained. (*Early Lantana,* 3)

1845—Florida admitted to the Union as a slave state counterbalanced by Iowa as a free state.

1855–1858—Third Seminole War. The war began when army engineers and surveyors were sent into the Great Cypress Swamp to make note of the Seminole villages and their crops. The Americans stole crops and destroyed banana trees belonging to the Seminole. Consequently, under the leadership of Chief Billy Bowlegs, 40 Seminole warriors began a series of raids known as the Third Seminole War. About 200 Seminoles remained in Florida after Billy Bowlegs and his people were removed to "Indian Territory" in Oklahoma.
(http://www.nativeamericannetroots.net/diary/594/the-third-seminole-war)

1859—Detailed U.S. land survey of the Lake Worth area including, for the first time, meander lines along the waterfront, prepares the way for homesteaders.

1860—Completion of Jupiter Lighthouse as one of six on the Florida Atlantic Coast.

1860–1865—Civil War has minimal impact on South Florida due to small local population. Confederate sympathizers disable the Jupiter Lighthouse in an attempt to thwart the Union naval blockade and to aid blockade runners.

1862—Homestead Act passes Congress, allowing settlement of public lands and requiring only residence and cultivation of the land. Any citizen or person intending to become a citizen, 21 years of age or older, and the head of a household could make application. With five years residence and improvements/cultivation, only a $15.00 fee was required to get 160 acres. The act remained in effect until 1976, although the last homestead in the Lake Worth area was taken up in 1903.

1861–1866—August Lang, Confederate sympathizer and deserter, lived as hermit on Palm Beach Island. He is rumored to have been involved in the raid on the Jupiter Lighthouse. Lang left Palm Beach and moved to Vero Beach as soon as he learned that the Civil War was over.

1863—Emancipation Proclamation. President Lincoln frees slaves in the Confederate States.

1865—Federal troops occupy Tallahassee. Reconstruction Era begins. Thirteenth Amendment to the U.S. Constitution outlaws slavery throughout the United States.

1866—Opening of "Lang's Cut," first attempt at Palm Beach Inlet from the Atlantic Ocean into Lake Worth. Voyage of Michael Sears, first known American to sail into Lake Worth.

1868—Fourteenth Amendment guarantees citizenship, due process, and equal protection to all people, including ex-slaves.

1870—Fifteenth Amendment grants voting rights to all citizens regardless of "race, color or previous condition of servitude."

1873—Congress passes several laws as supplements to the Homestead Act, including provision for "preemption." Preemption shortened the time a settler needed to obtain a patent on 160 acres of unoccupied public lands, provided that he built a house, physically resided on the property, cleared the land, and used it for agricultural purposes. Fees for preemption were $1.25 per acre.

1873—First permanent residents, Pierce and Moore families, move to the lake.

1876—Geer and Dimick families settle in Palm Beach.

1877—E. R. Bradley moves to the west side of the lake, north of Lantana (Lotus Cove).

1877—Attempt to construct permanent Palm Beach Inlet, south of Lang's Cut. The inlet proved unstable, continually silted up and migrated south.

1877—Federal troops end occupation of Florida.

1878—Michael Merkel moves to lake area, lives as a hermit in a lean-to on Lake Osborne.

1880—Fannie and Samuel James, with Lucy Jones, Fannie's sister, are in Tallahassee.

Circa 1880–1884—The Jameses move to Cocoa, Florida, perhaps following Rev. Butler Reed as members of Zion Orthodox Primitive Baptist Church of Jesus Christ.

1885—Jameses move to the lake, stake first homestead, and build their first Lake Worth home on the waterfront near the current South Bryant Park picnic pavilion.

1885—In September, Stites and Pennsylvania boys arrive from Newport, Pennsylvania. They engage in land dispute with the Jameses.

1885—In October, William Stephan stakes his claim in the College Park area.

1885—New Florida Constitution begins to roll back Reconstruction reforms, suppresses black vote, outlaws interracial marriage, institutes poll tax.

1885—Completion of the canal linking the Jupiter Inlet with the north end of Lake Worth.

1887—Jameses begin subdividing waterfront homestead with the sale of five acres to Harry Griswold.

1888—Lymans move to Lantana.

1889—Jewell Post Office opened with Fannie A. James as postmistress.

1889—Celestial Railroad begins to run between Jupiter and Juno on the north shore of Lake Worth.

1891—Samuel James files second homestead claim (160 acres), builds house near L Street.

1892—Lantana Post Office opened.

1894—Florida East Coast Railway reaches West Palm Beach.

1895—Canal from south end of Lake Worth to New River completed.

1896—FEC reaches Biscayne Bay, Miami.

1896—Start of train mail delivery to Jewell and Lantana.

1897—William Stephan dies. Samuel James appointed executor of his estate. Fannie James purchases 163-acre property from his heirs in Europe.

1903—Jewell Post Office closes.

1909—Dade County divided to form Palm Beach County on the north. West Palm Beach becomes county seat.

1909—Samuel James passes away after a prolonged illness.

1910—Palm Beach Farms Company begins acquiring land for the Town of Lucerne. Fannie James sells remnants of first and second homestead, moves to 12th Avenue South.

1912—Survey of the original town plat completed. Name changed to Lake Worth.

1912—"The Auction," agricultural acreage with 25-foot town lots awarded by lottery.

1912—Lake Avenue graded and rocked. Construction of 1,000-foot-long Intracoastal dock. The first edition *Lucerne Herald* published. Lake Worth stop added to FEC. Post Office, Public Library, Bryant Park, Union Church, Calvary Methodist Church, and Saint Andrews Episcopal Church established. First school opens. Lake Worth population stood at 38 in July and reached 308 before year-end.

RECAPITULATION

PERMANENT RESIDENTS.	
Men	115
Women	97
Boys (under 21 years)	55
Girls (under 21 years)	41
	308
Transients	65
Total	373

Houses cottages, dwellings, etc., built	77
Houses, cottages, dwellings, building	48
Total	125
Conservative estimate of cost of buildings	$ 92,421.00
Conservative value of furniture	22,135.00
Total	$114,556.00

PERSONAL PROPERTY.	
Number of fowls	876
Live stock (horses and cattle)	15
Wagons	10
Automobiles	7
Bicycles	36
Approximate value	$ 12,958.00
Miscellaneous property	4,875.00
Total	$ 17,833.00

Lake Worth population and financial data from *Lake Worth Herald*, December 12, 1912.

1913—Town of Lake Worth charter adopted on June 4, subject to the approval of the governor. Town Commission consisted of three appointed members, mayor, vice-mayor, and town clerk. Bank of Lake Worth and Florida Hotel open. Beach bathhouse built. Beach ferry begins operating. Construction of the municipal social center, called the Club House, was completed.

1914—City celebrates its first anniversary. Picnic plans were interrupted by incessant rains.

1915—Fannie James killed in an auto accident.

1918—Palm Beach Inlet stabilized at its current location.

1919—Completion of first Lake Worth Bridge, second school, first band shell, horseshoe pitch.

1922—Completion of Casino Building at Lake Worth Beach. Completion of Lake Worth High School. Construction of Gulfstream Hotel.

1924—Oakley Theatre opened, now the Lake Worth Playhouse.

1925—Opening of Lake Worth Municipal Golf Course.

1927—Opening of South Lake Worth (Boynton) Inlet.

1928—Hurricane batters city. Casino building spared.

1934—Municipal Auditorium dedicated, now City Hall.

1937—Florida Legislature repeals the poll tax.

1938—City celebrates its 25th anniversary.

1941—Building of current library and post office.

1942—During WWII, German U-boats sighted off the Lake Worth Beach.

1946—Construction of Osborne Colored School.

1947—Hurricane destroys Beach Casino.

1948—Casino redesigned and reconstructed.

1949—Enlargement of Colored District.

1954—Supreme Court decision, Brown v. Board, outlaws racial segregation of public schools.

1954—Lake Worth Pier opened to the public.

1961—Two black students, Johnny Greene and Theresa Jacks, enroll at Lake Worth High, the beginning of the end of school segregation.

1963—City celebrates its fiftieth anniversary.

1969—Closing of Osborne Colored School marks end of school segregation.

1982—Museum of the City of Lake Worth established.

1988—City celebrates its 75th anniversary.

1994—Mural of Unity transforms former Osborne segregation-era wall into a tribute to diversity.

1995—First Martin Luther King march and first Street Painting Festival held. First African American, Retha Lowe, elected to the Lake Worth Commission.

1996—Paul Blockson hired as Lake Worth's first African American fire chief.

2005—Construction of Pathway to Freedom and Martin Luther King Memorial in downtown Cultural Plaza.

2012—Renovation of Lake Worth Casino. 100th anniversary edition of *Lake Worth Herald*. Lake Worth Public Library centennial celebration.

2013—City of Lake Worth Centennial.

Appendix G: Historical Basis
for Details of Cover Art

The painting *Fannie A. James and the Jewell Post Office* is an artistic depiction of opening day at the frontier post office on August 22, 1889. No photographs of the Jameses or their first waterfront homestead exist. To the extent possible, the elements of the painting have been drawn from photographs and written records of the lake community during that period.

In the painting, the mail is being delivered by a barefoot postman in a sailboat. The design of the boat is taken from a photograph of an outing on the west shore of the lake.

Potter family with sailboat, *circa* 1890. Courtesy of the Historical Society of Palm Beach County.

It is uncertain whether the famous Barefoot Mailman personally served the Jewell Post Office. By the time that the Jewell Post Office opened, the official Star Route along the beach began at Hypoluxo, south of Jewell, and ran down to Miami. Nevertheless, the U.S. Post Office Department was an informal business in those days, with mail sometimes carried to the post offices by contractor Capt. U. D. Hendrickson by sail or steamboat. At other times, the small community of friends would fill in for one another and the Barefoot Mailman would go up to Palm Beach to pick up the mail. (PLSF 213) Regular steamboat service did not start until 1891. The method of mail delivery used on that first day at the new Jewell Post Office on August 22, 1889 is unknown, but the use of a small sailboat, such as was common on the lake during that period, is most likely.

Charles W. Pierce, himself a Barefoot Mailman for a time, described how small boats were landed. Few settlers around the lake had a dock for a boat landing; they would simply anchor their boats in water not more than knee deep, pull off their shoes, roll up their trousers to keep them from getting wet, and wade ashore. (PLSF, 102)

The mailman's hat is broad-brimmed for protection from the sun as shown in old photos, rather than the official mailman's cap shown in the famous post office murals in West Palm Beach.

One of six murals of the Barefoot Mailman from West Palm Beach Post Office, painted by Stevan Dohanos in 1939.

The Jameses' home served, for a time, as a small general store. A photograph of the Pierce house, located across the lake on Hypoluxo Island, was used as a model. The rustic building was constructed of salvaged lumber as was typical of the early houses on the lake, collected along the Atlantic beach from shipwreck debris washed ashore, and then roofed with palm fronds.

The Pierce Home, *circa* 1878.
Courtesy of Historical Society of Palm Beach County.

In the painting, Samuel James is depicted in the background, moving barrels of common food-stuffs such as flour or sugar. The coconut tree next to the house, the hunting dog on the porch, and Samuel's rowboat in the weeds are all details added in accord with the typical lifestyle of the early homesteaders.

James Henshall provided a vivid description of a hunting with Florida "deer dogs"—"mongrels, a mixture of cur and hound and trained to follow a warm trail very slowly… through the thick pal-metto scrub." In the painting, such a hound lazily stretches out on the Jameses' front porch.

The house is surrounded by sea grapes, mangroves, and other salt-tolerant plant species. By the mid-1880s, the formerly freshwater lake was already brackish as the Palm Beach Inlet had been in existence for over ten years. A spiked sisal is growing in the yard, an ornamental plant that was popular with early pioneers.

Even the chickens are based on the historical record. Bradley made reference to Fannie's hennery in his Lotus Cove column.

> **Mrs. Fannie A. James** has a hennery also a Samuel and a postoffice. Samuel has a new pair of shoes built in Baltimore.

Tropical Sun, September 16, 1891—Fannie's hens.

A tourist walking the entire 44 miles of the lakefront, took notes on everyone he met along the way. He refered to Fannie as "the lady chicken fancier." (Myers, "Newspaper Pioneering on the Florida East Coast," 62.)

Up until the time of her death, Fannie continued to raise chickens. The probate list of her estate's assets included 41 chickens and one rooster.

Citation Abbreviations

(Unless contained in this list, in-text citation abbreviations provide author's last name and title with full publication information in the bibliography.)

1896 Directory - Gardner, C. M., and Kennedy, C. F. *1896 Directory, Guide and History of Dade County, Florida including Broward and Palm Beach Counties.* Genealogical Society of Greater Miami, Inc. 1996 Reprint.

Early Lantana - Linehan, Mary Collar. *Early Lantana, Her Neighbors and More....* St. Petersburg, Florida: Byron Kennedy & Company, 1980.

Foundations of Faith - Norfus, Victor D. *Foundations of Faith – Early African Americans in Boynton Beach Florida.* Boynton Beach Historical Society, 2009.

Henshall - Henshall, James A. *Camping and Cruising in Florida.* Cincinnati: Robert Clarke & Company, 1884.

Hooded Americanism - Chambers, David Mark. *Hooded Americanism: The History of the Klu Klux Klan.* Durham, North Carolina: Duke University Press, 1987.

History of Fayette County - Allen, Frank M. *History of Fayette County, Ohio: Her People, Industries and Institutions.* Indianapolis, Indiana, B. F. Bowen & Company, Inc., 1914.

History of Juno Beach - DuBois, Bessie W. *A History of Juno Beach and Juno, Florida.* Juno Beach, Florida: published by the author, 1978.

Jewel of the Gold Coast - Koontz, Jonathan W. et. al., *Lake Worth – Jewel of the Gold Coast.* Lake Worth, Florida: The Greater Lake Worth Chamber of Commerce, 1997.

Lakeworth Abstract of Title - Lake Worth Title and Guaranty Company. *Abstract of Title to the Townsite of Lucerne in Palm Beach County, Florida, now known as Lakeworth.* Lake Worth Title and Guaranty Company, 1912.

Municipal Cemeteries of Lake Worth - Palm Beach County Genealogical Society. *The Municipal Cemeteries of Lake Worth, Florida.* Palm Beach County Genealogical Society, 1998.

Pioneer Days - Linehan, Mary Collar, and Marjorie Watts Nelson. *Pioneer Days on the Shores of Lake Worth 1873 – 1893.* St. Petersburg, Florida: Southern Heritage Press, 1994.

Prehistoric Peoples - McGoun, William E. *Prehistoric Peoples of South Florida.* Tuscaloosa and London: University of Alabama Press, 1993.

PLSF - Pierce, Charles W. *Pioneer Life in Southeast Florida.* Edited by Donald W. Curl. Coral Gables, Florida: University of Miami Press, 1970.

Tropical Frontier - Robinson, Tim. *A Tropical Frontier – Pioneers and Settlers of Southeast Florida, 1800 – 1890.* Port Salerno, Florida: Port Sun Publishing, 2005.

Tuskegee Institute Yearbook - Negro Yearbook Publishing Company. *Tuskegee Institute Yearbook, 1931-1932.* Tuskegee, Alabama: Negro Yearbook Publishing Company, 1931.

UF Digital Collection - *University of Florida Digital Collection: Miscellaneous Pamphlets and Brochures,* http://ufdc.ufl.edu/AA00000150/00011/1.

Underground Railroad - Calarco, Tom. Places of the Underground Railroad: Geographical Guide. Santa Barbara, California: ABC-CLIO, 2011.

Abbreviations for Digitized Homestead Application Files (Bureau of Land Management)

Bradley HA

Crenshaw HA

Earnest HA

Geer HA

Hoagland HA

James HA1 (First Homestead Application)

James HA2 (Second Homestead Application)

Porter HA

Stephan HA

Stites HA

Bibliography

Allen, Frank M. *History of Fayette County, Ohio: Her People, Industries and Institutions.* Indianapolis, Indiana, B. F. Bowen & Company, Inc., 1914.

American City Directory Company. *1915 Directory of West Palm Beach & County.* American City Directory Company, 1915.

Arnold, Bill. *Lake Osborne History : a monograph.* West Palm Beach, Florida: Publications of Palm Beach, 2005.

Bradbury, Alford G. and E. Story Hallock. *A Chronology of Florida Post Offices.* The Florida Federation of Stamp Clubs, 1962, reprint, Port Salerno, FL: Sewall's Point Company, 1993.

Bramson, Seth H. *Historic Photos of Palm Beach County.* Nashville, Tennessee: Turner Publishing Company, 2007.

Brown, Canter, Jr. *Florida's Black Public Officials, 1867 – 1924.* Tuscaloosa, Alabama: The University of Alabama Press, 1998.

Calarco, Tom. *Places of the Underground Railroad: Geographical Guide.* Santa Barbara, California, ABC-CLIO, 2011.

Chambers, David Mark. *Hooded Americanism: The History of the Klu Klux Klan.* Durham, North Carolina: Duke University Press, 1987.

Clarke, Everee Jimerson. *Pleasant City–West Palm Beach*, Black America Series. Charleston, South Carolina: Arcadia Publishing, 2005.

Commissioner of Agriculture. Third *Census of the State of Florida: Taken in the year 1905.* Commissioner of Agriculture, Tallahassee, Florida. Capital Publishing Company, 1906.

----------. *Fifth Census of the State of Florida: Taken in the year 1925.* Commissioner of Agriculture, Tallahassee, Fla., T. J. Appleyard Inc., 1926.

Curl, Donald W. *Palm Beach County-An Illustrated History.* Windsor Publications, Inc., 1986.

Drake, Lynn Lasseter and Richard A. Marcon. *Images of America West Palm Beach 1893 to 1950.* Charleston, South Carolina: Arcadia Publishing, 2006.

DuBois, Bessie W. *A History of Juno Beach and Juno, Florida.* Juno Beach, Florida: published by the author, 1978.

Ellis, Mary Louise, and William Warren Rogers. *Tallahassee & Leon County: A History and Bibliography.* Florida Department of State, 1986.

Gardner, C. M., and Kennedy, C. F. *1896 Directory, Guide and History of Dade County, Florida including Broward and Palm Beach Counties.* Genealogical Society of Greater Miami, Inc. Reprint.

Palm Beach County Genealogical Society. *The Municipal Cemetaries of Lake Worth, Florida.* Palm Beach County Genealogical Society, 1998.

Griffith, Gordon. *Black Diamond Minstrel Book – A Treasure Chest for Blackface Comedians.* Chicago: The Dramatic Publishing Company, 1930.

Hann, John H. *Indians of Central and South Florida, 1513 – 1763.* Gainesville, Florida: University Press of Florida, 2003.

Haynes, Melvin, Jr., and Vivian Reissland Rouson-Gossett, editors. *Like a Mighty Banyan Tree: Contributions of Black People to the History of Palm Beach County*. Palm Beach Junior College, 1982.

Henshall, James A. *Camping and Cruising in Florida*. Cincinnati: Robert Clarke & Company, 1884.

Dickinson, Jonathan. *Jonathan Dickinson's Journal or God's Protecting Providence*, editors Evangeline Walker Andres and Charles McLean Andrews with a New Introduction by Leonard W. Labaree. New Haven, Connecticut: Yale University Press, 1961.

Kelke, Luther Reily. *History of Dauphin County, Pa. Vol. 3*. New York: The Lewis Publishing Company, 1907.

Koontz, Jonathan W. et. al., *Lake Worth – Jewel of the Gold Coast*. Lake Worth, Florida: The Greater Lake Worth Chamber of Commerce, 1997.

Lake Worth Title and Guaranty Company. *Abstract of Title to the Townsite of Lucerne in Palm Beach County, Florida, now known as Lakeworth*. Lake Worth Title and Guaranty Company, 1912.

Lawson, Steven F. *Black Ballots: Voting Rights in the South, 1944-1969*, New York: Columbia University Press,1976.

Linehan, Mary Collar. *Early Lantana, Her Neighbors and More….* St. Petersburg, Florida: Byron Kennedy & Co., 1980.

Linehan, Mary Collar, and Marjorie Watts Nelson. *Pioneer Days on the Shores of Lake Worth 1873 – 1893*. St. Petersburg, Florida: Southern Heritage Press, 1994.

Littlefield, Daniel, Jr. *Africans and Seminoles – From Removal To Emancipation*. University Press of Jackson, Mississippi, 1977.

McGoun, William E. *Prehistoric Peoples of South Florida*. Tuscaloosa and London: University of Alabama Press, 1993.

----------. *Southeast Florida Pioneers – The Palm & Treasure Coasts*. Sarasota, Florida: Pineapple Press, Inc. 1998.

Mooney, James. *Myths of the Cherokees*, Smithsonian Institution, Bureau of American Ethnology, Washington, D.C.: Government Printing Office, 1900.

Motte, Jacob Rhett, *Journey into Wilderness*, Gainesville: University of Florida Press, 1953.

Mustaine, Beverly. *Images of America on Lake Worth*. Arcadia Publishing, 1999.

Negro Yearbook Publishing Company. *Tuskegee Institute Yearbook, 1931-1932*. Tuskegee, Alabama: Negro Yearbook Publishing Company, 1931.

Newton, Michael. *The Invisible Empire – The Klu Klux Klan in Florida*. Gainesville: The University Press of Florida, 2001.

Norfus, Victor D. *Foundations of Faith – Early African Americans in Boynton Beach Florida*. Boynton Beach Historical Society, 2009.

Ortiz, Paul. *Emancipation Betrayed – The Hidden History of Black Organizing and White Violence in Florida from Reconstruction to the Bloody Election of 1920*. Berkeley and Los Angeles, California, 2005.

Pedersen, Ginger and Janet M. DeVries. *Pioneering Palm Beach – The Deweys and the South Florida Frontier*. Charleston, South Carolina: The History Press, 2012.

Pierce, Charles W., *On Wings of the Wind,* unpublished manuscript.

Pierce, Charles W. *Pioneer Life in Southeast Florida.* Editor Donald W. Curl. Coral Gables, Florida: University of Miami Press, 1970.

Porter, Kenneth W. *The Black Seminoles – History of a Freedom Loving People.* Gainesville: University Press of Florida, 1996.

Robinson, Tim. *A Tropical Frontier – Pioneers and Settlers of Southeast Florida, 1800 – 1890.* Port Salerno, Florida: Port Sun Publishing, 2005.

Snyder, James D. *A Light in the Wilderness – The Story of Jupiter Inlet Lighthouse & The Southeast Florida Frontier.* Jupiter, Florida: Pharos Books, 2006.

----------. *Five Thousand Years on the Loxahatchee – A Pictorial History of Jupiter / Tequesta, Florida.* Jupiter, Florida: Pharos Books, 2003.

Tordesillas, Antonia de Herrera. *Historia General De Los Hechos De Los Dastellanos En Las Islas Y Tierra Firme Del Mar Oceano.* Madrid: Emplenta *[sic]*, 1615.

Tuckwood, Jan and Eliot Kleinberg. *Pioneers in Paradise – West Palm Beach, The First 100 Years.* Marietta, Georgia, Longstreet Press, Inc., 1994.

Woodward, Comer Van. *Reunion and Reaction: The Compromise of 1877 and the End of Reconstruction.* Oxford University Press, 1991.

----------. *The Strange Career of Jim Crow,* Commemorative Edition. New York: Oxford University Press, 2002.

Periodical and Other Articles:

Andrews, Charles M. "Florida Indians of the Seventeenth Century." *Tequesta, The Journal of the Historical Association of Southern Florida* (1944): 143–151.

Capron, Louis. "The Free Negro in North Carolina." The Citadel, Chapel Hill University, 1920, 5.

Dimick, Ella. "Transportation from 1876 to 1896." *The Lake Worth Historian: A Souvenir Journal*, published by the ladies of Palm Beach, 1896, reprint by Historical Society of Palm Beach County, 1973.

Dreyfus School of the Arts. "Kanu Broke Palm Beach School Segregation Barriers." *Muse*, October 11, 2011.

Myers, Ruby Andrews. "Newspaper Pioneering on the Florida East Coast, 1891–1895." *Tequesta, The Journal of the Historical Association of Southern Florida* (1983), 62.

Peters, Thelma. "The First County Road: From Lantana to Lemon City." *Update – Historical Association of Southern Florida*, December 1973.

Rivers, Larry E., and Canter Brown, Jr. "African Americans in South Florida: A Home and a Haven for Reconstruction-era Leaders." Tequesta, The Journal of the Historical Association of Southern Florida, 1996, 5-23.

Taylor, R. H., "The Free Negro in North Carolina." *The Citadel*, Chapel Hill University, (1920): 5.

Voss, Lillie Pierce. "Hypoluxo and Its History." *Lake Worth Historian: A Souvenir Journal*, published by the ladies of Palm Beach, 1896, reprinted by Historical Society of Palm Beach County, 1973.

----------. "Pioneer Mail Service on Lake Worth – A Pioneers' Memoir", Tustengegee, vol. 4, num. 1, Spring 2013, published by the Historical Society of Palm Beach County.

Wheeler, Ryan J., and James Pepe. "The Jobe and Jaega of the Palm Beach County Area." *The Florida Anthropologist.*" *Tequesta*, Vol. XXV55 (2002): 224 - 237.

Newspapers:

Daily Tropical Sun, West Palm Beach Florida

Fiery Cross, Indianapolis, Indiana

Florida Star, Titusville, Florida

Florida Times-Union, Jacksonville, Florida

Lake Worth Herald, Lake Worth, Florida

Palm Beach Post, West Palm Beach, Florida

The Gazette, West Palm Beach, Florida

Tropical Sun, Juno, Florida and West Palm Beach, Florida

Sun-Sentinel, Fort Lauderdale, Florida

Selected Newspaper Articles:

Bessette, Leni and Louise Stanton Warren. *"From Our Past:'First family' of Fleming Island included 15th Florida Governor."* The Florida Times-Union, May 13, 2006.

McCabe, Scott. "Mystery of the Lost Grave." *Palm Beach Post*, April 20, 1999.

----------. "First Settler's Grave Site Confirmed." *Palm Beach Post*, May 17, 1999.

----------. "Lake Worth to Honor Its First Settlers -- Ex-Slaves." *Palm Beach Post*, May 19, 1999.

----------. "Lake Worth Prepared to Dig Up Settler's Past." *Palm Beach Post*, May 30, 1999.

----------. "Lake Worth Cancels Dig for First Settler's Remains." *Palm Beach Post*, June 3, 1999.

----------. "Lake Worth History Gets Confusing." *Palm Beach Post*, June 4, 1999.

----------. "Pioneer's Will Reveals More Surprises." *Palm Beach Post*, June 10, 1999.

Powell, Nancy. "City's Too Crowded For 1911 LW Pioneer." *Sun-Sentinel*, August 15, 1966.

Selected Websites:

The American Religious Experience, http://are.as.wvu.edu/minges.htm#

Historical Society of Palm Beach County, http://www.pbchistoryonline.org.

Lake Worth Pioneer Association, http://www.lwpa.org.

Official Website of Seminole Tribe of South Florida. http://www.semtribe.com/History/BriefSum-mary.aspx.

United States Postal Service, "African-American Postal Workers in the 19th Century." http://about. usps.com/who-we-are/postal-history/african-american-workers-19thc-2011.pdf.

----------. "The Digitized U.S. Postal Bulletins, 1880 – 1971." http://www.uspostalbulletins.com.

University of Florida Digital Collection: Miscellaneous Pamphlets and Brochures, http://ufdc.ufl. edu/AA00000150/00011/1

Public Records:

Department of the Interior, Bureau of Land Management

Lake Worth City Clerk

Library of Congress

National Archives

Palm Beach County Clerk and Comptroller

U.S. Census

Oral Histories (from interviews):

Delorisa Brown, Lake Worth native and past principal of Barton Elementary School

Ed Deveaux, Lake Worth native

Mark Easton, editor of Lake Worth Herald

Helen Greene, past curator of Lake Worth Historical Museum

Harold Grimes, Lake Worth native

Retha Lowe, past Lake Worth Commissioner

Grady Lowe, Lake Worth native

Index

(Selected Entries)

A

Allen, James
120

Armour, James A.
6, 8

Anderson, Alonzo
13, 76, 127, 140, 159, 161-162, 164

Anderson, Eliza
159, 161, 162

Armed Occupation Act
2, 3, 214

B

Bahamians
167, 170, 175

Bessie B.
13, 97, 141, 161

Barefoot Mailman
26, 85, 86, 187, 196, 220, 221

Biscayne Bay
10, 12, 85, 97, 156, 217

Black Diamonds
xv, 13, 14, 40, 76, 103

Black Seminoles
xvi, 2, 5, 6, 40, 71, 150, 155,
156, 158, 187, 212, 213, 214,
227

Bradley, Edwin R.
12, 15, 16, 21, 25-28, 84-86, 141, 201

Bradley, Guy
94

Brelsford, Dorinda
47, 48, 55, 82

Bryant & Greenwood
107, 108, 115, 116, 118

C

Canova, Tony
17, 21, 167, 199

Celestial Railroad
9, 86, 197, 216

Cocoa, Florida
15, 74, 198, 199, 216

Cocoanut Grove Hotel
44, 168

Crenshaw, Ernest Linwood
95, 96

D

Deer Park
40, 43, 44

Dimick, Ella
11, 92, 110, 112

E

Earnest, Jacob
94

Earnest, Thurza Belle
94, 95, 110, 112

F

Fayette County, Ohio
103, 159, 160, 161, 223, 225

Figulus
12, 40, 41, 43, 86, 92, 158, 196

Flagler, Henry
6, 55, 152, 169, 196

Florida East Coast Railway
38, 175

Fort Lauderdale
4, 6, 10, 12, 152, 157, 228

Fulton, Orville
20, 30, 35, 36, 37, 39, 144, 203

G

Gainesville Land Office
13, 19, 25, 53, 141, 161, 198, 199

Garnett, Andrew
13, 85, 196

Gazette
14, 186, 189, 228

Geer, Harvey
77, 93, 110, 112, 144

Gildersleeve, Millie
168, 171

Granville County, North Carolina 103, 159,
161-162, 164

Gray, Emma Charlton

127, 140, 162

Griswold, Harry
17, 47, 57, 198

Gudmundsen, Olai
56-58, 110

H

Halifax County, Virginia
105-106

Hartzell, Willian
20, 35, 39, 53, 198

Hendrickson, Uriah D.
88, 220

Henshall, James
xii, 9, 151, 222

Heyser, Allen
196

Himes, Benjamin
20, 22, 35, 39, 198, 199, 202

Hoagland, John C.
21, 24, 52-54, 57

Homestead Act
xi, 3, 15, 30, 80, 92, 144, 215, 216

Houses of Refuge
26

I

Intracoastal Waterway
3, 4, 110, 148, 169

J

Jacksonville, Florida
228

Jones, A. T. B.
128, 140, 164

Jones, Lucy
57, 71, 72, 76, 100-102, 123, 138, 216

Jones, W. T. B
127, 128, 164

Juno, Florida
223, 225, 228

K

Klu Klux Klan
xvii, 174, 175, 223, 225, 227

L

Lake Osborne
ix, 3, 5, 26, 29-30, 59, 94, 110, 113,
120, 182, 190, 206, 209, 216, 225

Lake Worth Post Office
4, 7, 16, 85, 197

Lanehart, Benjamin
12, 26

Lang, Augustus
7

Lemon City
97, 228

Loxahatchee River
xv, 4, 6, 7, 214, 227

Lyman, George R.
57

Lyman, Morris B
25, 27, 57, 96, 97, 112, 156, 171, 197

M

Mangurn, Lucy
123, 164, 165

Merkel, Michael
21, 22, 26, 29, 34, 57, 59, 216

Metcalf, Guy I.
75, 77, 97, 186

Metcalf, William I.
128-130

Miami
xiv, 4, 6, 10, 12, 26, 79, 85, 86, 89, 97, 122, 144, 151, 155, 156, 196, 197, 217, 220, 223-225, 227

Ada Mitchell, Ada
140

Moore, Amanda Malvina
48, 82

Moore, William (Uncle Will)
8

Mosquitos
199, 201

N

New River
4, 10, 26, 97, 152, 156, 217

O

Osborne Colored Addition
xvii, 119, 120, 175-177, 181, 183

P

Palm Beach Farms Company
27, 30, 51, 54, 92, 93, 95, 101, 107, 108, 110, 112, 114, 124, 126, 143, 217

Pierce, Charles
6, 8, 13, 14, 26, 29, 32, 44, 53, 59, 76, 85, 150, 155, 161, 196, 199

Pierce, Hannibal
6, 8, 40, 41, 141, 167, 196

Pierce, Margretta
6, 167

Pineapples
22, 33, 54-57, 82, 94, 186

Porter, Owen S.
47, 54, 58

Potter, George
xii, xvi, 6, 11, 16, 40, 43, 44, 55, 113, 141, 156, 167, 196

Potter, Richard (Dr.)
92, 156, 168

R

Reconstruction
xi, 62, 63, 72, 74, 75, 77, 215, 216, 227, 228

Reed, Butler (Rev.)
73-75, 78, 80, 216

S

Sears, Michael
151, 215

Seminole Wars
2, 150, 155, 206

Seminoles
xvi, 2, 5, 6, 40, 71, 150, 155, 156, 158, 187, 212, 213, 214, 227

Speed, Walter
73

Stephan, William
13, 21, 32, 33, 34, 48, 52, 57, 66, 110, 199, 216, 217

Stewart, William G.
69, 72, 73, 80, 141

Stites, Harry (Dr.)
13, 20, 35-38, 110, 189, 198, 199

T

Tallahassee, Florida
74, 225

Titusville, Florida
47, 75, 228

Tomatoes
27, 167, 190

U

Underground Railroad
xvii, 160, 224, 225

W

Webster, Nancy W. P.
127, 140, 162

Worth, William Jenkins (Col.)
110, 150, 214

Mystery Still Unsolved
The Search for Samuel's and Fannie's Remains Continues...

Grave Disappointment

When Fannie James sold her Lake Worth property, she did so with the exception of a ten by ten foot plot where she said Samuel James was buried. There is no record of the Jameses' bodies having been exhumed and moved.

Recently, Mike Decosimo and his partner Robyn purchased the property. They agreed to allow a ground penetrating radar survey of the property.

Local Author, Ted Brownstein has written a book, *Pioneers of Jewell*, which delves deeply into the holdings of Samuel and Fannie James in the early days of civilization here. His research indi-cates the graves of Samuel and Fannie James were located on the property.

The ground penetrating radar (GPR) indi-cated a couple of anoma-lies underground. The first was around 3.5 to 4 feet deep and the second was about six inches deeper. The disturbances in the earth were about two feet wide, approxi-mately the width of a cas-ket. Having found indi-cation of disturbance of the earth at those depths in the location depicted by early maps raised a level of excitement in those present during the ground scan.

Since GPR only indi-cates disturbances in the earth, where some shift-ing of the ground or dig-ging has previously oc-curred, probes were used to feel around for any-thing that might be un-der the surface, probing to depths of about seven feet. Above one of the dis-turbance indications the probe encountered what appeared to be a water pipe about three and a half feet deep.

To the disappointment of City Manager Michael Bornstein, Ted Brown-stein and others who had congregated in anticipa-tion of finding the gravesite, a fairly thor-ough search failed to lo-cate any graves or head-stones in the area. The search for the Jameses continues.

Lake Worth Herald - June 20, 2013

TED BROWNSTEIN

About the Author

Ted Brownstein is a highly regarded researcher and popular writer with a broad background in diverse fields. He holds a master's degree from the University of Wisconsin in Biblical Studies and had a successful career as an economic analyst. Ted has dug deeply into subjects as varied as interfaith religious studies, the life insurance industry, the stock market, ancient Near Eastern history, Mayan archaeology and Florida history. His previously published works include *The Interfaith Prayer Book*, a compilation of prayers from six world faiths (2001) and *Sunshine Republic*, a futuristic novel set in Lake Worth, Florida (2010).

Brownstein is active in his community, serving on the Lake Worth Martin Luther King Committee and the Lake Worth Centennial Committee, is co-founder of the Lake Worth Interfaith Network, organizer of the Earth Day Peace Jam and past president of the Kiwanis Club. Born in New York City in 1951, Brownstein has been married since 1970, and has two married daughters and three grandchildren. He has been a resident of Lake Worth, Florida, since 1987.

Net proceeds from sales of *Pioneers of Jewell* will benefit the Lake Worth Public Library.